Like Grass before the Scythe

1. William Remmel, sometime after his promotion to sergeant. William Remmel Papers (MC 597). Courtesy of Special Collections, University of Arkansas Libraries, Fayetteville.

Like Grass before the Scythe

The Life and Death of Sgt. William Remmel, 121st New York Infantry

William Remmel

Edited by Robert Patrick Bender

The University of Alabama Press
Tuscaloosa

The University of Alabama Press
Tuscaloosa, Alabama 35487-0380
uapress.ua.edu

Hardcover edition published 2007.
Paperback edition published 2019.
eBook edition published 2008.

Inquiries about reproducing material from this work should be addressed to the University of Alabama Press.

Typeface: AGaramond

Cover image: Sgt. WIlliam Remmel; courtesy of Special Collections, University of Arkansas Libraries
Cover design: Paul Moxon

Paperback ISBN: 978-0-8173-5975-1
eBook ISBN: 978-0-8173-8147-9

A previous edition of this book has been catalogued by the Library of Congress as follows:
Library of Congress Cataloging-in-Publication Data

Remmel, William.
Like grass before the scythe : the life and death of Sgt. William Remmel, 121st New York Infantry / edited by Robert Patrick Bender.
p. cm.
Includes index.
ISBN-13: 978-0-8173-1552-8 (cloth : alk. paper)
ISBN-10: 0-8173-1552-7 (cloth : alk. paper)
1. Remmel, William—Correspondence. 2. Soldiers—New York (State)—Correspondence. 3. United States. Army. New York Infantry Regiment, 121st (1861–1865) 4. New York (State)—History—Civil War, 1861–1865—Personal narratives. 5. United States—History—Civil War, 1861–1865—Personal narratives. 6. New York (State)—History—Civil War, 1861–1865—Regimental histories. 7. United States—History—Civil War, 1861–1865—Regimental histories. 8. German American families—New York (State)—Devereaux. 9. Immigrants—New York (State)—Devereaux—Biography. 10. Devereaux (N.Y.)—Biography. I. Bender, Robert Patrick. II. Title.
E523.5121st .R46 2007
973.7'447092—dc22

2006024420

To Mr. Frank Douglas
Who taught his students the value of "the old infantry try"

Contents

Preface

Although it is natural to seek primarily military information from the letters of soldiers and to delve into civilian sources for content about the war on the home front, the letters of William Remmel offer an interesting mixture of both elements and, therefore, provide an opportunity to gauge the maturation of a typical young Union soldier in the context of both his military and familial roles.

The character of Remmel's letters develops gradually throughout the war in relation to his experiences, documenting the transition from recruit to veteran. As part of the Army of the Potomac's 6th Corps, the 121st New York Infantry served in reserve for most of its first year. The first section of letters, therefore, focuses on details of camp life, fellow soldiers and regimental officers, and Remmel's attempt to maintain emotional connections to home and family. The Chancellorsville campaign, however, marks the beginning of a transition. With his first direct experience in combat, Remmel begins to confront the complexities of war on a more personal level, including the changing nature of the conflict itself. Although he shares many racial attitudes of his fellow soldiers—viewing free and enslaved African Americans as generally inferior—he clearly opposes the institution of slavery and views it as the central cause of the conflict, an institution at odds with the ideal of a democratic republic. His opposition is typically expressed as a mixture of moral condemnation and socioeconomic beliefs about the negative impact slavery exacts on the free labor market. As the war evolves into a crusade to end slavery, Remmel supports this development.

In the aftermath of Gettysburg, as the 6th Corps shoulders a greater burden of combat, Remmel's letters reflect further personal loss and war-related frustrations. Letters from this period include observations on political and military commanders, operations such as Mine Run and the Overland campaign, hospital conditions (after being wounded at the battle of Spotsylvania), civilian attitudes about the war, as well as the developing character of "total war" (as a general concept and also as a specific development in the eastern theater during Philip Sheridan's controversial 1864 Shenandoah Valley campaign). Remmel's acceptance of hard war reflects a synthesis of his patriotic support for preserving the Union and his deep Christian faith, of the strategic need for such tactics as a means to undermine civilian support for the Confederate war effort and the need to rid the nation of a morally and economically crippling institution.

The letters, however, also offer interesting insights into the dynamics of a working-class immigrant family of the mid-nineteenth century. Indeed, this characteristic stands as a particular, if subtle, strength of the collection. Because his parents spoke a limited amount of English, for example, Remmel served an important role as a supplemental parental figure in his family. Within his letters he frequently offers advice on such family issues as education, work ethics, western migration, personal discipline, and morality. In addition, his reports on the military experiences of so many friends and acquaintances help to illustrate the collective impact of the war upon a series of small rural communities in upstate New York.

Finally, although the loss of individual family members was frequent during the Civil War, documentation of a family's extensive postwar efforts to find answers is not as common. This aspect of the collection, discussed extensively in the epilogue, connects the collection to recent scholarship interested in the war's impact upon entire family units, especially children and younger siblings, and the creation of a culture of patriotism in the late nineteenth century.

Acknowledgments

Sergeant Remmel's family faithfully preserved William's wartime letters after his death. The letters remained in the family's possession until March 8, 1986, when William's nephew Harmon Remmel Jr. donated them to the Special Collections Department of Mullins Library at the University of Arkansas. An enormous debt of thanks is owed to Mr. Remmel for his careful preservation of these letters; in addition, he proved an invaluable source of information on Remmel family history, and his generous assistance helped make this project more complete.

Thanks are also due to many other individuals who have helped shape my development as a historian. As a doctoral candidate at the University of Arkansas I enjoyed the opportunity to study under Dr. Daniel E. Sutherland, who offered support and valuable advice about the publication of these letters. Long ago, Frank Douglas inspired my interest in an academic career and continues to express interest in my ambitions. My friends and former colleagues in the Special Collections Department also expressed support and encouragement throughout the course of my graduate studies and during the completion of this project. Tod Waterbury of the Herkimer County Historical Society provided valuable information that helped fill in some gaps concerning the Remmel family's residency in New York. My parents and siblings, a growing army of nieces and nephews, and several close friends also provided much-appreciated encouragement.

Editorial Note

During the preparation of this manuscript, certain basic guidelines governed the editorial process. The letters have been altered as little as possible from the original text, in order to present William Remmel's wartime experiences in his own words, while also providing the level of clarity necessary for the modern reader. Although written in an articulate and intelligent style, Remmel's letters exhibit a lack of precise grammar, a common trait among letters of the Civil War; run-on sentences and other minor errors occur periodically throughout Remmel's letters. Spelling and punctuation have, therefore, been standardized when practicable; where place-names have been misspelled the original spelling has been retained, with a corrective notation. Bracketed corrections have also been kept to a minimum, used only to complete an important abbreviated word or when a necessary word or phrase has been omitted in the original text. Italics have replaced underlining for words or phrases. Beyond these basic necessities, the original text has not been altered. All parenthetical statements and the use of quotation marks are original to William Remmel's text.

Remmel mentions numerous individuals throughout his letters, both famous and obscure. Extensive efforts were expended to identify as many of these individuals as possible. Unfortunately, some of them remained unidentifiable.

The William Remmel Papers, held by the Special Collections Department of Mullins Library at the University of Arkansas, contain additional materials not included in this publication. These materials consist of letters, class assignments, and grade reports from Remmel's enrollment at Fairfield Academy as well as a significant collection of postwar correspondence produced during the family's search for answers about his death. These materials have been utilized to support analysis of the Remmel family history and particular elements of William Remmel's personality, as well as his wartime service and disappearance, and are discussed at length in the introduction and epilogue as well as in the relevant endnotes. In addition, the Remmel Papers contain two wartime letters written by other individuals. One, a letter addressed to Augustus Remmel dated May 1, 1863, is misidentified in the manuscript collection as a letter from William Remmel. This letter, signed in a small but still legible signature, was authored by Louisa Remmel Empie. The other, a fragment of a letter, was apparently written sometime in early December 1863 and contains information available in other letters of that period. Because this item is incomplete and contains no unique information, it is not included in this publication.

Introduction

William Remmel arrived in the United States with his mother, Henrietta, and five siblings in January 1851, a month prior to his eighth birthday. The transatlantic journey, still memorable more than a decade later as he served his adopted nation, reunited the young family for the first time since Gottlieb Remmel emigrated from Hermicke, Germany, two years earlier. The family first settled in Stratford, a small village in upstate New York, where the local tanning industry afforded Gottlieb sufficient labor to support a growing family. In addition to Charles, Louisa, William, Augustus, and Caleb, the Remmels had two more children in America, Harmon and Ada. After a fire destroyed their home in the mid-1850s they moved to the nearby village of Devereaux, where they purchased a small farm in 1859.[1]

Before the war, William worked on the family's farm and at jobs in various local industries, such as the production of molasses and the culling of hemlock tree bark for the tanneries. These experiences, along with the hardworking example of his parents, instilled a firm work ethic in William that remained an essential element of his character even after he joined the Union army. As his letters demonstrate, however, William also developed an early appreciation for the importance of formal education. During the 1861–62 academic year he attended Fairfield Academy, a nearby preparatory institution. The few extant letters and work assignments left from this educational experience reveal a bright and observant young student with a broad aptitude for many subjects. His wartime letters reflect his continued interest in academic pursuits, as he repeatedly emphasizes the importance of education to his younger siblings and encourages them to build careers based on their intellectual abilities. The letters from William's year at Fairfield also reveal a developing sense of self-confidence and a strong sense of self-reliance, qualities that would serve him well during his military service.[2]

William does not discuss his feelings about the war or other political issues in his letters from school; nor does he reveal the precise circumstances that influenced his decision to enlist in the summer of 1862. Because he was a young man of military age, however, the issue undoubtedly weighed on his mind. Two previous regiments, the 34th and 97th New York Infantry, both raised considerable numbers of recruits from the academy and the young men of Herkimer County—including many of Remmel's childhood friends and acquaintances. As part of the Army of the Potomac's 2nd and 1st Corps, respectively, these hometown regiments saw a great deal of combat in the war's first two seasons and suffered severe casualties. Many other regiments suffered similar losses, so that by the summer of 1862 the entire Union army required many new recruits to fill its ranks. As a result, President Abraham Lincoln issued a call for three hundred thousand additional volunteers. On August 22, 1862, Remmel enlisted in Company I of the 121st New York Infantry in answer to this call. The regiment—composed largely of young men from Orange and Herkimer counties—took its initial nickname, "The Orange and Herkimer Regiment," from its place of origin. Several of Remmel's friends also joined the new regiment, including his best friend, Alphonzo Casler of Company H.[3]

Mustered into Federal service in Herkimer on August 23, the recruits made their way to Camp Schuyler in German Flats, New York, and undertook their initial training. Shortly after taking to the field the regiment experienced its first significant change, with the resignation of Col. Richard Franchot in September. Colonel Franchot, a New York politician largely responsible for the regiment's recruitment, resigned in order to resume his political career and out of recognition for his lack of prior military training or expertise. Soon thereafter, the regiment came under the leadership of Col. Emory Upton, a brilliant young West Point graduate who shaped the regiment into one of the best-disciplined units in the eastern theater. Due to the perceptible difference made by Upton's regimen of drill, the regiment soon earned a more distinctive sobriquet, "Upton's Regulars." Remmel complained very little about this process and, in general, seems to have accepted the strict discipline as a matter of course; he quickly developed into a respected and dependable soldier, as evidenced by his promotion to sergeant prior to the regiment's first real battle at Salem Church in the spring of 1863.[4]

Blessed with excellent health throughout his service, even during long periods in camp when many soldiers suffered from a nearly endless variety of contagious and little-understood diseases, Remmel endured all of the regiment's hardships until wounded at the battle of Spotsylvania on May 10, 1864. Following a convalescent stay at Emory Hospital in Washington, D.C., and a furlough at home, Remmel rejoined his regiment in time to participate in Maj. Gen. Philip Sheridan's Shenandoah Valley campaign, in which the Army of the Potomac's 6th Corps served as part of an independent command known as the Army of the Shenandoah.[5]

During the Valley campaign, at some point in the climactic but chaotic battle of Cedar Creek, William Remmel disappeared—numbered among the missing in action. Despite their best efforts, neither his family nor his fellow soldiers ever heard from him again and, thereafter, assumed that he died as a prisoner of war at Andersonville. The epilogue examines the evidence related to this issue.[6]

The letters contained in this volume are all that remain to tell the story of a young soldier's life and service and the influence he exerted within his family. They provide a clear picture of a young man with a strong personal character and an intelligent and observant mind, showing his evolution from a somewhat naive small-town boy into a seasoned and disciplined soldier of the Republic. Remmel provides accurate and detailed accounts of some of the war's most memorable campaigns, descriptions of life in camp and on the march, and vignettes about his fellow soldiers and various commanders. He also expresses personal views about such important issues as the prosecution of the war, the institution of slavery, Copperhead sympathies among Northern civilians, the use of bounties and conscription to fill the army's depleted ranks, and the presidential election of 1864. His letters, therefore, provide a detailed look into every aspect of a common soldier's experience during the crucial middle years of the Civil War. Throughout his military experience, however, his family remained foremost in his thoughts, as reflected in his emphasis on family and community issues. Because of his leadership role in the family, these letters also suggest something about the long-term impact that such loss exacts on family dynamics.

I

1862
"On Our Way for Washington"

William Remmel wrote his first letter home a little more than a week after enlisting in Company I, as his regiment, the 121st New York, made its way from Camp Schuyler in German Flats to New York City; soon thereafter they received orders to proceed to Washington, D.C., by way of Philadelphia and Baltimore. Once in the capital city they joined the 2nd Brigade of the 6th Corps' 1st Division as part of the general reorganization that occurred within the Army of the Potomac after the failure of the Peninsula campaign earlier that summer; they remained with this unit for the length of their service.[1]

Although the regiment did not actively participate in combat during their first several months of duty, they did stand in reserve at several significant battles in the autumn and early winter of 1862–63; at South Mountain, Antietam, and Fredericksburg the regiment caught early glimpses of the fearsome realities of war. The carnage of these battles made a vivid impression on Remmel about the value of military drill and the need for effective officers such as Emory Upton and Egbert Olcott to lead the young troops through their "hard and dangerous work." As the regiment took to the field, they continued to acclimate themselves to their new environment and responsibilities.[2]

This first section of letters documents that process of acclimation, as Remmel and his fellow soldiers adjust to the rigors and demands of daily life in the Union army. In these letters the reader meets a young man whose views and experiences often typify the new Northern recruit. Like most immigrants he places a great deal of importance on family and community connections and individual work ethic, seeing those factors as the most significant influences in upward mobility and success in any endeavor. Like all young recruits, he is new to everything about the army but also filled with a spirit of adventure and a naive sense of awe for areas of the nation that he is seeing for the first time. As he and his comrades journey to the seat of war, Remmel is most interested in the lay of the land, the look and type of Southern agriculture, and the people he encounters. Above all, however, he attempts to maintain his presence in the family as a source of stability, guidance, and quiet strength and to assure his family of his contentment with "a soldier's life."[3]

New York
August 31, 1862
My Dear Parents,

You no doubt have been anxious to hear from me. I, therefore, take the present opportunity of addressing you. You will observe from the heading of this letter that I am writing to you from the largest city in America (New York).[4]

We have, dear parents, at last left our old campground at Herkimer and are now on our way for Washington. We started from Herkimer yesterday at one O'clock (P.M.). Many were the tears shed by relatives and friends at our parting and there could be seen, in the faces of all, an expression of deep sorrow at the moment of our departure. While at Herkimer campground, I enjoyed myself finely, yet was very anxious to leave for the seat of war during the whole time and finally that wish has been gratified.

While in camp we fared well. The board being of the best kind, although there was some complaining among some of the boys; yet, as far as my judgment would allow me to decide, I should say that we had good living. The drill was not very hard—there being no regular hours for drill, which, of course, will be different after we arrive at Washington. The only difficulty while there was the extreme heat of the weather, which effected the men very much. I witnessed several fainting while on drill, yet I was not in the least effected; yet, I know not how soon this may occur. Standing quiet in the scorching sun is different from laboring under such an exposure.

The ride from the campground here has indeed been a pleasant one to me. When we took our leave of Herkimer, hundreds of people greeted us. After a ride of 7 miles the cars arrived us safely at Little Falls. There the people could be numbered by almost thousands, the railroad being completely lined with men, women, and children. This being the only place along the route where I am acquainted, I cast a sharp look about me in quest of friends; and, as fortune would have it, I saw several; and among the number, saw George K. Rogers. I hailed him immediately and, having a check of $45 in my pocket which I wished to send to you, gave it to him, which he will give to you as soon as convenient. I also sent, by Mr. Kimble last Thursday, $50 and 2 Ambrotypes. The Ambrotypes you can send about as you wish, please let Louisa have 1 or 2. Mr. Kimble has, of course, paid you before now.[5]

At about 5 O'clock yesterday we arrived at Albany, where we took supper. From Albany we took the steamboat for New York, starting at 9 O'clock and arrived in New York at 8 O'clock in the morning. The ride from the latter place was a very fine one indeed; it reminded me of the time we crossed the Ocean. After remaining on board the boat about 2 hours we were ordered to march to the city barracks, which we did quickly and at this place we are now situated. We are ordered to start from here early tomorrow morning. The soldiers are all feeling well and anxious to start for Washington. I myself am feeling well and anxious to go and whip the rebels. I must now, dear parents, close this letter and wait till a more convenient time for writing another, which will be very soon.

We receive our guns in the morning and also our cooking utensils. So goodbye, you will hear from soon.

From your son,
Wm. Remmel

September 7, 1862
Dear Parents,

Today (Sunday) is one of great expectation and anxiety. We arrived at our camping ground near Washington and today we are ordered off to battle. The enemy have crossed in great numbers on the Potomac and there is a great battle expected. We may not have to fight, yet there is every possibility that we will. We shall start immediately. We hope that we will come out safe.[6]

I can write no more at present. Goodbye.

Your son,
Wm. Remmel

Get someone to read this for you.

State of Maryland,
September the 14th, 1862
Dear Parents,

You probably have had some anxiety about me since last I wrote you, for I told you that we were expecting a battle and that we should be engaged. And I will now say that we have not been in any battle yet, but are liable to be called into action at any moment.

We have been marching since last Sunday everyday, making heavy marches each day, which sometimes nearly exhausts our strength; and today (Sunday), we have been marching all the morning with the expectation of meeting the enemy. We came in sight of their lines shortly after noon today. We expected a fight immediately, but we [have] not yet gone into action.

While I am writing, the balls are whistling continually over my head and striking in an opposite field. We are lying at the bottom of a hill where the enemy cannot see us, so they will not fire upon us. We have a very heavy force, and think that there can be no doubt but we shall whip them yet.[7]

It is now night and probably we shall not go into the battlefield till morning. It is almost dark, and cannot write much more. I like a soldier's life as well as I expected. It is very hard and dangerous work, yet I think that I can stand it and have high hopes for coming out safe.

My last letter that I wrote you I gave to a Negro in Washington to mail for me, I not having time to do it myself when we were marching through there. I do not know whether he did the errand or not. If you did receive it, you, of course, saw that it was very poorly written and but little news. This I could not help, for I had no more than 5 minutes to write it.

You, of course, wish to know all the particulars. I have been in good health and fine spirits since I started from Herkimer, not having been sick a moment. We have to live principally on crackers and pork with a dish of coffee, with which we can make out a good meal. We have been able to buy things that we were not furnished with; sometimes going into a cornfield, taking a little corn and make a soup or stir some apples for sauce. When we started from Fort Lincoln on our march, we were ordered to leave our knapsacks at the fort, which we did, and it has deprived us of a great many comforts. We have since had to sleep out nights under our blankets, which sometimes has been very cold, for nights here are very cold; yet the days are very warm, which makes it very uncomfortable. Our luggage is very heavy that we have to carry, which makes it hard marching. We are now near Harper's Ferry, within 6 miles of the city and probably by tomorrow night we will be near the city if our army has good success.[8]

[*Unsigned*]

Near Williamsburg, Maryland
September the 22nd, 1862
My Dear Parents,

Your very kind and paternal letter was received last evening, and I was very glad to hear from you. The letter was read to me by one of the men in the company who is a German. I could understand all that you wrote to me. And I hope that hereafter you will do the greater part of your writing yourselves, which will, of course, be read for you just as well for me. Write as plain as possible, so it can be easily read and I will understand it better. [Next sentence illegible.] I am very happy to hear that all are well and hope that you will continue to be so.

You say Augustus is on a visit to William. Hope that he will have a pleasant time. Suppose Caleb is in the woods to work yet. Hope that he is well and will be careful not to meet with any accidents. Harmon, I suppose, is the principle man at home and Ada the lady. They will, of course, both be soon to school this winter. Give them all the chance that you can and they will both, no doubt, improve their time and be children you can be proud of. As for Louisa, I trust that she is well, also William. I have not heard from her yet, but hope to soon. I shall write her as often as I can.[9]

In reference to the boots, which you spoke of, I will say that I shall be very happy to have you send me a pair by Alphonso Casler when he comes. I hope you will have a good pair made with heels and long legs, the size will be 9's and have them wide at the bottom. I will leave for another time to writing the particulars.[10]

As for myself, must say that I am well. I have not been sick a day since we have come in camp, which is one great blessing to a soldier. Health is the most important blessing, without it a man *cannot* get along in the army. This I know from observation. A great many men in our own regiment are very unhealthy and most of them brought to that condition by being sick at home; and, for a sprinkle of advice, would say that no one except strong and healthy men ought to enlist to serve as soldiers.

Since last I wrote you, nothing any great importance has transpired in camp. You, no doubt, have had much anxiety upon your mind since last I wrote you; as well you might, for then I told you a battle was expected every day and that we were liable to be called into action. So I thought, and think yet, although some very heavy battles have been fought within our immediate vicinity. There will be more before the week closes and very heavy ones too.

The battle which I spoke of in my letter was fought in Hampton Gap, of which you probably have read. The commander was General Slocum, who is our division general. The battle was very short, but very heavy while it continued. We were lying within 2 miles of the field at the time. On that same day another great battle was fought at South Mountain, which was a complete victory to our side, though the slaughter was very great.[11]

From Monday till Friday noon we were encamped in Hampton Gap. Here we enjoyed considerable rest after heavy marching all the week. We also fared pretty well. Which, not from the Quartermaster's stores, however, but from the rich planters, which lives here in great luxury, although most of the things we obtained we bought. You may think this all foolish to spend money in this way, thinking, of course, that the government furnishes us food good enough and aplenty. Well, I must say that they furnish us enough of such as it is, sea crackers and pork and coffee, but of this soldiers will becomes tired after a while, when it is eat[en] weeks in succession. And so it is with us; whenever we have an opportunity, we buy something to gratify our hunger; and in this way many soldiers spend their money, for which they ought not to be censured. I myself have spent nearly $10 dollars for provision, which I consider perfectly right.

When at Fort Lincoln, we had tents, but since then we have had none. When we left there, we left our knapsacks and all that we could get along without, thinking that we would receive them soon, but we have not seen anything of them since and probably will not. This deprived me of a rubber blanket, rubber leggings, and all the little necessities, which I needed in mending my clothing. Since then we have had a blanket for a covering, which makes it rather unpleasant sometimes. Last night we marched from 12 O'clock till 7 in the morning, which has been the worst of our night marching. You may believe that it was a sleepy march. It reminded me of the time when I worked to Burrell's; used to walk there and back. The reason of our marching in the night was because a battle was expected this morning, but the enemy crossed the river. The battle of last Wednesday was terrible one. The loss of life was immense, yet the loss for the enemy was much greater than our side. On the whole, it was a complete victory and hope that it maybe followed by others. The 34th, in this battle, suffered severely and many poor fellow breathed his last in that engagement. We will probably tomorrow cross the Potomac and make Virginia the battleground once more. This is not generally liked by the soldiers who have fought there.[12]

You may think me rather shiftless, my scribbling such a dirty letter. I can do no better. We have to carry our paper with us and not possible to keep it clean. Next time, I will try and write upon clean paper. I also have to write with a lead pencil, having no chance to get pen and ink. I can write no more at present; besides, I have given you all the news which would be of interest to you. I hope that Alphonzo Casler will be able to come and join us soon. Give him my best wishes and all the other boys.

I will now close this lengthy letter and hope that it will be interesting to you. Please write as soon as you can. So goodbye dear parents.

From your son,
Wm. Remmel

Camp near Bakersville, Maryland
October the 8th, 1862
My Dear Parents,

I now take my pen and paper to write you another short letter. I intended to have written you a few days before, but have delayed it until now. And I trust that this letter will be welcomed by all of you.

You will, of course, first wish to know whether I am well and whether I have been in any battle since last I wrote you. I am happy to say first that I am enjoying excellent health, and have been since I have been in the South. I have not yet been in any engagement, and have met with no bad luck. I believe that in my last letter I wrote you that our regiment had been very near several battles, and so it has, but we have been fortunate enough not to be called in. At the time that the battle of Wednesday near Sharpsburg was fought, our regiment was lying about six miles [from] there in a mountain. The place where we were is called Crampton Gap, where a few days before a battle was fought by General Slocum, which I wrote to you about at the time it took place.[13]

We have, for the last two weeks, been encamped about 2 miles from the Potomac River and about 16 miles from Sharpsburg. We are very pleasantly situated here and should like to stay here some time; but probably in this I will be disappointed, for I think the army will move from here into Virginia before long. We have, up to the present time, lived without tents. But today we have received them and we are happy enough too, for before this we have had to take rails, or anything else, to make shelters of to protect us from the weather. And sometimes we have had to sleep out with a blanket for a covering; but these things have passed over, and I feel none the worse over it.[14]

The weather here at present is very pleasant, though rather warm at times, sometimes very uncomfortable. The weather here is much different from yours at home, it is much more steady weather. Since we have been here, we have not seen one day when it has rained during the whole time, and not more than two or three times have we been wet at all. The nights have been very cold here and we have, for the past 2 weeks, observed frost upon the ground early in the morning.

The people here have harvested most of their grain. They have just cut their own corn. The corn here is different from that at home. It is the large Ohio corn and will not ripen as quick. Apples are very plenty here and the boys buy a great many of them. We have also bought many peaches.

Our living here at present is composed of the following things: 1st sea crackers, 2nd pork, 3rd coffee, 4th sugar and 5th fresh beef twice a week. When we want anything else, we have to buy of either of a farmer or a sutler. But we have found that it will not answer to buy much, or we will have no money. I have got but $5 out of $17 left now, so you see it costs me something to live.

Yesterday and the day before, we were out on the picket along the Potomac. We saw several rebs across the river picketing, but they did not shoot at us so we did not fire on them. We had a very fine time and met with no accidents. Last night we went over to the river and caught a lot of fish, and this morning we had a very fine breakfast. Today we came back to our camping ground.

One word about the regiment; there are at present a great many sick. Out of 1146 men, officers included, that started from Camp Schuyler, there are only about 800 men fit for duty. About 250 men are sick out of that number; but one has died. So you see that soldiers are more liable to die of sickness than on the battlefield. The boys, most of them, are pretty fine fellows, though some of them are pretty tough.[15]

You probably would like to know something of the 34th reg. Some of the boys were over here the other day. I was away and did not see them. Those that saw them said they were feeling well. None, I believe, from our neighborhood were killed in the last battle. I saw Captain Thompson a few days since, from the 97th. He was well and looked very healthy, and he is very fleshy. He has been in several battles, but has not been hurt yet.[16]

Alphonzo Casler has not arrived here yet. I expect to see him soon and hope that he will bring the boots along. I received a letter from Louisa a few days since. I think she is well. I also received one from Anna Tuesday. She is enjoying herself. I hope this letter will find you all well and hope that Augustus' eyes will get better soon. Suppose Caleb is in the woods yet. Suppose he will go to school this winter. Harmon and Ada, I hope, are well. I will try to write them all. I will now close my letter, hoping that I shall hear from you soon. Write German. I can get it read for me. Goodbye for the present.[17]

From your obedient son,
William Remmel

Camp near Bakersville, Maryland
October the 20th, 1862
Dear Brother Augustus,

I am very sorry to think that I have not written you before and you have been very much disappointed, no doubt, in not receiving any news from me; but I will endeavor to do better in the future. Only excuse me this time. You probably have heard from me as often as Father has received a letter from me, and probably read them all.

Father's letter dated October the 3rd has but just been received. It must have been delayed on the road, for it takes only four days for letter to arrive here in camp. I was very happy to hear that you were all well, but am sorry to know that your eyes have been troubling you so badly of late. I hope you will get help soon, that they (eyes) may get well. Be careful of your health and not expose yourself more than is necessary, for exposure to the weather is very bad.

You probably would like to hear how I am getting along, and whether we have seen any fighting yet. As for myself, am happy to inform you that I am well and getting on as well as could be expected in my present circumstance. I have not yet seen a sick day, though have been very much exposed to the weather. We have as yet seen no fighting and we have great doubts about seeing the rebs this fall. We expect to go into winter quarters before long and commence fighting again in the spring. Nothing of importance has transpired since I wrote Father last.

We are at present situated about 10 miles from Hagerstown, which is our nearest advance station and about 2 miles from the Potomac River. We have received our tents and are quite comfortably sheltered. Our knapsacks, which were left at Fort Lincoln, have just come and we will soon be prepared for winter. And this is very necessary, for I have found that we shall have to go farther south than Maryland to escape the cold weather. For even now the nights are so cool that we have to bundle on all that we have to keep warm.

Our regiment is at present very much reduced from sickness. Not over 700 men can now be brought out to drill. Most of the boys from our way are now in good health, except about five. Allan Jennings has been sick some time, and has been in hospital, but is now slowly recovering. With proper nursing he will soon get well. His people need not worry about him. Charley Tomkins is also sick and has been dangerous, but is recovering. All the other boys, I believe, are well. Jake Pram, who lived near the South schoolhouse, shot himself in the hand about 2 weeks ago while the regiment was out on picket. His hand had to be taken off. He will soon return home.[18]

About one week ago I had the pleasure of seeing Alphonzo Casler, who had just come from home. The boys that saw him were all happy to meet him and a hearty good shake we had too. He told us that he had been on the road about 3 weeks in search of the regiment, until he at last found us. He is well and was glad to see us.

Since I have been here I have seen several of the boys out of the 97th regiment. Captain Thompson has been here too and, since he is the same old boy, he looks healthy and is very fleshy. He has seen some pretty hard times, but has come out without a scratch every time. Our old friend and clown, Austin, has been here to see us. It would have done you good to have seen him. He looked natural as day and to all appearances he was the same Austin that used to entertain us so highly winter evenings in dancing and telling yarns, for which he was well cut out. He wore a hat, which was about as big as a Hoghead. I wish you could see him. I have seen more of the boys of the 34th, but am told that those who yet remain are well. Many, I believe, killed in the last great battle. Do you know whether John McDougal is safe?[19]

Please write me in your letter. Yesterday I received a letter from Louisa. She writes that all are pretty smart; but William, who has been quite ill, is recovering. As there is nothing more of importance, I will now close. You must write soon. Please address your letter as follows:

Washington, D.C.
121st Regiment New York Volunteers
In care of Capt. Kidder[20]
Company I

From your brother,
William Remmel

Goodbye. Give my love to our people.

Camp near Bakersville, Maryland
October the 26th, 1862
My Dear Parents,

Your very kind letter has been timely received and I was glad to hear from you, and much happier to know that you are all well. I am, as heretofore, well and enjoying myself.

We are still encamped on our old ground and know not how long we may stay here. It is generally thought that we will soon go into winter quarters. Yet this will depend on the weather. If the weather should continue warm and pleasant, the army may make a forward movement again. Should it, however, prove the contrary, we will have to prepare for winter.[21]

The weather for the past few weeks has been very cold, especially at nights. We have had several heavy frosts and some very cold winds, which has made it very unpleasant for us soldiers, especially those who were unprovided with clothing in sufficient amount. But I am happy to know that a good share of the army has been newly clothed and have no occasion to complain.

In my letter to Augustus I wrote that our knapsacks with our clothing, that which were left at Fort Lincoln, had arrived and that they would be safe, but in this some of us have been disappointed and I among that number. My knapsack has been either lost or someone else has taken it. It contained everything I brought from home and half the clothing which the government furnished us, besides a rubber blanket, leggings, and oil cloth for cap. The private property I will have to lose, but that of the government they are responsible for. Today I drew an overcoat, knapsack, and shirt. The deficient articles I will soon receive.

The general appearance of things here at present is that of desolation and ruin, and this is becoming every day more apparent. Farms, which one month ago were in a high state of culture, are now to be seen without a sign of cultivation, cut up everywhere with rails and paths and fences almost entirely burned for firewood. But such are the effects of war. Destruction follows in every form.

The boys from our neighborhood are, most of them, enjoying good health and show no signs of discontent. Alphonzo Casler is well and takes a great interest in our drills. I regret that he is not in the same company with me, yet we have ample opportunity for chatting together everyday and this privilege is improved. Albert Jennings, Merton Tanner, Norman Goodwin, Nathan Wood, and a host of others from our vicinity are all well. Charley Jenkins and Allan Jennings, who have been sick so long, are still confined to the hospital and recover but little. Allan came over to camp yesterday, but soon returned. He looks very weak and haggard. He told me that he got no better and would not until he received better nursing; and this, I fear, is so true with most of the sick. They are much neglected.[22]

Our hospitals are composed of barns and old worn out log huts, deserted by even Negro families. But our Colonel appears to be a humane man and I understand that he is a going to remove the invalids of our regiment to a brick church not far off and have them at last comfortably sheltered, if not medically treated. Our regiment is very much reduced from sickness. The companies can hardly muster fifty men for duty.[23]

In your last two letters you wished to know whether you should send the boots, which I desired to have made, and also many little necessities which you mention. I must say that I should be very glad to have the boots and other things you have prepared for me, for I need them, but I think it is unsafe to send them now for fear they might be lost. But wait a few weeks until our quarters are established for the winter. Then our address can be depended on and everything come safe. Have patience, I am not suffering, and get the things ready and I will write you when I want them. Please excuse this miserable writing this time. I will now close, hoping that this letter will find you all well.

Goodbye.
From your humble and obedient son,
William Remmel

Camp near White Plains, Virginia
November the 8th, 1862
Dear Parents,

Augustus' kind letter was received about one week ago; was glad to hear from him and also glad to hear that you were all well. I would like to have written him before, but I have been unable to do so in consequence of our marching. We have been on the move since last week Thursday and not one day since that time have we laid still in camp, and it is almost a miracle that we are not on the go today; but the reason why, I suppose, have been occasioned by a severe hailstorm, which set in early this morning and has continued up to the time that I am writing. But it is rumored in camp that we start again today, but the truth of this I doubt and hope that I may see this impression confirmed.[24]

I am as usual in good health, though have been in the possession of a sure cold for the last week, which also not as yet loosens its hoarseness. With this exception I am well as ever, which you know cannot be excelled, and I am thankful enough that I am blessed with good lungs and strong constitution; were I not, I am afeared that I could not endure the hardships to which I have been exposed. The weather has been favorable for our marches, thus far, and hope that it may once more clear up and be pleasant again.

You will observe from the heading of this letter that we are no longer in Maryland, among a good number of loyalists, but in Virginia, almost in the very heart of rebellion, where hardly one in a hundred is a Union man. But I think that with the immense force that we are bringing to bear against the confederacy we can soon bring them back under the old stars and stripes. There is a united movement on foot. The whole peninsula army is on the move and undoubtedly a long and heavy battle will take place somewhere in this state and, if rightly managed, will I think be the deciding blow of the present campaign.[25]

While we were in Maryland we were all greatly disgusted by some of the orders which were issued in regard to protecting the property of the inhabitants. Which were that each (planter) should have his property guarded and any soldiers who, without permit, took anything from planters—whether Union or secesh—should be punished accordingly. But since we crossed the river this law has not been strictly enforced. Though some of the prominent houses and farms are even now guarded, yet the officers are more indulging.

We have, since we have been in this state, been quite free with the four and two legged property of the Rebs and, had you been here some of the nights this week, you might have seen, between dusk and daylight, animals from the size of two year old heifers down to fowls as small as hens coming in camp by scores. I, of course, have been perfectly innocent of such mischief, having helped to bring in only one yearling heifer and a respectable fat sheep and hope next time to capture a good fat hog. This is, I believe, the true way of prosecuting this war. We have been protecting rebel property too long. We must show our enemies that we can destroy as well as they.

The boys that are now with us are all able to do good marching. Those that were sick and ailing have been left behind in the hospitals. There are, at present, 53 effective men in our company out of 77 that started with us. All the commissioned officers are absent, Captain and Lieutenants. The Captain and one Lieutenant are sick and the other one has been promoted to aide on general's staff. Alphonzo Casler is well and says that he is agoing to write home.[26]

I had the pleasure, a few days since, of shaking hands with DeLoss Perkins. He is the same old boy. He looked rugged and healthy and no doubt has experienced hard times.[27]

You, no doubt, would like to know something about whether I desire to have those things sent to me. There is but one thing that I would like to have you send me. That is a pair of gloves. I should like it if you can send the same. I wish you would do so. If father measure them on his own hands, I think that they will fit me. Do them up snugly in the form of a letter. The boots you may keep for me till I send for them. Send the gloves the same that you would a letter, with the same direction. Let the gloves be lined and have long wristlings. There are many Germans in our regiment who I can get to read letters for me. Please write often. I must now close.

Good bye from your son,
Wm. R

Camp near Warrenton, Virginia
November the 15th, 1862
Dear Parents,

As it has been some little time since last I wrote you, I improve the present opportunity by addressing you. I am well as ever, and enjoying myself as well as

I can. We have marched but little since last I wrote you. One day, I believe, has been all the marching that we have done within the past week, which was last Sabbath. Sunday's we are sure to march and we have become so accustomed to it that Sunday is thought to be more of a laboring day than any other in the week. Preaching with us seems more like a Christmas holiday than like an everyday affair. There has been but 2 sermons preached in the regiment since we have been out here and those were more like lectures than sermons.

I have had the pleasure of meeting several of my old friends within the past few days. The night before crossing the Potomac, while walking about over our camping ground, who should I meet but DeLoss Perkins. He was riding his horse and just about to leave for his camp when I hailed him. We were both greatly surprised at seeing each other after so long a time. After holding an interesting conversation for some time he departed for his quarter. He is in good health and likes soldiering.

This week I have had several calls from boys in the 34th and 97th regiments and among them were John McDougal and Moses Bliss. They were both well and were glad to see me. John said that he had seen some pretty hard times and came several times near being killed, that his comrade had been killed by his side; yet, amid all the dangers, he has come out without a scratch. He hopes that in the spring he may be able to go home with his regiment, which will then be discharged. There are about 300 in his regiment, which shows how severely they have suffered. Moses Bliss came five miles to see me. He is at present quite well, but looks very poor. He has been sick several times since he left home. He says that John Satterly is in the hospital, but that his father is coming after him. Moses, like all others, is anxious that this war maybe closed so as to be able to return home again.[28]

The weather here at present is very pleasant, something like September weather at home. We have seen but little rainy weather yet. Last week Thursday was the stormiest day that we have seen, it commenced raining in the morning and continued until night. The snow melted nearly as fast as it came, so that the next day it all disappeared, yet it was very disagreeable to us. We were not prepared for it and consequently suffered much from the cold.

While in Maryland we had aplenty of money and lived pretty well, but since crossing the river we have not fared quite so well. Our pockets have become empty and we have been unable to buy anything to satisfy our hungry stomachs, so we have to take up with government fare, which is pork and hard crackers with an occasional piece of fresh beef. But the paymaster will be here soon and then we will be all right again. You need look for but little money at home if I receive no more than thirteen dollars, for I shall need it all. If, however, I receive more you may look for some.

In my last letter I spoke of having you send me a pair of gloves. If you did not receive it, I will mention it again. The weather will soon be cold and then I shall want something warm on my hands. I could buy a pair here, but they would cost too much. You can buy a good pair at home for 10 or 12 cents that would cost $3 here. Many of the boys have sent for them and some have already arrived. Besides the gloves send me some postage stamps and also a few needles and some thread, for we cannot procure these things very well. If you send a pair of new boots father and you can wear mine. Put them in, for I know not when we shall stop marching. It will not be safe to send for them until we get into winter quarters, which will not be very soon. As I am writing, orders have arrived at headquarters that we must prepare to march again tomorrow, which order has been expected all the week. As I said before, Sundays we are always marching and I think it will soon change to fighting. I would like sometimes to write to Harmon and Ada and I suppose Caleb would be glad to hear from me, but I am unable to do so for I can hardly procure paper and stamps enough to write to many others that write to me. I hope that Ada and the boys are well. How are Augustus' eyes getting along? Are they getting better? He must take more care not to take cold, or he may lose them.

There is nothing more that I could write worthy of note. We expect that in the next battle you will hear of the 121st regiment being engaged. The regiment, at present, is under the following commanders: Corps, General Franklin; Division, General Brooks; Brigade, General Bartlett. I will now close this letter, hoping that these ill-written lines will find you all well. Let Augustus, or someone else, read this for you.[29]

From your son,
Wm. Remmel

Camp near Stafford Courthouse, Virginia
November the 29th, 1862
My Dear Sister [Louisa],[30]

Your kind letter of the 20th instant has been timely received and its perusal afforded me much pleasure. I had long desired to hear once more from you, a sister who is so affectionate, so kind, and so anxious to look after the welfare of her brother now living and serving in the Army of the U.S. It is indeed a consolation and a joy to me to know that I have left relatives and friends behind who can sympathize for me, while enduring the many trials and hardships to which a soldier must necessarily be exposed while leading such a life.

I have been quite anxious of late to know how our people were, not having heard from home in nearly a month. Judging from your statement, of letters to me and received by you, many letters have been lost on the road and gone to the dead letter office at Washington. I am glad to know that our people are all well and that things are generally going on right. As you did not speak of your own health, I trust that it is better than when I last heard from you. William, of course, is well and [so are] the friends at Ephratah. Annie's letter to me I think has been miscarried, for I have received but one letter from her. I have also received none from William, which is strange to me for I have written twice of late. Please remind him of me and I doubt not that he will write. I cannot hear too often, for you cannot imagine how deeply a letter is appreciated by a soldier. It is a consolation and a comfort to hear from those that are dear to us.[31]

I am, as usual, enjoying the same good health. I have not been one sick day in the Army yet and trust that this blessing will long remain unimpaired.

I am very sorry that father has sent me a box of articles of so great variety and value as you spoke of; they have not been received by me, which, of course, could not be expected. They consequently have been left at Washington in the express office and from there will have to be ordered on by me. I hardly know how to manage about it, but will do something soon. May have to wait some time before anything can be done of any use. Am glad to think that father is going to send a pair of gloves. I need them much. Woolen ones will do just as well as leather ones.

We are at present lying in a barren country, where very little cultivation can be seen. The country is almost destitute of any kind of sustenance. 2/3 of the land here is covered with forest and it is now and then only that a cultivated field can be observed. The people are almost in a starving condition, especially the poorer class, for the husbands have been either forced or gone voluntarily into the Confederate army. The wealthier class have wisely moved their families to Richmond or elsewhere, where they are properly cared for.

It has often grieved me sadly while out foraging to see the unpleasant condition in which the people are here placed. Although their sentiment is contrary to ours in most instances, yet this would naturally be so. I often witnessed soldiers immediately after forming new encampments, directly after a march when very hungry, go into houses and take everything in line of edibles that could be found—if having to take it out of children's mouths. Hogs and chickens killed before the owner's eyes, without any interrogations.

Our quarters here are only temporary and it is rumored in camp that we are under marching orders. For the last week we have been drilling continually, hardly having time to cook our food. Our new Colonel, who is a regular officer, will make the 121st a very efficient regiment if only he has a chance. The only thing with which the boys are discontented is the living, not because of the small variety, but of the small rations. Many do not have enough without buying or trading in some manner. I think that home living will be better appreciated by all, should they return to their homes again.[32]

The boys from our place are well. Alphonzo Casler is well and in *good* spirit. I saw John McDougal and Moses Bliss while staying at our last encampment. They were both well. They are anxious to return home again.

Had it not been for the postage stamp you sent me, I could not have written this letter. Please send them. Place two or three in the letter and also speak to our folks (please) about it. We have not been paid off yet, and I have not one penny in money. As there is nothing more of either interest or importance, I will close hoping that this will reach you safely and find our people all well.

From your brother,
Wm. Remmel

Camp near Fredericksburg, Virginia
December the 18th, 1862
Dear Brother William,[33]

Your interesting letter of the 8th instant has been received by me and I improve the present opportunity of writing you a short letter, to give you some idea of my whereabouts and a few facts which will be of interest to you. First, will say that those gloves which you sent me were received the same evening that your letter to me [arrived]. I cannot say enough to you for the kindness you have shown, and trouble and expense you have been to, in procuring and sending on such a beautiful and well finished pair of gloves. They are excellent and a more desirable fit could not have been made. They will be carefully used and, if possible, bring them back home with me.

For the past few days you probably have felt considerably anxious about me. For, according to newspaper correspondents, a great battle has been impending for sometime past and one in which the whole Potomac Army would be engaged, which would of course include our Corps commanded by Gen. Smith, which forms a part of the Left Grand Division under Franklin. Therefore, as a matter of course, the 121st regiment would have to take its chance with many others of engaging the enemy.

Those plans which Burnside had fully matured for annihilating the rebel army near Fredericksburg have been, I think, in part defeated by the strategy of the able reb generals, which I think last Saturday's fight will go far to prove.

For it was, without doubt, a decisive victory for the rebs. Our loss must have exceeded theirs by several thousand.[34]

Our regiment, luckily, was not called into action. Yet we were, during the engagement and the remaining part of the time that our division was across the river, on the further picket line on our side; which, of course, gave us a fine view of the battle. We were none of the time more than one mile from the conflict on the left and at one time much nearer. Our position was mainly between the left and right of the left wing, so that we were between two fires of our troops. Although we did no fighting, yet we lost 4 men killed and 3 wounded from the enemies shells and sharpshooters' bullets. Our boys manifested great coolness while in so exposed a condition. I have not a doubt but, had we been called into action, we would have discharged our duty honorably.[35]

The retrograde movement across the river unquestionably saved our whole division from annihilation, or an unconditional surrender. The retreat was made last Monday night between 12 O'clock and daylight which, of course, completely surprised the rebs for every move was made with a death like stillness.[36]

The slaughtering on our side was awful. Regiments that had, heretofore, suffered but little were in several instances almost wholly destroyed. Defeat after defeat seems to follow our Army and unless our generals make better moves in the future the Confederacy, in my opinion, will be recognized by foreign powers ere another six months roll around.[37]

I am, at present, in good health and the regiment, generally speaking, is fast recruiting from the crippled condition it was in one month ago. No more at present. Give my love to all our people and request them, at my wish, to write to me.

From your faithful brother,
Wm. Remmel

Camp near White Oak Church, Virginia
December the 31st, 1862[38]
My Dear Parents,

Your kind letter was received this afternoon and, as our regiment is ordered on picket for 2 days, I thought I would write you this evening. I am still in good health, which thus far has been one of my greatest blessings.

Our regiment is at present encamped about 5 miles from Fredericksburg, near a place called White Oak Church, where our brigade has since laid. Nothing of importance has transpired about here since last I wrote you. A shot from the artillery may be heard now and then to break the stillness, nothing new.

It is rumored in camp that the enemy have been trying to cross the Rappahannock, but have not as yet succeeded. And also the rebels are making their appearance near Harper's Ferry again. I trust that this latter rumor may not be true for, at present, we have enough in front to tend to without looking in our rear.

The weather here at present is delightful. It is one continual sunshine and starlight. Our days are warm and pleasant, much like September weather in [New] York State. Consequently, the roads are dry and hard, making it easy to supply the troops with abundant rations.

We fare very well at present, for we have had quite a variety of articles for food. Within the last 10 days we have drawn potatoes twice and rice and beans twice, which we think here is quite extravagant living within so short a space of time. For during the 4 months before that we drew but 2 rations of potatoes, so that when we saw them again we hardly knew what use could be made of them. Some had almost forgotten how they looked, but I for one can say that it did not puzzle me long to know what they were, whither I had quite forgotten their good qualities. I had lived too long in Stratford to be thus deceived.

Our regiment at present is very greatly reduced by sickness, and many of our brave and noble boys are fast going to their long homes. Within the last week no less than six or seven have died and many are now in the hospital. Albert Jennings is very sick and is in our regimental hospital. I hope that he will soon recover, but unless he has good care I am afraid it will be a lingering sickness and, perhaps, finally result in death. Alphonzo is well, as usual, and plays his part of the soldier well. I think that he is quite contented and enjoys himself as well as any of us; yet you may be assured that even that is not so very great joy, for there is not a soldier in the regiment but what is tired of this business.[39]

The dollar, which you sent me, came safe and it was very acceptable to me just at present, for I have been without money some little time. You said if we were not paid very soon I should write you, you would forward 5 dollars more. We probably will not be paid off until about the middle of January, which is about 2 weeks, when we will receive 4 months pay. Therefore, I would like to have you send me 2 dollars more, if you can conveniently, in your next letter, which will be enough until we are paid off. I want to buy some little articles, which I need. Do not send more than $2.

If we are paid for 4 months I think of sending you a check of 25 or 30 dollars, perhaps more, for I find that it is not necessary to live on one's own funds. For we would all be better off to confine ourselves to government food. Yet it is necessary to always have some money to buy butter, syrup, or other little dainties which we do not have. I am glad that you have been wise enough to order that box of provision and other articles therein back home again. For I think that it would have been very unsafe to have tried to order them to our regiment at present and you may yet have an opportunity of sending it on, but be sure not to do this until you know it will reach me. Should we get into permanent winter quarters I will send for it, not before, and then I will tell you what to send.

I will now close my letter, hoping that these lines will find you all well. I trust that Caleb will soon be well again. Tell the boys that they may look for a letter from me in a few days and have Ada send me one of her used knives. Farewell for the present.

Your affectionate son,
Wm. Remmel

2

1863
"Like Grass before the Scythe"

Through the spring of 1863, William Remmel's first nine months of service consisted primarily of camp activities, drill, review, marches, and fatigue duty, as well as periodic conversations with friends in some of the more seasoned regiments. Even these limited experiences, however, produced a subtle but perceptible change in his correspondence, as his letters gradually illustrate the process of maturation undertaken by a relatively new recruit. With the start of the 1863 campaign season Remmel and his comrades took an active role in battle for the first time, at Salem Church, Virginia, during the Chancellorsville campaign, marking the completion of their transition from recruits to experienced soldiers. The "anguish and sorrow" of this experience quickly became apparent to Remmel, particularly after the death of his close friend Alphonzo Casler.[1]

The most obvious symbol of Remmel's development as a soldier also occurred at this time when he earned promotion to sergeant in April 1863. As Remmel's military experience increased, so did his expression of personal opinions about such issues as the need for a military draft, the morale of the troops, the varying abilities of his successive commanders, and the need for hard measures "to blighten the hopes" of the Confederates. By the end of the year Remmel spoke with the voice of a weathered, but still committed, soldier of the Union.[2]

Despite the distance from home and the dangers inherent to the life of a soldier, Remmel continued to write regularly and always expressed great interest in the education and employment of his siblings, especially the two youngest—Harmon and Ada. In this manner, despite the distance, he exercised a considerable influence over his family. By emphasizing such values as sacrifice, hard work, and the necessity of gaining an education, he helped instill in those younger siblings a strong sense of patriotism and ambition that lasted well beyond his own life. In doing so, Remmel and other soldiers like him helped to reinforce a developing national ideology and culture that served as a foundation for tremendous prosperity and stability in the postwar era. With his attentions thus focused simultaneously on his duties in the field and his responsibilities at home, Remmel continued to typify the Union soldier in the middle years of the war.

Camp near White Oak Church, Virginia
January the 5th, 1863
My Dear Brother Augustus,

I am very sorry indeed that I have not written you before and I must confess that I have done very wrong in delaying it so long and, no doubt, you have felt a harshness toward me in consequence. But Augustus I shall have to beg this one more pardon and, I assure you, I will do better in the future. My letters to father and mother were probably all read by you, so that you as well as they know what I have been doing and what places I have visited since my arrival here in Dixie. And I have no reason to believe that they were not read with interest by you and all of the others of our family.

You probably have seen from my statements in one of father's letters that we came near going into battle while across the river (Rappahannock), near Fredericksburg, on the day that the terrible disaster took place when we lost so many men. It was a lucky escape for us for, had we been called into action, the 121st would now be, I am confident, but a shadow of its former greatness.

At the time the battle was fought our regiment was lying in a road running parallel to the enemies breastworks, the latter which were about ¾ of a mile from the place of our encampment, which was not far enough to be entirely safe from the rebs' shells. But directly beyond the road was a little crest running the whole distance of our lines, which in fact sheltered us or at least prevented the rebs from seeing us. Yet withstanding all this, the shells were constantly exploding over our heads or else before or behind us. At the time that these deadly missiles were flying so thickly there was some tall dodging among our boys. It would have done you good could you have stood off at a distance and seen us go through these motions. All that I can compare it to is to behold a lot of chickens drinking water, heads constantly going both ways. So with us, only that our heads instead of going into the bottom of some kind of dish, bowed respectfully to some mud hole or other place for safety and many were the boys that I think had some injured part about them occasioned by these mighty gestures. The battle was, in truth, an awful affair and has, in fierceness of fighting and daring among officers and men, not been equaled in the present campaign. Yet, notwithstanding this boldness and good fighting, we gained nothing and lost much. I trust that the next movement will be carried on by with a different leader, or different management. For such sacrificing of life, all for nothing, this will I know not be endured by the people of the North much longer and ought not to be.[3]

The 34th, I learn, has suffered much from the battle for the regiment was in the hottest of the battle, making several charges on the enemy. The 97th regiment was also in the engagement, but did not suffer much. I saw Captain Thompson after we crossed the river. He visited our camp. He looked well and said he enjoyed the best of health. From him I learned about the 34th. He had at the time been to see the boys. He said that Jack was safe, but quite ill. He went into the fight after coming off a bed of sickness, yet determined to fight the rebs. Andrew Smith was killed. He was hit by a cannon shot and died almost instantly. He was mangled in a horrible manner, the ball taking off both legs and shattering one arm; the latter which was done either before or after the 1st. His people must feel awful about it.[4]

Our regiment at present is encamped near what is called White Oak Church about 5 miles from Fredericksburg. We are pleasantly located in a beautiful piece of woods and have got things arranged very nicely. All that we want now is to receive orders to go into winter quarters, for we have got tired of visiting for at least this fall and will willingly wait until spring before measuring swords and muskets with the enemy. For we think that if we wait until that time the dispute will be settled in a different manner.

There are a great many sick in our regiment and more or less are constantly dying. Hardly half the boys that started with us are here now. Many have died and many more are lying in hospitals. Charley Tomkins has not been with us in a long time. Allan Jennings is very ill in the hospital. Alphonzo Casler is in good health, as is Merton Tanner. As for myself, am in good health. No more for the present. Give my love to our people and all the family. Please write me soon and tell all the news at home Augustus.

[*Unsigned*]

Camp near White Oak Church, Virginia
January the 18th, 1863
My Dear Parents,

Your kind and very interesting letter was received yesterday morning and it afforded me a vast deal of pleasure to hear from home once more and to know that parents, brothers, and sisters were all well. How gladly would I desire to step upon a father's threshold again and kiss the maternal lips of a mother and talk stories to the children—but a wish. Space intervenes between my present habitation and old Salisbury and an oath that is stronger than the distance is great holds me in my place. Therefore, it is no use wishing or thinking of what will not [be] granted. I have sworn to obey the laws of U.S. and serve if need be a certain length of time, and until that time arrives, unless sickness prevents, in no way except through dishonor can I return. Yet I trust and hope that 3 years will not elapse until that hour may come and we shall be gathered at the same table and seek shelter in the same house.

I was glad to hear that Caleb had fully recovered his health and going to school, as I suppose with Harmon and Ada. Augustus, in his last letter, spoke of the school in the village, saying that the teacher this winter was a poor one and thought that the children would learn but little. I am very sorry to hear this, for it is essential to have good instructors in any school, whether it be composed of large or small scholars. Caleb is old enough to know the necessity of an education and I hope that he will improve his time this winter and study diligently, and not take advantage of the teacher's slackness and play mischief. Harmon and Ada will, I think, do best to learn and [I] hope that they will be good children. Augustus, I know, will try to learn if he only has an opportunity, which I hope he may have.

I was very much surprised on hearing that our old friend and neighbor John S. Hyatt had married. Please tell him and his bride that I wish them a great deal of joy and a long and happy life.[5]

You spoke much about the box, which you sent me; that you had been to considerable trouble to try to ascertain where it had been left in order that you might have it returned home, but had been unsuccessful. I am most happy to be able to relieve your anxiety for its safety, prevent any further trouble on your part. Imagine my surprise last Monday when on returning from a brook, where I had been washing, to my tent to find a box directed to me, which had been brought from the commissaries by one of the boys. Quickly did I grab it in my hands, to know it[s] weight, for I knew not but that it might have been opened and everything taken out; but happy to say on opening it found the box full, everything was well packed, and think that they had not been disturbed. The cakes were all spoiled, having come moldy by lying so long on the road. Alphonzo came and got his things, but his cake was also spoiled. I think that everything which you sent came safe. The boots are an excellent fit and think they will do me good service. The stockings are very acceptable. They are much better than government socks. All the other things will be appreciated. You need send me no more articles until I write for them. If some of the neighbors or friends desire to send a box to the boys you can put in a few cakes, if your desire, for now they will come through directly and provision will not spoil. As I said at the beginning of this letter that your letter had come safe, I also acknowledge the receiving of $2, which you so kindly sent me.

Our regiment, the 121st, is still encamped where it was 3 weeks ago. At the time of the fall back at Fredericksburg we moved about six miles from the city into a beautiful oak forest, where we have laid ever since. Since our stay here we have been drilling almost the whole time. Our officers are becoming pretty well acquainted with tactics and the men learn very fast. The boys in our company do not like their Captain very well. I think that he had better go home.[6]

The weather thus far this month has been very fine, but is getting cold now. The boys in the regiment, most of them, have built comfortable log huts with 4 or 5 in a tent. I and 3 other of my camp are tenting together. We have a good time. Our house is made of logs principally. It is about 4 feet high and dug in the ground about a foot. Probably we shall not stay in here long, for I think we shall move in less than one week; probably cross the river *again.* The men do not like this very well and many of them are deserting. 2 nights ago 15 left the regiment and but 3 have returned. They are running away all the while. I would rather stay than go, for it is so very cold. If we go into battle and I come out safe I shall write you immediately. My love to you all.[7]

From your son,
Wm. Remmel

Camp near White Oak Church, Virginia
February the 16th, 1863
My Dear Parents,

Thinking that you would be anxious to hear from me and to know my present whereabouts, I sit me down to write you a short letter.

Our regiment still remains in its old quarters near White Oak Church and there is every prospect of remaining here until the weather becomes settled, which will not be short of 4 or 5 months, for I think that General Hooker will not venture a move until the weather can be depended upon. The weather for the last few days has been of the finest kind, but this morning has commenced raining and the air is quite chilly. It may change to a snowstorm before it is over with. The almost perpetual fine weather so far this winter in this state (Virginia) is said to have been unequaled by any within the recollection of the oldest inhabitants. We have had but one snow storm of any account this winter, but the snow only remained one day, when the ground was again bare and the sun again shedding its genial warming rays over the whole landscape.[8]

The most of importance that I have to write you is that our regiment has just been paid off. Yesterday morning the Paymaster made his appearance at the Colonel's headquarters and in a short time the Captains secured orders to march their companies in order to headquarters to acquire pay. Nothing ever rejoiced our boys so much since enlisting in the service as did the sound of that one word, pay. For we had labored for nearly six months for U.S., suffering from hardships of all kind and entering near privation, without receiving the least compensation. Many men in the regiment were very much discouraged from not receiving pay, for their families are in an almost destitute condition at home, and many more have deserted from this account. But, now that we have been paid, the men will again be contented and willing to remain. We drew from the first of January, but before leaving Camp Schuyler we were paid 1 month's pay in advance. I drew $40.33. This was the amount due me up to the mentioned time (January), reckoning from the 22nd of September, which was just one month after I enlisted.[9]

I intend to send you $25. $5 of which I enclose in this letter and the remaining $20 I have given to Capt. Galpin, of Co. A, who is going to send home the whole amount of money that his company desire to send to their relatives and by procuring a draft for the whole amount endorsed by the Paymaster, and sending it to his brother at Little Falls, who will draw the money at the bank and distribute it to those who have been designated by the men to draw the same amount. As Capt. Galpin is a gentleman, as well as a soldier, I thought it would be a good opportunity to send the amount I desired to let you have in this draft. I found, upon inquiry, that he was willing to assist anyone who would make application to him. I, therefore, gave him $20 to place in the draft and the amount to be drawn by Mr. William Dutton, who would call for it or draw it on his order at Galpin's own depot—Little Falls. As I thought I could spare $2 more and not be able to send it with the other, I have enclosed it in this sheet—hoping that it will reach you safe. The $20 probably can be drawn by the time you receive this letter. Speak to Mr. Dutton about it and he will probably arrange the affair all right. There is no doubt but that it is all right.[10]

As for myself, am well and in good spirits. I will now close. Hoping that you are all well and in easy circumstances so far as money is concerned.

William Remmel

Camp near White Oak Church, Virginia
February the 18th, 1863
Dear Brother Augustus,

The very interesting letter you wrote me last was received in due season, and the perusal of it afforded me a great deal of pleasure. How much joy I appreciate upon receiving a letter from a brother, sister, or a parent, and learn that all are well at the Old Homestead. And how wishfully I look forward to the time when, if I am spared, shall again be able to assemble with you all to form—I had near said—one unbroken family circle, but a second thought prompts me to think different. For I fear that are you all at home—as well as here abroad—spared to see that time, there will still be an absent one. And that dear cherished and loved one will quickly flash to your mind as I write this and you will quickly say it is Charlie, and you are right, it is of him I speak. It has now been about 4 years since he left us and, though we have heard from him once since that time, I fear that he will never write another letter. For if he was living I am sure that he would write to some of his young friends with whom he used to associate at home, even if he desired not to let any of his relatives know his whereabouts. Notwithstanding this opinion I have, it is not impossible that he should be living now, for there are many young men who are absent from home many years, without being heard from and finally return wiser and in many cases wealthier and more virtuous than when they went. I hope that Charlie will some day return, if he is yet living, for it would take a great burden off the anxious minds of father and mother, and what a joy it would create within us to see our lost brother again.[11]

The lead pencil, which you sent me in the paper, was very thankfully received. It is a very fine, as well as serviceable, one and cannot be too highly appreciated.

Father's letter, dated the 4th was not received until the 15th instant. It must have been delayed on the road. I wrote father a letter the same day, but mailed it before his letter arrived. Shortly after receiving it I had it read, for you know that I am unable to read German myself. Father spoke much on the subject of drinking liquor and cautioned me against using the poisonous article. I have never written him my thoughts on the subject, but I will here say that I am as much opposed to drinking intoxicating drinks as he is, for I have too many times seen the evil resulting from it. I have not tasted liquor but once while in the army and that was at a time when it was, in my opinion, beneficial. It was the night we had returned from the Rappahannock, marching through mud knee deep all day. This is the only time I ever drank in the army.

Father spoke of wishing to send a box of provision to me in great variety and in Louisa's letter, which I received yesterday, he also spoke of wishing to send me a lot of luxuries in the same box. I have thought the matter over and think it not be safe to send one, for it is getting near spring and before I would receive it, I fear, we should have to move. Many boxes are now on the road for the regiment, and some of them were sent 2 months ago. Tell them not to send anything until I write for it.

The weather, which has been so pleasant, has now changed to storm. It snowed and rained at intervals yesterday. The snow was about 6 inches deep, but now it is raining fast. Goodbye.

Wm. Remmel

If father has not received my letter, tell him I sent him $5 and he can draw $20 more of Mr. S. Galpin, depot Little Falls, on Mr. Dutton's order.

Camp near White Oak Church, Va.
March the 27th, 1863
Dear Brother Augustus,

Your very kind letter of the 22nd was received this evening. I was happy to hear from you and learn that you were well and enjoying yourself. In your present position, I think that you will ever be treated with kindness and respect. Lucinda is a very fine woman and I am sure she will always care for your wants and look to your welfare.[12]

You said that Mr. Hyatt was going back to Pennsylvania to spend the summer. He probably can do better there if he has business, than in Stratford, especially if he intends tilling soil, for I know of no poorer land unless it is here in Virginia where the soil has been robbed of all its riches by the tobacco weed.

You said that Nathan Wood was at home on a furlough, but would return to the regiment the next day. I did not know that he was agoing home, or I would have seen him before he started. I hope that he will return to the regiment and not try to desert, for in father's letter, which I received last night, he said that mother had sent me some very necessary articles by him. I cannot think that he would take articles intended for soldiers and not return.

I suppose that now you are busily engaged making maple sugar, if the weather is favorable for such business, which it must be by this time. Hope that you will have good luck and make a large quantity. Do not attempt to do too much, for nothing has ever been gained by over exertion; and besides, you are not the stoutest man in the world and you might, by being thus imprudent, destroy what might have been a long life of happiness. Always think before you strike and it may save you your health and many unpleasant hours. Probably you will think about commencing spring work before long, although the ground will not be suitable to be tilled in some time, but there are many kinds of work that will have to be performed before that time.

There is nothing of particular importance of which I could write you. The weather for the past few days has been anything but pleasant, excepting 2 or 3 days. March, so far, has been anything but pleasant. It has been the worst month for bad weather of any I have witnessed since my short stay here in the South.

The regiment is in better condition now, so far as health, good feeling, etc. is concerned, than at any time since winter set in. We have fared well all winter and have drawn bread, potatoes, and onions a good share of the time. And so [far] as I am concerned [I] have had no occasion to find fault with our victuals. We are also clothed very neatly and I think that you would not be disappointed, if you should be able to see us. I am still enjoying good health and in good spirits. Probably the regiment will have a chance to test its fighting qualities before long and hope that, if that hour ever arrives, it (regiment) will do honor to its name. I will now close hoping to hear from you soon. Goodbye.

W.R.

Camp near White Oak Church, Va.
April the 5th, 1863
My Dear Parents,

Having a few minutes casual time, I thought I would improve them by writing you a short letter. The army has not yet moved and we, therefore, are still laying in our old quarters near White Oak Church, Virginia. I have thought heretofore that perhaps we might by this time have seen some hard fighting, but this has not proved to be so. Even if it has been the intention of the commanding officer to move the army as early as now, he has been unable to do so from the bad weather which has prevailed the greater part of the time. I doubt not but it will be as much as one month before we will make our advance, though it may take place in a much less time. Spring to all appearances is no earlier here than at home and, so long as the ground remains unsettled, we will be unable to accomplish anything by way of fighting, for the army under such a condition cannot maneuver with ease or success.[13]

The weather here this spring has, the most of the time, been anything but pleasant or desirable. We have had some very fine days, but the greater part of the time has been either cold or stormy. Last Saturday night we had a severe snowstorm and the snow the next morning was 4 or 5 inches deep. From this you can form some idea of our sunny South. It is not as warm here this time of the year as I think it ought to be, but we will not have occasion to grumble upon this subject after this month, and May will afford abundant scorching weather for us. A little experience in last September marching has proved this to satisfaction to us, as soon as the change is completed (for summer) it is too warm to be agreeable.

I received a letter from Mr. Shaver's people last night. It was an interesting letter to me. I am glad that they are not agoing to move far away, for they are good neighbors and very fine people.[14]

You wrote me that you had sent a lot of articles to me by Nathan Wood, but I fear you could not have placed them in a meaner man's care. He has not yet returned and probably will not, for I have learned that he has been playing some of his old games around home such as passing counterfeit money and the like. He is a villain and deserves a rope around his neck. I do not care about seeing him again, but I am sorry about those little necessaries, which I so much needed.[15]

Albert Jennings has returned back to the reg. He looks well. Alphonso is in good health. I saw Moses Bliss the other day. He was feeling well, but does not look first rate; is quite poor. The same day saw Charley Northrup and Merton Tanner, and yesterday Capt. Thompson made us a visit. In your next, I wish you would send me $2 if you [can], to buy bread with.[16]

Your Son,
W.R.

Camp near White Oak Church, Va.
April the 21st, 1863
My Dear Parent,

Your kind and interesting letter of the 13th instant has been received. The money came safe. The short letter which I wrote you last Tuesday morning you must have ere this time received, and I am afraid it has created some sorrow and many unhappy hours, especially with mother. But this morning I write to relieve your anxious minds of the great burden, which has fallen upon you so heavily.

In my last letter I said that we were agoing to move the next day, that we were to procure 8 days rations and take along such clothing as would be actually necessary for comfort. But that order was countermanded the next day, for at night it commenced raining and the next day the sound of rain came with such fury that it would wet a person to the skin in a short time. Under such circumstances it, of course, would not be prudent to move an army, for the roads were made almost impassable for either footmen or horses to get along. We have, therefore, laid here until now and it is not impossible that we may stay here longer. The weather since the storm has subsided has been very fine, and the roads once again dry and hard. I do not think that we will remain here much longer if the weather is good, but it is not for me to say when we will move, so I will pass that subject by.

You wished to know of me about the papers which Mr. Dutton send me every week, whether I receive them or not. In reply, will say that I have received more or less papers every week, though I think that I have not acknowledged it in any of my letter but one, in which I said that you need send me no more, unless it was very convenient to do so. For I thought that it would be quite an expense to you to send them. Besides, if we have any money we can buy papers here the day after they are printed in New York, so that we have much later news than what could be obtained from papers sent from home. But if it is not too much expense, I would like to have you send me Mr. Dutton's papers, for in them I find much good reading to pass away the dull hours in camp.

Nathan Wood has not yet arrived and I doubt very much whether he ever will come back. I do not think that he is in New York (sick). He has committed a great wrong and it will not be safe for him to come back in the regiment, for almost all know what he has been doing at home.

I said in my letter in which I asked for $2 that I desired to buy bread with it. You have thought from that that we did not get food enough here. I will tell why I buy bread. The government has provided each regiment and brigade with ovens, in which to bake bread for the soldiers, but it is not always convenient to supply the men with bread the whole week. And at such times the deficiency is made up with hard crackers. And I assure you, it is not very pleasant to eat bread 4 or 5 days in the week and eat crackers that are hard as a stone the remainder of the time. But we have the privilege to buy bread from the bakers at 5 cents per loaf, which is the government price, and those that have money would rather buy bread at that price than eat crackers a part of the time, and this is my opinion. That is the reason why I sent for money, so to be able to buy bread when we did not draw any.

I hope that we will be paid off again soon, and then I shall be able to send you some money. It is a poor place to think of laying up money in the army, especially among those soldiers who have no wives or children to provide for at home. I do not consider myself a spendthrift, but there is one thing certain, I shall not lay up much money in the army, for I think more of my stomach than of glittering gold; but no more on this subject.

In your letter, you said that Caleb had returned from Mr. Carry's.[17] I am very glad that he has got back home, for I do not think that it was a good place for him. There are too many rowdies in the place to make it a desirable place for such a boy as Caleb. I hope that you will find a good place for him. Augustus, I suppose, is hard to work making maple sugar. I am afraid that he is not strong enough to gather the sap and boil the sugar alone, but I suppose that he does not have to do the whole alone. Harmon and Ada, I hope, are enjoying themselves. They probably will have a nice time, with their rabbits. You have never said anything about the cattle, but suppose you have got all the cows yet. You must have a quantity of milk this time.

Everything in nature, here in Virginia, has assumed the appearance of spring. The peach trees are in full blossom and the apple trees are budding. The ground has been in good condition, for the past month, to cultivate. We have been kept pretty busy all the spring in drilling and target shooting, and our Colonel says that we are as well disciplined as any of the regular army. He thinks, that if we are called into a battle, that we will do good execution. The regiment at present is in a good condition; but very few are sick. All the boys from around home are well. I have had some very interesting talks with Albert Jennings about home. Albert looks well and rugged and I think that he will go through with us. Alphonzo is well. He is promoted to Corporal. As for myself, have but little to say. I am well as usual, have a good appetite and am full of fun, and ready to meet the rebs when called upon to do so. I have no more to tell you at this, so good bye.[18]

From your son,
Wm. Remmel

Camp near White Oak Church, Va.
April the 28th, 1863
My Dear Parents,

We have again received orders to prepare for a march, and this time there is no doubt but that we will go. We probably will move this morning. We, of course, do not know where we are going. If we do not go it will be because of a rainstorm, for it looks very much as though it was agoing to rain. I am well as usual and think that I will stand the march well. We have 8 days rations, crackers and meat, and there may be something done before the close of that time in the way of fighting. But there is no telling what will be done, if the weather should prove unfavorable for marching within the next 10 days. Enclosed in this I send $11, part of the pay that I drew yesterday from the Paymaster. I drew $28, but

I have bought a rubber blanket and other articles, which cost considerable, and besides I owed about $3 among the boys. Please accept of the small sum that I send you and next time will try and send you more. Hoping that this will reach you safe. I will close this brief letter, hoping to hear from you soon. You will hear from the daily papers in a very few days whether the army has made an attack. I hope that we will have good success if we move. Goodbye.[19]

From your son,
Wm. Remmel

Camp of the 121st Regiment
Above Falmouth, Va.
Afternoon, May 5, 1863
My Dear Parents,

It is with feeling of anguish and sorrow that I sit me down to write you these few lines. Our regiment has been in action and we have lost nearly half of the men, 267 men including officers have been either killed, wounded, or missing. We went right into the fight Sunday afternoon about 5 O'clock. The fight lasted about 20 minutes. 4 regiments of our brigade were in action. We attacked the rebs in a strong position. It was behind a piece of woods in rifle pits that we attacked them. We were unable to get at them on account of their strong works, while they could fire upon us in open field. The regiments all fought well, until the ranks were killed almost half, when they were driven back by the rebs about ½ mile. Our regiment then rallied round the flag and our brave Colonel, and we soon drove them back into their holes, with the assistance of artillery. When we rallied around our flag, there could not have been more than 100 men out of the regiment together. After the fight was over, we fell back to our brigade where we found about 200 more, making in all 300 men that now belong to the regiment. I did not get a mark, but the bullets whistled pretty close around my head. I expected every minute to be hit, but kind Providence saved me. 8 officers out of 20 were either killed or wounded. 3 of them we know are dead.[20]

I will give a list of those that are either killed, wounded, or missing, that I think you know or have seen. I am grieved to tell you that Alphonso Casler is missing and nothing is known of him. It may be that he is a prisoner and it is not impossible that he is killed. I hope that he is all right, of course, no one knows. I inquired of the boys of his company very particularly whether they had seen him, but they said they had not. Merton Tanner, at the tollgate, is badly wounded. Nathaniel Lamphere is badly wounded. Jenks Perkins is wounded in the arm. Charley Tomkins is reported killed. These are all that you are acquainted with. Albert Jennings came out safe. The Captain and 1st

Lieutenant of Co. H, to which these boys all belong, were both killed. Gransberry, of Emmitsburg, is also wounded. In our company we lost one officer, or rather, he was wounded. Company I went in with 53 men and came out with 27 men. Our whole corps, which is the 6th, has all crossed back over the river. We are lying about 2 miles above Falmouth. I will now close. I hope that this will reach you.[21]

Wm. Remmel

Camp of the 121st Regiment
Near White Oak Church, Va.
May the 16th, 1863
My Dear Brother Augustus,

After much hesitation and long delay, I again take a few moments of leisure time and devote it to writing you a short letter. I suppose you have been waiting in anxious suspense to once more hear from me and convince yourself that I am still alive. Father's letter, or rather, the letter which I wrote to our people, if forwarded with the usual promptness and not miscarried, must ere this time have reached you or them. The letter was written either the first or second day after we had re-crossed the river (Rappahannock), after being compelled to retreat. I, at the time, gave all the particulars of the casualties in our regiment, so far as I had learned. I gave the number killed, wounded and missing, as near as I could ascertain. I think it was something like 270 men, including officers, but this number has been reduced a very little. About 250 will come nearer to the true number.

The contest was a very severe one. Regiments that had often faced showers of lead and walked up to the enemy, with gleaming bayonets pointed at their own hearts, as if destruction seemed inevitable, declared that the firing during the action eclipsed anything that they ever heard in point of noise and destruction. About every other man in our company was either killed, wounded, or missing. The loss in each of the companies was in about this same ration.

The engagement lasted about 20 minutes. It was brought on in about the following manner. At the time that the heights opposite Fredericksburg were taken our division (Brooks'), about 7,000 strong, was lying about ¾ of a mile below the city. General Brooks immediately received orders to march his division upon the heights and follow the panic stricken rebels. The column was soon in motion and after a very fatiguing and weary march we arrived upon the top of the hill. We halted just about long enough to restore a long breath. When we were again just in motion, we had gone but a short distance before the rebel shells came booming over our heads and exploding just beyond where we were marching.

The rebels effected but little by their random firing, for they could not see us, being hidden behind a dense thicket of woods. But one man was hit by this shelling, but he was literally torn to pieces. Our batteries were got in position at a double-quick, which soon silenced them. After they had been dislodged from their position, they fell back to where we fought them. Here they had picked a strong position behind a ridge, directly in rear of a piece of woods. When we advanced upon them it was believed that nothing but the rear guard were here, but we soon found different, for we were mowed down like grass before the scythe.

The following is a list of those who were hurt in the fight. M. Tanner, wounded 3 places. N. Lamphere, wounded in arm. C. Tomkins, wounded in arm. C. Gransberry, wounded and reported having died. Alphonso Casler, missing, reported dead. Hoping this will reach you.

Wm. Remmel

Camp of the 121st N.Y.S.V.
Near White Oak Church, Va.
May the 19th, 1863
My Dear Parents,

Confident that my last letter reached you with perhaps 1 or 2 days delay, informing you of my safety, I thought it needless to write another until I had heard from you. Your letter, I am happy to inform you, was received about 1 week ago.

I was happy to learn that my money had been received by you. The money I sent you was rather a small sum, but it gratifies me to think that you were satisfied with it and would not have complained if I had sent none. I think that it is very necessary to have more or less money in one's possession in the army, because a soldier's life is imperiled almost the whole time. And if it should be his fortune to be wounded and not killed, when taken to the hospital, there are many delicacies that a sick man needs and can be had, but not without the patient has money to buy them.

I would have spoken of your letter in Augustus' letter had I thought of it, but being busily engaged in giving a description of our fighting and the manner in which it was brought on, it passed my mind. Shortly before the letter was received I received a package containing a small towel. I knew not at the time from whom it had come, but your letter informed me that mother had sent it. It is a very nice one and hope it will do me good service. Ere this time you, of course, have ascertained all the particulars of the hard fought battles on the Rappahannock. How terribly the troops suffered on both sides. According to the official report sent by the commander (Hooker) to the War Department, and which has been publicly disclosed, our loss is much smaller than the enemy's. But, while we are flattering ourselves that this loss is much heavier than our own, the enemy are jubilant over what they term achievements, or series of successes and Lee informs his clique in Richmond that the loss of the Yankees must be double his own. If we are to judge from their reports what either side has accomplished or lost, we are left in the dark and suspicion and doubt arises with regard to the true issue. For it shows a disposition in both commanders to smooth his own loss and make the enemies as large as possible. Be this as it may, the ground was furiously contested by both sides. But there is no doubt Hooker would have whipped Lee had it not been for the disgraceful conduct of the 11th Corps, which broke and ran when it could have held its strong position if it had stood with firmness and determination.[22]

There is nothing of importance taking place, or has transpired, worthy of note in the regiment. We are in the same encampment that we were in all winter. Have drills as usual and prepare ourselves for another fight, for we expect to meet the rebs again before long. The weather is very delightful. It has been one continual sunshine, except when the moon interferes. For about 2 weeks it is not so warm as to be uncomfortable during the day and at night is very cool and beautiful sleeping.

One word about Alphonso. I wrote to his folks that I thought very likely that he was wounded and taken prisoner, but since then have learned from pretty good authority that he was killed. I talked with a Corporal in Co. H this morning about the fate of Alphonso and he told me that his brother, who was wounded and taken prisoner but since sent over to our lines, informed him that he went upon the field the next morning with someone's assistance and saw Alphonso and 2 others lying upon the ground dead. They were all from the same company and he knew them. Please write a little coarser next time.[23]

William Remmel

Camp of the 121st Regiment
Near White Oak Church
May the 24th, 1863
My Dear Parents,

Your kind letter was received 2 evenings ago and, being ordered to go on picket tomorrow and remain 3 days, I thought I would write you this Sabbath afternoon. I wrote a letter to you a few days ago and, probably ere this time, it has been received. I wrote you all that I thought would be interesting to you to hear.

There can be no doubt but that Alphonso was killed in the late fight, for I have made particular inquiry and the statements all agree as to his fate. This sorrowful announcement must have made a sad impression upon Alphonso's people. I know that they must all naturally mourn very much over the death of their beloved son. Alphonso was a noble boy, always kind, generous, and friendly. He became an idol among his associates. He was loved by all his company and his loss is deeply felt by all who knew him.

Our regiment has changed its quarters, but we have not gone more than 40 rods [220 yards] from where we were encamped before. We have moved out into the open field without as much as a shrub to form a shade. The ground is very hard and sandy, for we have dwelled upon it all the spring, and I can tell you that it is not very comfortable to have a hot and almost burning sun reflecting its scorching rays through our thin shelter tents. This change was ordered by the doctors, who thought it very injurious to our health to remain longer in our winter tents that would be so very warm in the summer besides containing much filth.[24]

Judging from your letter someone has informed you of my recent promotion to a Sergeant. You are to be proud of this mark of honor bestowed upon me, and I hope and trust that it will never be recorded of me that I shrunk from my duty or retarded my progress to a higher position. I rank as 4th Sergeant, receive $17 per month.[25]

Augustus wrote me that you had planted and sowed a considerable [amount] this spring. I am glad of this, for all produce I think will be very dear next fall. You, of course, cannot raise enough to have any to sell, but if you can produce enough to avoid buying that will greatly lessen your expenses.

With regard to the money, $20 at Galpin's Store at Little Falls, of which you wrote me, I have the following reply to make. Sometime last February I sent, by Capt. Galpin of this regiment, $20 to his brother the stove dealer in Little Falls. It was sent in a check and in care of William Dutton at Devereaux. The money I sent to Caleb Remmel, I supposed that you had received it shortly after the $5 came at hand—for I sent it before I did the $5. There can be no doubt but that the money belongs to you. I did not direct it to Mariah Remmel. You had better call for it, either through someone or go yourself. You will get it I am sure.[26]

The regiment is out on picket 8 miles from camp. We are having a fine time. I commenced the letter in camp and finish it here.

From your son,
William Remmel

Camp of the 121st Regiment
Near White Oak Church
June the 1st, 1863
My Dear Parents,

I again embrace the present opportunity by writing you. Having been paid, I concluded to send a part of my money to you. I have received $28, and shall send $15 to you in this letter. I have also had 3 Ambrotypes taken, 1 of which I am going to present to you, 1 to William and Louisa, and the other to a young friend who roomed with me at Fairfield.[27]

The pictures are not as good as I could wish that they might be, but considering when and by whom they are drawn, they give very good satisfaction. We cannot expect that artists can do the justice to their practice here as at home, for their rooms are prepared in good style and every facility afforded to produce the first quality of material for the work. But here in the army, rooms are taken in some poor canvass tents or ruined house or barn. All dirt and the poorest article furnished, with unskilled hands to use it. I send you the most natural one of the 3.[28]

The money that you spoke about, I think, can be no other than that I sent by Capt. Galpin in a check. If you have not received any money from Mr. Galpin, I know it must be mine. I sent it in care of Mr. Dutton.

Nothing of importance has transpired in camp since I wrote you while on picket. We returned from picket last Thursday, and since that time the regiment has been to work cleaning and arranging this new quarters. Everything is now in good shape, and probably we will commence to drill again in a day or 2. The days here are very warm and, were it not for the high winds that we have had for the past few days, it would be rather uncomfortable living upon the open plain.

No movement so far as I can learn has taken place in this army, but it is expected that some move is in contemplation either to offset the intentions of Lee, or take the offensive again. The boys in our regiment are in fine spirits and enjoying excellent health. The wounded are getting along finely and many will be able to do duty again ere long. Charley Tomkins and Nathaniel Lamphere are getting along finely. It will be some time before Charley will be able to return to duty again, but his arm will not be crippled. Our regiment has been filled up with 3 year recruits from 2 year regiments and it has created considerable trouble, for the boys refuse to do any duty. They say they are not agoing to stay in the army after this regiment have gone home.[29]

I have nothing more of importance to write you. I will, therefore, close.

Please write me as soon as you receive this letter, to inform me whether you have received all that I sent you.

From your obedient son,
William Remmel

Camp of the 121st Regiment
Opposite Fredericksburg, Va.
June the 7th, 1863
My Dear Brother Augustus,

Your kind letter was received a few evenings ago. I am happy to hear from you and to learn that our people were all well and that Louisa would remain at home some time. I am writing you this morning under rather peculiar circumstances. The army has moved, or at least a part, and one of the divisions is already across the river. Our division is lying on the north side of the river ready to move at any moment.

We are all puzzled as to the move. Some think that General Hooker is merely making a faint to keep the rebels in Virginia and prevent Lee from reinforcing the western generals. Others that a general engagement will be brought on in order to strike with Grant and make the expected victory in the West a more decisive one. I do not pretend to know what is to be done, but everything indicates that no battle will be fought here.[30]

The boys in the regiment are in good spirits and feeling as cheerful as when in camp. But, notwithstanding the buoyant spirits and good cheer of the boys, they all to a man have antipathy against going across the river and would rather fight anywhere else than at this place, for we have never had success and always meet with heavy slaughter.

Our boys met with very little opposition going across the river, but a few were killed, while many of the rebels lost their lives and a goodly number taken prisoner. Howe's division of our corps is across the river and holding a part of the plain.[31] I saw Capt. Northrup yesterday. He is looking well. He says their regiment will go home Monday, unless the movement prevents. I would like to visit the regiment, if I could, but I will be unable to do so for no passes are given.[32]

I have nothing more of importance to write you. I am very nervous this morning and find it difficult to write. I fear you will be unable to read a half of this botch of a letter, for I have made such unreadable scribbling. Pick out the words as best you can. Hoping that this will reach you and find you well, I close.

From your brother,
William Remmel

Please do not let any but our people look at this,
For I am ashamed of it.

Camp of the 121st Regiment
Opposite Fredericksburg, Va.
June the 12th, 1863
My Dear Parents,

Having aplenty of leisure time, I thought I would improve a part by writing you a letter. Louisa's letter will reach you, I think, tonight and you will know that up to the date of my letter I was alive and well. No doubt you experience great uneasiness for my safety at the present time, for the 6th Corps, to which I belong, has again undertaken a great task. The corps has lost hardly any men as yet. How long I shall be able to speak so favorably, I know not. No fighting has yet occurred. Our regiment has been across the river 8 days this week, doing picket duty and working on fortifications. We have possession of about 30 acres of territory across the river, with a front toward the enemy of about 2 miles. We have thrown [up] a very formidable earthwork, which I think will save many lives. Our regiment is on the north side of the river, opposite Fredericksburg. We expect to move somewhere before long. It may be across the river again. Everything looks favorable on our side. A great battle will come off, I think, before long.

I saw Emerson Northrup last Sunday, and also John McDougal. I suppose they are now at home. The weather is very warm, and makes quite uncomfortable marching. The very neatly packed budget you sent me, I received last night. I am much pleased with the presents and feel very thankful for them. They are articles that are much needed by a soldier, and are indispensable. If wounded on the battlefield and left to take care of yourself a handkerchief would be excellent to bind up the wound and perhaps, thereby, save your life. I can write no more this time, the letters are going out.

Goodbye,
Wm. R.

Camp of the 121st Regiment
Fairfax Station, Va.
10 miles west of Alexandria
June the 17th, 1863
My Dear Parents,

I again take permission to drop a few lines to you this morning. Our corps has been on the move for 3 days and 2 nights and we are now encamped about

½ mile west from Fairfax Station on the Orange and Alexandria Railroad, when we stopped last evening after marching 20 miles since early dawn. You will have seen from my last letter that we have been to work on fortifications across the Rappahannock.

Our corps, the 6th, held its position across the river until Saturday night, June the 13th, when orders were received to abandon our fortifications and re-cross the river. This order was strictly carried out during the night. The troops also re-crossed the river safe and the pontoons were all taken up before the break of day. Our regiment, except 4 companies, were out on picket camp. I was not out, having, with the other 3 companies, done fatigue duty the day before on the earthworks. The troops commenced their march shortly after dark. It rained very severely fast at night, which made it very muddy and bad marching. We commenced to march about 9 O'clock (P.M.). The night was very dark and we could see but little, which made it still more difficult to get along. The boys would often stumble down and become all over besmeared with mud. We marched until about 3 O'clock in the morning when we halted, slept until morning, rose, pitched tents, and stayed all day. At dark, we again commenced our march, marched all night, stopped about daybreak, rested about 2 hours, got breakfast, and again took up our march, marched until night, making a distance of 30 miles in a little more than 24 hours.[33]

The men were so tired in the afternoon from the fatigue, for the sun poured down upon us with intense heat, that they lay down along the road by the dozens. Many were sunstroke; rested all night and yesterday, before daylight, was again on the move. We are now at Fairfax Station, about 20 miles from Washington. It is now about 6 O'clock and we have received no orders to march. May stay all day, and also liable to move at any moment. The rebels are again in Maryland, and it is thought that we will move to the defenses of that state as soon as possible. We expect to see hard times, but we are ready to drive them from any position they may have in Maryland or Pennsylvania. The hellish traitors must be dispensed and we will do it, if they give us proper management. I will now close. Please excuse this poor writing.

From your son,
William Remmel

Please send me $5, for I need it much.

Camp of the 121st Regiment
Near Fairfax Courthouse, Va.
June the 20th, 1863
Dear Brother Augustus,

Your kind and interesting letter of the 14th instant was received last evening. I was very glad to hear from you and to learn our people were well. If my letter to our people has been dispatched without delay, you will tonight know where were our whereabouts last Wednesday, which was at Fairfax Station, about 4 miles south of here.

There has been a very great change in the positions of the two opposing armies within 1 week. At that time nearly the whole of our army was lying along the bank of the Rappahannock, above and below Fredericksburgh, while that of the rebels to a great extent was in the northern part of Virginia. Now our army has by almost superhuman exertion concentrated its strength in the vicinity of Bull Run (Manassas), while Lee, with an overwhelming force, has marched into Maryland, invaded Pennsylvania, and threatens to carry desolation and sorrow to every Union home in that vicinity.

Affairs for the present look dark indeed. How long this state of things will last time alone will disclose. I have always been in favor of action and energetic war measures and am today in favor of that same policy, but such management as has been conducted by our chief leaders for the past 2 years to crush this awful civil strife is shameful indeed. We have so far accomplished but little in this army to blighten the hopes of rebels, though in the West have accomplished more.[34]

I would be vain to censure any particular actor engaged in the struggle, for it appears to me as though there was a lack of action, confidence, and support manifested by all of our high officials. I think incompetent and unskilled generals, at the head of our armies, has caused many of the reverses that have overtaken us of late. Our present leader (Hooker) has lost the confidence of the army by the last fruitless slaughter on the Rappahannock and in allowing Lee to deceive him, by marching his troops into Maryland and Pennsylvania, while he (Hooker) supposed that he was holding the whole of their forces in the front of him. I will not dwell longer on this subject, only hope that the future will grow brighter.[35]

Our regiment has nearly recovered from its crippled condition so far as number is concerned, for a great many recruits have been sent from other regiments that were two year regiments, which makes our number nearly as large as before the battle. Most of the wounded men are getting along finely. Charley Tomkins is in Washington and will very likely go home. Nathaniel Lamphere is with the regiment and doing well. We expect to see some hard fighting within the next month and in this, I think, we will not be disappointed. It is impossible at the present time to procure a furlough. As soon as there is a chance, I will try to get one. We are liable to move from here at any moment. I do not think that we will stay here long. No more this time, so goodbye. I will write Caleb in a few days.

From your brother,
William Remmel

Camp of the 121st Regiment
Near Fairfax Courthouse, Va.
June the 21st, 1863
Dear Brother Caleb,

It has been a very great while since last I wrote you and I must acknowledge that I have done very wrong in not writing to you oftener. But we are all liable to commit faults and more especially the soldier, who has so much to take his mind from all important duties. I hope that in the future, should I be slack in performing my duty in this respect, you will act your part and write me often for I shall at time[s] be happy to hear from you. Augustus writes me often and I assure you that it affords me much pleasure to peruse a letter from a brother.

I have nothing of particular importance to write you at the present time. We are still encamped where we were when I wrote to Augustus, which is about ½ mile south of Fairfax Courthouse. We have laid here since we stopped our march from the Rappahannock, which is 1 week ago today. We are encamped in a very pleasant piece of woods, which forms a very beautiful shade. All the objection there is to remaining here is that the water is too far off, which makes it rather inconvenient for us. We have had to drill almost everyday since we came here, which makes pretty busy work for us.[36]

Our regiment has been recruited by men from the New York regiments who enlisted for 2 years and whose time is now out. There are about 125 in all. This makes our regiment quite large again. The boys are in pretty good spirits and I think that the regiment would do good fighting again, if they should be called into action.

It is thought that we will not remain here more than a day or two longer. Artillery has been moving all night and General Stahel's Cavalry, 6 or 7 thousand strong, has also taken up its line of march. There appears to be a general movement going on throughout the whole army toward Maryland. There will, undoubtedly, be another great battle fought within a short time. It is thought by many that the 6th Corps, to which our regiment belongs, will be kept as reserves with Hooker and not called into a fight unless it be actually necessary so to do.[37]

The boys that are with the regiment from around home are well. With the exception of a severe cold, I am well and in good spirits. If father will procure a light woolen hat and send it to me, I should like it very much. Caps are too warm in the summer. Tell him to procure a dark colored hat about your fit, very light and soft. I have nothing more to write you this time, so goodbye. Please excuse this bad writing.

From your brother,
William Remmel

Give my love to all of our people and tell them I will write soon.

Camp of the 121st
In field 2 miles south of
Hagerstown, (MD)
July the 3rd, 1863
Dear Brother Caleb,

Your very kind and interesting letter received yesterday morning. I was pleased to hear from you and gratified to learn that you were well. It seems that your attention has been taken up with various employments since spring, none of which seem to give you satisfaction. I would advise you as a loving and well wishing brother not to change employers so often, for I do not think that it will be for your interest to do it. A studious and diligent young man is much more respected by good society than one who is shifting from place to place thinking of doing better, by receiving a dollar or two extra per month. If I were you, I would find a good place to work, where the people are kind and pleasant, and make my stay more permanent. I know it will be for your interest to do this. One thing more Caleb and I am done with advice. I beg of you, as a brother of mine, not to mingle anymore than you can possibly help with those who are low and mean. Do not connect yourself with bad society. It has been the ruin of many a young man who bid fair to be a promising and prosperous man. I have not time to dwell longer upon this subject, for I am liable to be called up at any moment to take my gun, ready for a fight.[38]

Our whole army is drawn up in line of battle at, or in the vicinity of, Hagerstown. We are entrenching ourselves and expect a heavy battle. It may commence or may not in 2 or 3 days, but a fight is certain. We are all confident that we can whip Lee's army and hope to take a part of it prisoners. Our corps was fortunate enough at the battle of Gettysburg not to be called into action, except 1 or 2 brigades, but this time we will have to take the front and take the brunt of the fight. But we do not complain, for we think it our duty to go where we are ordered. If we destroy Lee's army, I think the Confederacy must soon fall.

Since we left the Rappahannock we have [been] under one very severe hardship, often marching days and nights in succession. But we do not regret that we [have] done this now, for by our fatiguing marches we gained one of the greatest victories of the war. I saw Moses Bliss while at Gettysburg. He had been in action the night before and looked much fatigued. He, however, felt well and felt highly pleased over our success. He came near being hit by a rebel bullet. It passed through a part of his clothes, into his side pocket, and struck his bible. It was narrow escape.[39]

The 97th N.Y.S.V. was badly cut up. There are about 80 men in the Regt. Colonels Wheelock and Spofford were taken prisoners. Lieut. Frank Murphy was also taken prisoner. Fred Munson and James Styles of Salisbury were killed. I know nothing of Austin Ferrell or Capt. Thompson. There are many things that I could write you if I had time, but must forbear under the circumstances. I must, therefore, close. Goodbye, I hope that I will pass through the battle.[40]

W.R.

Excuse this bad writing, as I wrote hurriedly.

Camp of the 121st Regiment
Near Berlin, (MD)
July the 17th, 1863
My Dear Parents,

I once more sit down to address a few lines to you. I am far away from where I last wrote you, and many more miles will intervene before another week rolls around. Our regiment did not go into action, as we expected that we would when at Hagerstown. Had Lee offered battle, there is no question that now there would not be as many living and well in the regiment. Lee's escape has no doubt for the present saved many lives for us, but I fear that in a very few days we will have to face the rebels again and perhaps under different circumstances. For I fear Lee will have his accustomed ground to fight on, where our reduced army will have to attack him.[41]

While at Hagerstown we threw up breastworks and made our position very strong, thinking the rebels would attack us, when we would give them a warm reception, but they also worked with the spade and raised strong works with the purpose to deceive our generals; which they did. As soon as we learned that the rebel pickets had fell back, we advanced upon them until we got to the river, when we saw that all our efforts had been in vain. The rebels made a very successful crossing, nothing but a few wagons and some old horses and mules were left behind. We remained on the bank of the river during the remainder of Tuesday. Wednesday morning we were ordered out at 3 O'clock in the morning, cooked our breakfast and started on the march at daylight, marched until 2 O'clock afternoon making a distance of 14 miles. Remained there during afternoon and night, and yesterday started again. Marched about 17 miles and are now encamped about 3 miles from the Potomac, and about 6 miles below Harper's Ferry. Today we have laid in camp. It seems like a kind of Sunday to us, for we are almost constantly on the move and have but little time to rest. Since we left the Rappahannock I think, safely speaking, our corps has marched 250 miles and there is a fair chance of marching as much farther before the summer's campaign will close. It is thought here that Meade intends to head off Lee at Richmond and give him battle. Meade moves very rapid and he maybe able to carry out his design. The country through which the army passed is almost desolated. Grain, to a great extent, is destroyed. Fields all cut up with roads, fences nearly all destroyed for cooking and other purposes. Farmers have in many instances not a cow left; the rebels having taken them all. Hardly a good horse was to be seen. I am enjoying good health, but our heavy marches wear upon me. I am so tired that I can hardly stand up, but still we have to keep doing, for keeping up with the regiment we must or be punished. Many men are deserting the army now. They think they can get away.[42]

Moses Bliss came to see me today. He looks rugged and healthy. How pleasant it is to shake hands with old acquaintances. I will not attempt to write anymore at this time.

From your affectionate son,
William Remmel

Camp of the 121st Regiment
Near New Baltimore, Va.
August the 11th, 1863
Dear Brother Augustus,

Your very kind letter of the 31st instant has been duly received and had I had time I would have answered it before. Our regiment only last night returned from a 3 days scouting tour, which has made it impossible to write any for several days. I trust that through kindness and sound consideration you will again pardon me.[43]

The last letter I wrote you, I believe, was dated Snickersville, Virginia; now we are far from there and much nearer Washington. The place near which we are now staying is called New Baltimore. The place is an insignificant one, there being not more than 4 houses in the place. This, together with half a dozen old barns and some nigger huts, forms the proud city of N B [New Baltimore].

N B is not the place at which we halted after our late march. Warrenton was the [place] at which we first stopped; a once thriving little town on a branch of the Alexandria and Orange Railroad, about 40 miles from Washington. We stopped at this place about one week and was then ordered to our present position to guard the different roads leading to the place, to prevent the capture of the supply trains of the rebels under the noted guerrilla Mosby. Trains [are] agoing to our cavalry along the Bull Run Mountains and in the vicinity of Thoroughfare Gap. The distance from here to Washington is about 5 miles and, although there is almost a continual travel going on between here and there, yet it is some risky to venture from here with supplies without an escort of guards to prevent attacks from prowling guerrillas.[44]

I will now tell you a little about a scout, which our regiment, together with 8 cavalrymen, had since early Saturday morning last. It is now Tuesday (P.M.). Our Col., who has been acting Brigadier General for about 4 weeks, returned to the regiment a few days ago and, being a very energetic and spirited man, he asked permission of his superior officer to allow him to go out with his regiment on a scout and ascertain, if possible, something about the whereabouts of the noted Mosby and his gang. This request was granted and early Saturday morning we were on our toes, packed and ready for a start. About daylight we put out. We marched to White Plains a distance of about 8 miles without anything of interest to attract our attention, for marching had become a common thing with us. As soon as we entered the town, which is a fraction larger than N B, we surrounded it and allowed no man to escape. We could, however, find no traces of any rebels in town.[45]

Company I was sent out a short distance out of town and took possession of a strip of woods containing a number of milk cows. It being our policy to confiscate everything of our own use, we took the liberty to strip these noble and useful animals of their delicious milk and appropriate it to our hungry and rather abused stomachs. I also during the day, with a squad [of] 7, went and partook of a resplendent dinner at a sick lady's house. Brought away a quantity of cream in a large jar and churned it with a sort of ladle.

At night we were summoned to the regiment and there received orders for future operations. The regiment was to be divided nearly equally. The right wing to be in charge of the Col. and the left by the Lieut. Col. They were to go respectively to Salem and Middleburg, rather to M[iddleburg] and S[alisbury], surprise the places by surrounding them before daylight and, if guerrillas were there, capture them. Search every house for rebels and guns, take all able-bodied men fit for service, capture all horses and supply yourself with rations from the houses of the secesh. This order was rather a strenuous one, but every man was ready to abide by it and carry it out to the letter. The Colonel forbid very strictly any man abusing the civilians, especially the women and children.[46]

The Colonel and Lieutenant Colonel possessed themselves of trusty guides, who were thoroughly acquainted with the country, to lead them to the respective places. We started about 9 O'clock (P.M.). Middleburg, where we were agoing, was about 9 miles distant. We found the road very rough and the march a wearisome one. We arrived near the place about 2:30 (A.M.), halted and slept until near daybreak when we started for the work. It was about ½ mile and we were soon there, surrounded the place without opposition, and a party entered to commence search, while the others were guarding the village. Houses were ransacked from top to bottom, but no Mosbies, as we call them, could be found. We, however, at last caught a single one in the following manner. In searching a doctor's barn, a U.S. horse and saddle were discovered. The boys became at once suspicious that the man was fostering a rebel, entered his house and demanded an explanation. He said he knew nothing about it, whereupon he was arrested and taken to the Colonel as prisoner. It brought him to terms, for he told us where the rascal was (*hid in the garden*). That morning we dined at secesh tables. Started back for White Plains at noon, searched every house on the road, and had a very great time generally. Drank what milk we wanted, and filled our haversacks with bread and meat. We arrived at *White Plains* just dark, with about 20 horses of all ages and diseases, all loaded with something good to eat. Fowls of every description. We also had captured one guerrilla and 7 or 8 citizens. Remained all night at White Plains and started next morning for camp, which we reached about noon, where we found the Lieutenant Colonel having had nearly the same luck we had. Thus ended up our first grand infantry raid.[47]

The horse the Quartermaster has taken in charge and the prisoners, after an examination, except the guerrilla, has been released and sent home. Next time we prefer to go mounted, and in the manner we can triumph. Were it not for the notorious robber and murderer Mosby, the people would not be molested. As it is, this is the course to pursue.[48]

There is nothing of particular importance going in camp. Our regiment was paid yesterday, and today sutlers will be once more patronized. I received a letter from William yesterday. I shall answer it very soon. Also received a hat father sent me. There are but few boys from home in the regiment. I hear we are agoing on picket tomorrow. I will not attempt to write anymore at this time, for I am afraid I will weary your patience. Am happy to hear you are getting along so well in your new house. Hoping that you will always succeed. I bid you a hearty good bye.

This from your brother,
William Remmel

Give my love to William and Louisa. Excuse this poor writing.

Camp of the 121st Regiment
Near New Baltimore, Va.
August the 12th, 1863
My Dear Brother Caleb,

Having a few moments of leisure before we start out on picket this morning, I thought I would drop a short line to you. Everything is quiet in camp and there has been little of interest going on for several days in the vicinity of camp. Our regiment, however, has performed important service for the government for last 4 days. And I think you would like to know in what respect that we have done so. I will tell you.

There are many guerrillas in this vicinity, who light on government supply trains and sutlers going to the various camps, destroy the train and appropriate the provisions and whatever articles they may be to their own use. Our Colonel last asked permission of General Bartlett to go out in search of the gang who commit these depredations, and the request was granted. This gang of robbers are under a villain by the name of Mosby. Early last Saturday morning we packed up, eat breakfast, and started for our work about daylight. We marched to a place called White Plains, 8 miles from here, without meeting any opposition. No rebels could be seen or heard from. As soon as we arrived in town, companies were sent out to keep the citizens in town, which was successfully accomplished. Our regiment stayed in town through the day, and we had a very fine time. Milked all the cows we could find, procured dinners, brought cream in camp, churned it with a ladle, picked string beans and had a good supper. Started about 9 O'clock at night for a place called Middleburg, about 9 miles. The road was very rough and the march was a very severe one. Arrived near the town about half past two in the morning. Our orders, when we started, was to search every house for rebels and firearms, take every able-bodied man and every horse. On our march the Colonel had a Negro for a guide, who knew the country well. On the route, we took one man along. He was in bed, but he had to come with us. We surrounded the place just as day was breaking and entered it. We found but one guerrilla. He was hid in a garden. Several citizens were arrested and taken along with us.

We staid in town until nearly noon, had a fine breakfast made up of bread, milk, &c. Started for White Plains about noon. Searched every house along the road and provided ourselves with rations, such as we could find. We arrived at White Plains about dusk, where we put up for the night. Next morning started for camp. Arrived at camp about noon. Here we found the Lieutenant Colonel having had about the same luck that we had. The whole raid summed up about as follows. Captured 1 guerrilla, 20 citizens, about 50 horses, and a great many fowl.[49]

I was not able to finish this letter in camp, and am now writing on picket. We are in a very cool shady place, and expect to have a nice time here. It is very warm now, but we stand it well. I have not yet seen a sick day. Our regiment was paid yesterday. I shall send father some money soon. There is hardly a boy from home in the regiment now. I will now close. My love to William and Louisa.

From your affectionate brother,
Wm. Remmel

Give my love to our people and tell them I will write soon. I am agoing to write Harmon and Ada in a short time, if I can this time, without fail.

Camp of the 121st Regiment
Near New Baltimore, Va.
August 26, 1863
Dear Brother Augustus,

Having a little leisure time, I thought I would address a few thoughts to you, for I suppose that it is sometimes very lonely for you at your new place and more especially if William and Louisa have taken their departure from Ephratah. For Louisa says that they were agoing to leave very soon. If you are a little lonesome you must not mind it, for you must expect someday to go among strangers and why not now commence? If you have got a good man to work for, one that will treat you kindly, I am sure you will get along.

There is not much of importance going on in the army just now. The infantry is all lying quiet. The cavalry go out scouting occasionally. Our brigade, as I have written you before, is entirely separated from the rest of the army. We form the extreme right of our lines. Our position, would you look on the map, you would find about midway between Thoroughfare Gap and Warrenton, Virginia. There are 4 regiments and one battery where we are.

The regiments perform their regular tour of picket, which is 3 days out of every 12. Our regiment is now out, and the boys are having a fine time. We always rather be on picket than in camp, for when we are in camp we are always drilling, which the boys are perfectly sick of. And more than this, we have a much greater variety of food when we are out from around camp. The way we manage when we are out on this kind of duty and want something good to eat, 6 or 7 of the boys take their guns and go out and take what they can find, and the squad never comes back without having captured something good. Either a hog, sheep, or some kind of a fowl, and perhaps a quantity of vegetables. Milk we have in abundance. Sometimes we milk the farmers' cows and then again we buy it, paying from 5 to 30 cents per canteen full, which holds a ½ quart. Corn is just right to eat boiled and, I tell you, we lay in for it at a great rate.

There are but few boys at present with the regiment from around home. Albert Jennings is, I believe, the only one. Merton Tanner is yet in the hospital and so is Charley Tomkins. Nathaniel Lamphere is at home on a furlough. Louisa has written me of several that were drafted in Stratford.[50]

The last letter that I received from home spoke very favorably of father's crops, which I am glad to hear. My health is excellent and I trust that this will find you as well. You must be very careful of your eyes and try to doctor them, if you can. I will not attempt to write more at this time, so goodbye.

Your affectionate brother,
Wm. R.

On picket near New Baltimore, Va.
September the 7th, 1863
My Dear Parents,

Having plenty of leisure moments I once more improve this opportunity to address you.

We are out on picket and, at such a time, hours are not as precious as in camp, for there we are constantly doing something to employ our time; either drilling, preparing for inspection, or something else. We felt more like ourselves when out on picket duty, for we have liberties which we could not think of getting in camp. We are at present, however, enjoying ourselves quietly in camp or outside. Everything appears to go off with life, hope, and cheerfulness. We are living in fine style. Have soft bread each day and vegetables, such as potatoes, beats, and beans 2 or 3 times per week, and to top off we draw pickled cabbage once a week. And besides all those dainties, for such they are to us, we have access to the cornfields around town, which opportunity we do not fail to improve. So you see, on the whole we do not fare so bad after all.

The weather here at present is very fine indeed. The days are very pleasant, though the nights are rather cool. I do not think that it is as warm here now as many times at home this time of year. We expect, however, to experience a severe wet weather yet, for I well remember how it was nearly one year ago. The heat was so great that many of our regiment fainted by the roadside from sheer exhaustion and heat.

I suppose you are aware what we are stationed here for. It is to keep the guerrillas from troubling or molesting our trains of wagons, as they pass to the various depots for supplying the troops that are stationed there with provision. Everything had passed off very quietly up till last Friday evening since we had laid here and the pickets had, in consequence, become rather careless and unwatchful and would many times sleep when they ought to be awake. The guerrillas, through citizens I suppose for they are all secesh, had found this out, for they are constantly prowling around camp and determined on making a midday attack on our lines and come through. The time, it appears, had been appointed last Friday night between the hours of 12 and 1 (A.M.). There were 3 regiments in camp at the time. I happened to be awake at the time. As soon as the first shot was fired, I pounced out of my roost and helped give the alarm. The whole camp was now in a bustle, some dressing, some loading guns, and others rallying the men. We were now in a line with loaded muskets and gleaming bayonets, ready for the music. But the cowardly gang, about 20, on hearing us, fired several rounds into our general's headquarters and dashed back unharmed. 3 men were wounded. Should they again attempt it, we hope to be prepared for them. Please write whether you have received the $15 I sent you. Goodbye for the present.[51]

Your son,
William Remmel

Camp of the 121st Regiment
Near New Baltimore, Va.
September the 11th, 1863
My Dear Brother [Augustus],

I very thankfully acknowledge the receipt of your very kind letter, which was received last evening. It afforded me much pleasure to hear from you and to learn that you were bearing your taxing labors so patiently and, although all that are near and dear to you were far away from you, yet you endured all manfully and with fortitude. I fear, dear brother, that I do not sympathize with you sufficiently, for your new home must indeed be a very lonely and embarrassing one to you at times, now that Louisa and William, as you say, are gone. But, Augustus, you must cultivate patience and try to be contented. Your trials will seem severe to you for a time, but they will gradually pass off and then your future will, I am sure, look bright and there will be, as I am sure there is, a rich reward in store for you.

Of one thing I want to call your attention, which I am happy to say you yourself spoke and that is bad company. Always shun bad society. Do not, I beg you dear brother, allow yourself to be led astray by the low and depraved men and boys of Ephratah. I am sorry to learn that there are so many vices existing in that small place. Shun them all as you would the sting of a serpent. Though the temptation maybe a severe one at first, but when your comrades find out that you have resolved not to indulge in carousing and blaspheming, they will think all the more of you for your nobleness.

I received a letter from father a few evenings [ago]. Our people are all well and their crops are looking finely. I wish that I might go and make them a visit, but this is impossible for the present for I am unable to obtain a furlough. Of this I am confident, although I have not tried. The time is too precious to allow furloughs to be given. As soon as there is any chance for procuring a furlough I shall do so, I assure you, but it would be vain for me to try now.[52]

Today we received the glorious news that all of Morris Island was in our possession and that Charleston must very soon fall, and also that Rosecrans had occupied Chattanooga. The rebellion, I am sure, is on its last legs. The other night, the guerrillas made a dash into our lines in the night, wounded 3 men, and escaped. It is now quite late and must close.[53]

I am very affectionately,
Your brother,
Wm. Remmel

Camp of the 121st Regiment N.Y.S.V.
Near New Baltimore, Va.
September 12, 1863
My Dear Parents,

Your kind letter came to hand a few evenings ago, and it afforded me much pleasure to hear from you. I was glad to learn that you were all well, and that everything appeared to prosper. And while you were rejoicing over your excellent health, crops, &c, we too are made happy by the glorious news from the South and Southwest. Yesterday the papers announced to us the evacuation of Morris Island by the chivalrous Beauregard and the possession of Chattanooga by Rosecrans, together with the capture by the latter of 2,000 prisoners belonging to Bragg's army and the possession of Cumberland Gap.

These brave and daring achievements by our brave soldiers had made our hearts glad and almost too full for utterance. We are all now confident that the rebels cannot hold out much longer. All that the Potomac boys want now is conscripts. If you will only send them, we will, in a few weeks, again beat back Lee's demoralized hordes, mangled and bleeding toward Richmond and again cover ourselves as at Gettysburg with honors such as can never be erased. I do not say this for flattery, for it is my honest opinion. I am confident that with equal numbers on both sides, and equal footing otherwise, we can whip them anywhere and at any time.[54]

And could I have my wish, I would have every Copperhead in the North in the army. They are nothing but a curse to the nation. They are opposed to the Administration, to the war and, I can say, to the Constitution. They are now crying for peace. They would like to see every rebel back as he was in the beginning, without being punished in the least. They even say now that, as soon as Charleston falls, the North can acquire measures of peace with them, but every true soldier in the army is opposed to this. They will tell you that they have fought two years, and can fight two more if it is required, to bring the traitors upon their knees. And this, with the help of God, we are bound to do.[55]

Everything here in the army at present is very quiet. The other night the rebels made a dash into our camp, rode to our general's headquarters and fired into his tent, and then wheeled about and rode back without being harmed. They wounded 3 men. The pickets were nearly all asleep and without loaded guns. I think it will occur again. The weather is cool and pleasant. We drill a great deal. Please send me a good large towel as soon as convenient. I must forbear writing now.[56]

From your son,
Wm. Remmel

Camp of the 121st Regiment
Near Rapidan, Va.
October 9th, 1863
My Dear Parents,

Your letter was received by me some days ago, but for want of time and other difficulties I have been unable to answer it before. Our corps is now holding the front along the upper part of the Rapidan. We moved to the front last Monday. We relieved the 2nd Corps. Our regiment has been out on picket 3 days. We came in last night. We had a very pleasant time out. The Johnnies, as we call them, were very friendly. I had several chats with them. They appeared to be much delighted at the interview. They said that they would always like to meet the Yankees on as friendly terms. I changed papers with one of them and found much that was interesting.[57]

We are having a very fine weather, although the nights are quite cold. This was the case last night and it is so cool this morning early that my fingers are quite stiff as I am writing, which makes it difficult to write this morning. I do not intend to write much this morning, for we have got to go out and see a deserter in a Jersey regiment shot very soon. This I think a very painful duty, but we have to witness it, for that is the orders and orders in the army have to be obeyed. It seems hard to have to shoot men of our own army, but it is the only way to stop desertion. If there was no check of this kind made, the army would in a short time be reduced to a very small standard.[58]

One reason why I write you today is to have you order a pair of boots made for me, for it is most time that a soldier should look out for dry feet. I would like a pair of boots such as you sent me last fall, with this difference, have the heels and toes plated to prevent the heels from running over and the toes wearing out. The legs should be long enough to admit the pants; the in-step pretty high; have a double row of nails placed around the soles; the heels should be large and square, the leather kipskin, the size No. 9. I do not know exactly how to get them here. If Charley does not come down here to see me, you had better send them by Adams Express Company to Washington and in care of Samuel Miller, sutler for the 121st Regiment, N.Y.S.V. Have them made as soon as you can. Also send a couple of pair of socks. Write me as soon as you send them and tell me where you have sent them. There is some talk that we are agoing to fall back to Washington. I will not attempt to write more at this time, so goodbye.[59]

From your affectionate son,
Wm. Remmel

I would not advise Charley to visit just now. If he is drafted, it will be time enough.

In the field
Seven miles North of
Centreville, Va.
October the 16th, 1863
My Dear Parents,

Knowing that you are ever anxious to hear from me, and especially in time of expected danger, I take the present opportunity to drop a few lines to you.

You see from the heading of this letter that the army is again in the vicinity of the memorable Bull Run ground and, in truth, we are here. Ere this reaches you, you will undoubtedly have learned of the results of the past few days fighting in the army. A great battle was expected today, but we have been disappointed, which I trust is for the best. But if Lee should attack us in our present position, we are confident that we will come out victors. Our corps is holding the extreme right. We are strongly entrenched, having thrown up heavy earthworks all along our lines. And I can say, with hardly an exception, that the army is anxious for Lee to attack us, so great is our chance for success. We are all in fine spirits and think that, if we are to face more battles, we had better stand in rifle pits than on the open plain.[60]

There was heavy fighting going on yesterday on our left. We have not learned the results. The day before yesterday there was considerable fighting in the rear. The rebels evidently trying to capture part of our trains, but they were foiled in their attempt and were beaten back with heavy loss in prisoners and artillery. It is now generally thought that the rebel general will not dare to attack us in our strong position, but must attempt to invade Maryland. But it is getting too late, I think, for such a movement and there may not be much done after all. It is not impossible that a battle maybe fought tomorrow. Today it has been quite rainy and not favorable for a fight.[61]

But it is getting dark and I must close. Do not think that I am by any means troubled about the expected battle. I am ready and willing to stand and take the storm, for it is in a just, holy cause that I [am] struggling. I will write again as soon as circumstances will allow me.

I may drop Charley a letter in a day or two. I now bid you an affectionate good night, and hope to hear from you very soon. I send my love to all.

From your distant son,
William Remmel

Near Centreville, Va.
October the 17th, 1863
Dear Brother Augustus,

It is a great while, I suppose you think, since I last wrote to you. And I fancy that, by this time, you are desirous of hearing from me again, especially ere the present time, for you must by this time have learned of the activity in this army for the past few days.

The army, which 10 days ago was lying sixty and seventy miles from Washington on the route to Gordonsville, has fell back to a new base on the old Bull

Run ground. On our retreat back we were continually harassed by the rebels. Our corps had, a few days before we fell back, gone to the front and relieved the 2nd Corps. Our position was along the Rapidan, 12 miles beyond Culpeper. We arrived near the river Monday afternoon, Sept. 5th, and were immediately ordered on picket. We were out 3 days and had a gay old time, there was no picket firing while we were out. The rebels were very friendly and would often come half way to change papers, trade coffee, and have a soldier's talk over the war.[62]

There was also a cornfield mid-way between the picket lines, and neither side was at all backward in supplying themselves with corn. But our pleasant times were to last but a short time, for the next Saturday we were ordered to move, we knew not where. We laid all day with our things packed, but did not get the order to move until dark, when we started. We marched that night as far as Culpeper. After we had eaten a scanty breakfast and had taken a little rest, we started again to the rear and arrived at Rappahannock station along in the afternoon. As is always the case, when there is a retreat, the cavalry brings up the rear and often they are compelled to show fight to keep the enemy back. This was the case this time, but the dashing and impetuous Kilpatrick cut his way right and left through the rebels with comparatively small loss.[63]

The next day, Monday, which was the present week, General Meade offered battle, but they would not accept. Next morning, one O'clock we were again ordered up to skedaddle and we have since found out that it was a strife between the two generals to see which would get at this place first. Luckily, the Union army was the winner. Had Lee got here first, he would have cut us off from Washington and possibly destroyed our army. We are now in full possession of the old Bull Run ground and can hold it at all events. We are strongly entrenched and can hold twice our own number in check. If they attack us, we will drive them back. But I must close this long and ill-written letter, so goodbye for this time.

From your brother,
Wm. Remmel

Camp of the 121st
Near Warrenton, Va.
October the 26th, 1863
Dear Brother Charles,

Your kind letter was received last evening and I was much pleased to hear from you once more. But I confess that I am ashamed that I have not answered your other letter, which I received while at Culpeper about 3 weeks ago. I received the letter and intended all the while to have answered it, but sorry to have to acknowledge that I did not do it. It is no use now grieving over what I have not done, but I assure you that in the future your letters will be promptly answered. I doubt not that some of the family, especially mother, has worried some about me since I wrote my last letter. If this has been the case this letter will, I think, take that anxiety from her mind.

I take pleasure in announcing that the army did not become engaged, which I presume ere this you have learned. I expected at that time that a battle would take place, but Lee did not dare to risk an attack when he learned that we were prepared for him.

The bulk of the army is now encamped in the neighborhood of Warrenton, about 50 miles south of Washington, where it will lay, I think, several weeks to await the repairing of the railroad and the rebuilding of railroad bridges.[64]

You appear to have left the decision of your coming to make me a visit with me. I would like very much to see you, but I have my doubts about your being able to procure a pass at Washington at the present time. I would on the whole not advise you to come this fall, but wait till winter when you will have less difficulty.

You say that you are agoing West. I hope that you will be successful should you buy. I think, however, that with your experience you can make a good strike. I am glad that you intend to return to stay at home this winter, for it will be quite lonesome for our people unless you do.[65]

You say Louisa and William are agoing West, which will make it very lonesome for mother. The boots you say were being made or, rather, a second pair. I am glad of this, for I need a pair very bad. My shoes are nearly worn out. Instead of sending them to Washington in care of Samuel Miller, send them by the Adams Express Company, and direct them to the 121st Regiment N.Y.S.V., 6th Corps, 1st Division, 2nd Brigade. Tell mother to send me some thread, needles, and pins.[66]

My health is excellent. I saw Hiram Cady today, from the 152nd Regiment. He looks natural. I have not seen Moses Bliss in some time. I trust this will reach you before we start. Goodbye.[67]

From your affectionate brother,
Wm. Remmel

Camp of the 121st Regiment
Near Warrenton, Va.
October the 28th, 1863
My Dear Brother Augustus,

Your letter was received a few days ago and I was much pleased to be able to read another of your interesting letters. I wrote a letter to you a few days before I received your last and probably before this you received it.

The army at present is at a standstill and not until the destroyed railroad has been fully repaired can any very important advance be made by this army. We had expected a few weeks ago that a great battle would be fought between Meade and Lee sometime during the present month, but we have in one sense of the word been happily disappointed. For, had a battle been fought, the loss on both sides would naturally have been heavy, as is always the case when two such armies as Meade's and Lee's meet. But if this army is to do more fighting, which we all expect, we had rather meet them on the ground we occupied one week or more ago, than meet anywhere else in Virginia.

Our regiment is lying within sight of the renowned village name Warrenton. It is a very pretty place at a distance, but close inspection will disclose many imperfections in the buildings in many of them. There are, however, many pretty houses in the place. The village has seen as much wear and tear from this war as any of equal size in Virginia. Many of the houses have been torn down by the soldiers and appropriated to army use, such as firewood, hut frames, &c.[68]

All of our supplies have to be brought on wagons a distance of about 12 miles from a place called Gainesville, which makes it very hard for our team and teamsters, who have to be out a good share of the time on the road. To add to this arduous labor, they have to be exposed to any attack that the guerrilla Mosby or his band choose to make upon the trains. A few evenings ago, he made a dash upon one of these trains and captured about 20 wagons with their teams and provisions, teamsters included.[69]

But I must not dwell too long upon these different topics, for I fancy you want to know something of myself. My health, as always I inform you, is good. I am tough and rugged, and bid fair to stand my 3 years as a soldier, if some careless bullet does not waylay me. We have, of late, had little or no drill in our regiment, which none of the boys will acknowledge they are sorry over. It has until very recently been drill, drill, whenever there was the least chance for it, ever since the regiment first stopped at Bakersville a year ago.

The weather of late has been very cold and rather unpleasant, especially at night, for cold weather leaves its mark upon a soldier more than hot weather while in camp. While on the march, the former is much preferred. Want in a few days to take a peek at the country and, perhaps, buy a piece of land.

Hear William and Louisa are agoing. Our people are well. But I must bring this lengthy letter to a close, so goodbye brother.

Wm. Remmel

Camp of the 121st Regiment
Near Warrenton, Va.
November the 4th, 1863
My Dear Parents,

As I sit me down this beautiful November morning in my little rude cabin, built of logs and covered with white canvass, my mind wanders to the far off North and I think of home and all that a son would love and cherish. How gladly would I like to make you all a visit if it were not more than a day, but oh! if it could be for an indefinite length of time, leaving you and me to decide how long. But I must not dwell on this rather painful topic, but suffice it to say that, as I thought of these things, I determined again to write a few lines to you.

If I remember right, my last letter was written near Centreville, Virginia, and, as I thought then, at a rather critical time. But time has changed the aspect of affairs and now where we are lying everything wears a look of quiet and stillness and one would hardly dream of a battle for months to come. While at *Bull Run* and thereabouts a battle we were quite sure would take place, but our position looked dangerous to Lee and he dared not attack us. So he cowed back like a whipped dog.[70]

The greater part of the army have gone into temporary winter quarters, which few expect will last long for it is the general impression that the army will yet advance and perhaps fight a great battle. The rebels, we learn from the papers, are still on the north side of the Rappahannock and it is General Meade's intention, we think, to at last drive them across the river. With that, we had force enough to advance on Richmond and take that treasonable city. We could then release our noble soldier brothers, who are pining away and dying in the loathsome prisons there from woeful neglect.[71]

About one week ago I made a visit to the 152nd N.Y.S.V. and I saw several boys that I know from around home. Among them was Hiram Cady, Swift Roback, and James Monk. The latter said that he was home all summer and worked for Palmer in the bark woods a part of the time, and said that Caleb worked with him a month. He spoke of Caleb as being a pretty lively boy, but would not drink whiskey. When I heard this last remark, I felt glad within myself to think that Caleb had taken so firm a resolution in this direction. For nowadays it is getting very fashionable to step up and take a glass of rum.[72]

I received a letter from Augustus 2 nights ago. He informed me that he was well, but did not attend school yet. Augustus is a steady and intelligent boy and, if he retains his health, he will make his mark.

I was very much pleased with a letter from Ada, which she sent me. She writes and composes splendidly for a child so young. I hope to receive a letter from both her and Harmon. Please write me in your next where you have sent the boots. Remember me to Eliphelet Shaver, as I learn that he cannot live long.[73]

Goodbye
Wm. Remmel

Camp of the 121st Regiment
Near Warrenton, Va.
November the 4th, 1863
My dear Brother [Augustus],

I am happy to acknowledge the receipt of your kind letter, which came to hand two ev[enings] ago. Your health, you say, is very good and I trust that your eyes will fully recover, as I think they will by proper treatment. I hope that you will soon attend school, for this is very important. If you are not able to go regularly, on account of business in the store or otherwise, you must inform your employer that this will not answer, that you can do better. I hope that you will get along with this without any trouble.

Everything is very quiet in the army at present. The railroad is nearly repaired and a movement is talked of, whether true of not, time alone can tell. Our regiment is very comfortably quartered and most of the boys are building log houses. My two tent mates and myself have just finished ours and we think a great deal of it. We have a very nice fireplace and a good bed. On the whole, it is a very comfortable house for a soldier, for we have learned to take our quarters wherever and whichever way we can. All that troubles us now is that we will have to leave our pleasant camp and bivouac wherever night overtakes us.[74]

The weather here at present is very mild daytimes. The sun shines brilliantly and its cheering rays refreshen and warm the earth. But the nights are extremely cold, which makes sleeping quite uncomfortable unless there is plenty of clothing on hand.

While on a visit to the 152nd New York the other day, I saw several boys from our vicinity. Among them the following: Hiram Cady, Swift Roback, and James Monk. They looked hearty and robust. Monk took a furlough last summer and thought to stay for good, but was arrested and brought to his regiment then in New York City. He said that he worked with Caleb in the bark woods for Palmer.[75]

I was much pleased with Ada's letter. It shows that she does not idle away her time in school, but tries to learn and progress, as her letter gives ample proof. The letter is well written and finely composed.

It also gave me pleasure to read how abundantly father had stored in of his different crops. And what gratifies me most of all is that father is now sole owner of his little farm. And as you say, he ought to possess the strip across the road and then he could live on its products and enjoy himself. Well, we will hope for the best, for that time may yet come.

Charley, I suppose, has taken his departure and William and Louisa will, I suppose, start soon, which will leave our people almost alone again. Under the existing circumstances, I have my doubts whether the family will ever all together meet again. It grieves me much that Eliphlet Shaver cannot live long. He was respected by many. But I must bring this lengthy letter to a close, so goodbye for this time.

W.R.

Camp of the 121st Regiment
In the field
Near Brandy Station, Va.
November the 9th, 1863
Dear Parents,

Having a little leisure this morning, I take the opportunity to address you with a very few lines. Our regiment left Warrenton Saturday morning for Rappahannock Station. We arrived to within about one mile when we found the rebels in force. Our generals immediately sent out skirmishers and fighting commenced. The rebels were in severely strong works, which had been built sometime before, and our corps had got to drive them across the river.[76]

Our batteries kept pouring into the works all the afternoon and there was also considerable musketry. Just dusk, the 3rd brigade of our division and 2 regiments in our brigade were ordered to charge the works. The 2 regiments were the 5th Maine and the 121st, our regiment. We charged the works most handsomely at the point of bayonet. The rebels made but little resistance. They fired but few shots. We captured, in all, about 2,000 prisoners and took 7 pieces of artillery. Our regiment had 4 killed, 22 wounded, and 2 missing. Our company lost one man killed. He fell dead by my side.[77]

We crossed the river yesterday on pontoon bridges and offered battle, but they declined. Our corps will probably push on this morning. I do not think there will be any battle here. For the rebels will not dare to risk a battle this side of the Rapidan. There may be no more fighting here this fall. It is not impossible that a great battle may yet take place.[78]

But I will close this letter. Hoping to be able to write you again soon.

From your son,
Wm. Remmel

Camp of the 121st Regiment
Near Hazel River, Va.
November the 19th, 1863
My Dear Brother [Augustus],

Your letter dated November 13th has been received and, having a little leisure time, I thought I would improve it by answering your letter. I was happy to learn that your health was yet good, and hope that it may long remain unimpaired. You say that you are agoing to have a talk with your employer, which I trust will result in your favor.

You said that William and Louisa had come down to Ephratah. I suppose they have by this time taken their departure for the West. I am sorry to learn that Charley has concluded not to buy, but return again to California. I suppose that from what I had heard from home that Charley would conclude to settle down, after wandering so long far from home. If I have an opportunity to write him, I shall try and discourage such a second enterprise.[79]

You said that your clothing was not yet finished and that you lacked $1 of having enough to pay for the suit. Your request, desiring a little assistance to pay for the whole from me, I willingly concede to. You will find enclosed in this the desired amount.

There is nothing of importance going on here, but a forward movement is looked for. No doubt we will move in 2 or 3 days. It is generally thought that it will be a movement to capture Richmond. This has been tried so often that such an event would astonish the whole world. Although we have at each previous time failed to accomplish anything by such an undertaking, yet we may now nevertheless accomplish what is by many considered an impossibility. Should our expectations be realized (the capture of Richmond), this rebellion will soon have to tumble to atoms.[80]

We have had some drilling to do this week. The weather is very mild and pleasant. It resembles our Indian summer at home. No doubt ere this letter reaches you will have received by previous letter, which I sent a few days ago (Sunday). It is about time for dress parade and I must draw this letter to a close. I received Maria Empie's letter some time [ago]. One letter on my part will finish our correspondence. I will prepare it soon. Do not show this to any of William's friends. Hoping this will find you well, I will close.[81]

From your affectionate brother,
William Remmel

Camp of the 121st Regiment
Near Hazel River, Va.
November the 21st, 1863
My Dear Parents,

I herein send a certificate from the commanding officer of the regiment, Col. E. Upton, to show that I have been honorably appointed Sergeant of Co. I, 121st N.Y. Vols. All of the non-commissioned officers have received them in the regiment. You will please preserve it until I call for it, or until I arrive home. I have nothing new to write you.[82]

Yesterday there was a grand review of our corps, the 6th, by the corps commander, Sedgwick, and some Russian Naval officers, among them Rear Admiral Lavoski. The review was very fine one and very highly spoken of.[83]

There has been considerable talk of a march this week, but I do not know whether we will move or not. It would seem as if this army ought to make another strike before winter sets in and it is generally believed that there will be more fighting before January. Time alone will disclose these things, for we cannot tell much about what will be done, although [we are] right in the army where all has to transpire.[84]

My boots and other articles have not yet arrived. I do not know exactly where you have directed them. I gave two different directions. The first was to Washington, DC, in care of Samuel Miller the sutler to our regiment. The last was ordered through to the regiment by the Adams Express Company. Please write me in your next about it.

Have you received the $17 sent you last Sunday? It is very rainy, so goodbye.

From your son,
William Remmel

Camp of the 121st regiment
Near Hazel River, Va.
November 24th, 1863
My Dear Parents,

It gives me great pleasure to be able to inform you that my very much desired and expected package has been received. It arrived at headquarters yesterday. I was on picket during the day and, therefore, did not receive the package until this afternoon, at which time I arrived off from duty. I am very sorry, indeed, that some of the valuable articles sent me were picked out of the bag, which has a large hole in the side. The socks, peppers, and nutmegs have either been taken out or else lost out. The boots, which are of the greatest importance, are all right. They fit well and I think that they will do me good service. I would like to have had steel plates upon the heels and toes, but I suppose it is difficult to get them to have. The needle-book, given me by Ada, I think very much of and I shall always think of her as I look upon the useful present. The berries are very nice and the bread was excellent, though a little hard. The butter is also wholesome and good and, on the whole, I am very thankful that the articles came as safe as they did.

But I cannot fill this sheet for want of time. The army received orders to move this morning, but in consequence of a rainstorm it has been countermanded and we will probably start tomorrow or day after. It is very muddy and will be very hard marching. I do not know which way we are agoing, but probably it will be toward the Rapidan.

I sent a company record to you 2 days ago and I trust that by the end of the week you will receive it. I think that you will like it. You can procure a frame for it and it will make a nice ornament in the sitting room. It has all the names of the company upon it that came with the regiment. There were some mistakes made, which are covered with strips of paper. Those names which contain no remarks after them are the names of those men which yet belong to the company that have remained uninjured. The names of those killed, wounded, taken prisoners and where, in our battles are also down and those that are discharged. I hope that it will be much liked.

Have you received the $17 I sent you the 15th instant in a letter? Please tell all about it in your next letter. I do not feel much like writing and did not expect to write as much as I have. You will please excuse this poor writing, for my hands are very numb from the cold. I can only say of the package you have sent that I am very thankful for your kindness and will always remember these gifts. Goodbye.

From your son,
William Remmel

Camp of the 121st Regiment
Near Hazel River, Va.
December 7th, 1863
My Dear Parents,

I thought I would write a few lines to you to let you know that I am among the living and well. I shall not attempt to write much at this time, for I want to fix up my tent, for cold weather makes it uncomfortable to cook outdoors and besides a fireplace will make our little kitchen, bedroom, and parlor, which are all made up of one room, more comfortable.

You have, of course, learned from the papers that our corps did not become engaged across the river, consequently no accidents happened from shells or bullets. The weather, while over the river, was very cold and it was difficult most of the time to keep warm. Had there been a great battle fought, many men would have perished from the cold. I, for one, am glad that we returned without fighting a very great battle.

It is too late to capture Richmond after the 1st of December. It is nonsense to think of it. If these newspaper proprietors, and others north, could live and endure with us awhile they would know the reason why something is not done. It makes me mad to see so much faultfinding in the papers about our army here. This army and its generals do all that men can to capture that infernal city (Richmond) and it is wrong to find fault; but enough of this.[85]

The weather is very cold and the whole army is preparing for winter. Our regiment will have to change camp to get good quarters, where wood is handy.

My health is excellent. I felt better. The boots are doing me good service and the other articles are, or have been, appreciated. I received your letter with $1 enclosed. Have you received my last 3 letters? One had $17 in and the other one a company memorial. The postage stamps I have received. I have received a letter from Louisa and Charley. They are all well. Augustus has written me several letters. He is also well. I will write you again in a day or two, so goodbye from your son.[86]

I send my love to all,
Wm. Remmel

Camp of the 121st Regiment
Near Hazel River, Va.
December 9th, 1863
My Dear Brother [Augustus],

I am sorry indeed that I have not written you before, since I returned from our late campaign across the Rapidan. The truth of the matter is, I have been so busy in changing camp and fixing up log shanties, &c., that I have been unable to write to anyone. My letter tonight will be quite short, for want of light to write by, for you must know that I am sitting on the ground and scribbling by the light of a fireplace.

Our regiment, while over the river, did not become engaged, although twice drawn up for that purpose. The weather the most of the time while across the river was very cold and, had there been a great battle fought, many of the wounded would have perished before they could have been brought off the field. I think that General Meade was very wise in withdrawing his army, for there would have been a terrible loss of life had any assault been made on the enemy's position. The army has, I think, gone into winter quarters, although a change in position may yet be ordered.[87]

Nearly the whole army is lying on the south side of the Rappahannock. Our brigade moved to the north side of the same river yesterday. The boys have all been very busy today in building up log houses for the winter, for we will remain here until spring.

There are four boys in our tent, which is rather more than ought to try to winter in one small log tent. I have not yet raised my canvass house, for all of my partners were away today. Two on picket and the other gone home on a leave of absence. Probably tomorrow night I shall be all right.

That package that father and mother sent me I received a day or two before starting on our last advance. Some of the articles were taken out. There was a large hole in one corner of the bag in which the articles were packed, where the things undoubtedly found out by some shrewd villain's hand. Two pair of socks, writing paper, envelopes, and other articles had been taken. Mother sent me a pair of socks a few days ago, and I received them all right. Father wishes me to give him a list of the articles lost, and he will hold the Express Comp. responsible.

Our people were all well except mother, who was sick but not serious. I trust that she will soon recover. Caleb, Harmon, and Ada are all attending school now. I have heard from Louisa and Charley. Louisa said that she became very much exhausted riding on the cars. She is much pleased with the city (Fort Wayne). Charley is very much discontented and wants to return to California. He is coming home soon to spend New Year's. This letter is longer than I intended, but do not feel discouraged. Wishing you a happy good night, I will close. I will write again.

W. Remmel

Camp of the 121st Regiment
Near Hazel River, Va.
December the 12th, 1863
My Dear Parents,

I am glad to be able to acknowledge the last two letters that you have written me. Your last one, dated December 6th, I received last night and was much pleased to learn that you were all well.

Your other letter came to me about 1 week ago. The same day that I wrote a letter with lead pencil to you. The pair of socks you sent me came through all right and I appreciated them much, for the weather is very cold and good socks are needed by every soldier. The money you sent me, which was $1, I received, as I stated in my last letter. I do not need it now, but can send perhaps more next on that account. We draw pay very regular every 2 months, unless on a summer's campaign, when sometimes we have to wait a little longer. In the winter a soldier need not be out of money, if he uses it right.[88]

I was happy to learn that you received the $17 I sent you, also the company memorial and the certificate. It gives me much pleasure to know that you think so much of the splendid little record of our company, which gives the names of our regimental and company officers and also the names of the men belonging to the company (I). The men killed, wounded, died, deserted, taken prisoners, and those that have not been injured. Also the list of men promoted to Sergeants and Corporals. The battles that the "Compy" have participated in. I think it is very nice and will be a beautiful token of remembrance in the family, if I should not return. And if I participate in any more battles and survive them and finally return home, as I hope to, I can have the record remodeled or changed as circumstances require.

You say that you have put part of the money, $20, on interest in the Little Falls Bank and intend to place more therein. This is perfectly satisfactory to me. But if you need the money in the family I do not want you to dispose of a penny in the bank, but use it. For money is no object to me now. Not until I return from the war. I say once more, if you need the money, I want you to use every cent of it. If not, then you have used it right. The bank is the right place for it. One word about postage stamps. It is difficult to get them here and I wish you would send me about 50 cents worth every month.

The following are the articles received in the box or bag. 1 pair boots, 1 lump butter, 1 bag of berries with cake, 1 loaf of bread, 1 needle book, 1 bunch thread with thimble, 1 paper of sugar, and 1 bag of salt. This is all that I recollect of now.

Nathan Wood has not yet arrived. The death of Eliphelet Shaver is certainly very sad. It causes grief almost to tears within for I loved him, though he possessed faults which none are free from. I hope he rests in Heaven.

We are preparing good quarters and I should in a few weeks like to have you send a box. I shall let you know when furloughs are given for 10 days. Shall I try to get one?[89]

Goodbye for the present,
Wm. Remmel

Camp of the 121st Regiment
Near Hazel River, Va.
December 30th, 1863
Dear Brother [Augustus],

It is a service of great pleasure to me to be able to write you occasionally, for from you more than any other one do I look for unhappiness and grievances. For you are away from home and among entire strangers, except such as you have in your short stay, by business transactions, become acquainted with. I am exceedingly glad that, though your lot is a trying and grievous one, you bear all so cheerfully and make the best of it. There is nothing that is more worthy of admiration than a persevering and contented mind. The man that is ready and willing to make sacrifice, endure disappointments, and bear afflictions to support himself, and be dependent on his own earnings for a livelihood, cannot at last avoid being a prosperous and perhaps wealthy man. It no doubt seems at times to be under the absolute rule of a stranger, though now, of course, you have made a full acquaintance with your employer, but bear all with cheer and you will at last have learned a valuable lesson. One which will lead you on the road to prosperity and wealth. I am glad that you are at last attending schooling and, if you are only permitted to go steady, spring, I am sure, will see you far advanced in your studies. Strive to learn all that you can and, I assure you, you will never regret having been diligent and studious in the schoolroom. Tell me in your next letter what you are studying this winter.

I received a letter from Charley and Louisa a few days ago. They are both well and in fine spirits. Charley says that he has given up all ideas of going back to California and has come to the conclusion that he will marry before long and settle down. This, I think, will be a very wise move in him and, if he follows this course and invests his money safely in some kind of stocks and commence in business, I cannot see why he cannot make an easy livelihood and enjoy himself too. I think Louisa enjoys herself as well as could be expected. William, I suppose, has gone into business by this time. I hope that he may do well.

One word about the army; the troops have all gone into winter quarters and the Potomac army will do no more fighting until spring, and this rest will be deeply appreciated by every soldier in this army. For both officers and men are sorely in need of rest. Our corps is a beautiful one and we pride ourselves on having the best camp in the army. We live pretty well and there is nothing to mar a pleasant and highly delightful winter vacation, as we call it. I trust this finds you as well. Nathan is not here. No more for the present.[90]

Goodbye,
Wm. Remmel

2. Horatio Wright succeeded to command of the 6th Corps after Sedgwick's death and led it through the end of the war. Library of Congress, Prints and Photographs Division.

3. Lt. Delevan Bates served in Company I until promoted to colonel of the 30th United States Colored Troops in March 1864. He earned a Medal of Honor for actions at Petersburg in July 1864. U.S. Army Military History Institute.

4. John S. Kidder served as captain of Company I and held Remmel in high regard. U.S. Army Military History Institute.

5. Maj. Henry Galpin served in the ranks of the 44th New York and helped recruit the 121st New York during the summer of 1862. U.S. Army Military History Institute.

6. Lt. Frank Foote mustered into Company I as second lieutenant on August 18, 1862, and succeeded Delevan Bates as first lieutenant on March 16, 1864. He was wounded and captured during the regiment's assault at Spotsylvania. U.S. Army Military History Institute.

7. Egbert Olcott succeeded to command of the 121st New York after Upton's promotion to brigadier general in July 1864. U.S. Army Military History Institute.

8. John Sedgwick, the beloved commander of the 6th Corps. A Confederate sniper killed "Uncle John" on May 12, 1864, at Spotsylvania Courthouse. Library of Congress, Prints and Photographs Division.

9. Philip H. Sheridan brought the tactics of total war to the Shenandoah Valley during the summer of 1864. Library of Congress, Prints and Photographs Division.

10. Emory Upton, shown at the rank of major general, served as colonel of the 121st New York for nearly two years. His strict discipline made a significant difference in the regiment's development. Library of Congress, Prints and Photographs Division.

3

1864
"Should I Ever Return to Your Fireside"

In 1864 William Remmel began his second full campaign season with the Army of the Potomac, then under the leadership of Lt. Gen. Ulysses S. Grant. During this year the 121st New York participated in the costly Overland campaign, including battles at the Wilderness and Spotsylvania. Although the regiment sustained heavy losses in these battles, they continued to distinguish themselves. At the battle of Spotsylvania, "Upton's Regulars" realized their defining moment of glory in their courageous but unsuccessful assault on the "Mule Shoe," a vulnerable salient within the entrenched Rebel rifle pits. Wounded in the forearm and hand during this assault, Remmel spent the next three months in Emory Hospital and on convalescent leave at home. Always conscious of a soldier's vulnerability and the importance of good health, William reflected deeply at this time upon his mortality amid the perils of war in relation to sacrifices already endured. During his recovery he openly hoped that the wound might result in an honorable discharge from the army. A strong sense of familial responsibility and concern for the potential burden of grief to his parents also influenced his disapproval of the proposed enlistment of his three brothers that fall, though he remained committed to the terms of his own enlistment.[1]

Like many other Union soldiers at this point in the war, Remmel remained committed to the cause but also felt increasingly frustrated with some of the political and military leaders who were directing the effort. The lack of commitment and sacrifice expressed by various elements of the Northern civilian population proved an equal if not greater source of frustration. His experience in the field as well as his confidence in the abilities of Grant and Lincoln allowed William little sympathy for civilians and politicians who continued to question the army's ability to achieve a full victory. His own commitment to final victory is reflected in his support for the tactics of "total war." Despite his strong religious inclinations, Remmel continued to favor harsh policies designed not only to defeat the Confederate army but also to destroy the will of Southern civilians to continue the war. As a participant in Sheridan's Valley campaign, he put these beliefs into action in his final engagement of the war.[2]

This final group of letters concludes with the arrival of sixteen-year-old Pvt. Caleb Remmel on October 16, 1864, just three days before William's disappearance.[3]

Camp of the 121st Regiment
Near Hazel River, Va.
January 3rd, 1864
Dear Parents,

Your last letter was received 2 evenings ago and was delighted to learn that you were all yet well. My health is excellent this winter and I think that I shall enjoy myself finely through the winter months. The weather here at present is very cold. This change has taken place within the last 2 days, for a week before that it rained nearly every day. I have seen snow just one morning this winter and there was hardly enough to cover the ground.

The troops in this army are now all in good quarters and the cold weather can have but little effect upon them. We are living in good style, have plenty of soft bread and other articles in good proportion. I think that this army will come out in good fighting twine next spring. Our quarters are very comfortable and we enjoy ourselves as well as soldiers can expect to in the field.[4]

Many of the old regiments are re-enlisting and we shall stand a chance of getting most of the old soldiers to stay till the struggle is over. I have but little news to write to you at this time. We received an order the other night that we were agoing to start for Washington the next morning by railroad, but we did not go. We have since learned that the reason of this order was an expected raid near Harper's Ferry, by a portion of Lee's cavalry and infantry.

As you desire to have me come home this winter, I will try to procure a furlough, but I think that it will be no use, for about ½ of our brigade is going home for 30 days after having re-enlisted for 3 years. This will make a great deal more duty for our regiment and it is thought that no more furloughs will be granted until these men get back. I can tell you before long whether I can come home or not. If I should not be able to come, I will write you and then you can send me the box.

I went and saw that German, Russ, and told him what you wrote me. He said that he had wrote one letter to his brother, but that he had never answered it and he should write no more until he heard from him. He said that his brother need not send me anything, for he has got enough himself. Having no more news to write, I will close.[5]

From your son,
Wm. Remmel

I send my love to all.

Camp of the 121st Regiment
Near Hazel River, Va.
January 10th, 1864
My Dear Parents,

I received your last letter a few evenings since, and sit me down to reply. I am well as ever and from present indications think that I will enjoy myself, and in fine style, this winter. The snow is about 4 inches deep and lays on frozen ground and there is a prospect of its remaining for several days, unless the sun comes out warmer and the air grows milder than it has for several days past.

Our quarters are very comfortable and, so long as we are permitted to remain in them, there will be no danger of complaint about cold weather. But we have to go out on picket once a week and sometimes four, and there we find it quite uncomfortable, especially at nights, for we have no covering. Nothing but a few pine brush thrown up to keep the wind off a little. But one day in the cold is nothing for a healthy soldier, and we think but little of it after having endured so much that is much worse. Many of the old troops are re-enlisting and by spring there will be a larger army in the field, ready for the work which will be laid out for them through the winter.

We soldiers all feel confident that the war will not last more than one year longer, if the army is managed right. I think that next summer campaign will wind up the rebellion. The troops are all in excellent spirits and are all anxious to see the draft come off, if the troops (soldiers) cannot be raised by volunteering. I hope that the quota will be filled up by volunteers, but if it cannot be quickly done then resort to the draft. For it is no use putting off 2 or 3 months longer and, when the men are wanted, not have them ready for the work.

I am sorry to say that I will hardly be able to come home on a furlough this winter. There are others that have families, who will have the first chance of going. If I can come along in the spring, I will do it. Many of the old troops in our brigade have re-enlisted and gone home, which makes a great deal more duty for our regiment and, consequently, no more furloughs are granted in the regiment until these men get back.

If you choose to send the box, you can do so. It will come through safe. If it will be much trouble to you, do not trouble yourself with it. Should you send one, have small bands fastened around the edges, so that it cannot be well opened, and write when you send it. Place the same directions upon it that I gave you. We expect to be paid off in a few days, and then you may look for a few Greenbacks.

I am glad that you are agoing to send me postage stamps, for I want a few very much. I have nothing new to write, so will close for the time. Goodbye.

From your son,
William Remmel

I send my love to all and keep a part for yourselves.
Tell Charley to write me often, also Caleb, Harmon, and Ada.

Camp of the 121st Regiment
Near Hazel River, Va.
January 18th, 1864
My Dear Brother [Augustus],

Your letter was received last evening and now I sit me down to reply. I am, as usual, in good spirits and feeling well. The weather for the past few days has been quite mild and most of the time pleasant, but this morning it set in to raining and has kept on almost increasingly until about ½ hour ago. It is now about 4 (P.M.). The roads and camps have consequently become very muddy, and it is difficult to step out far from camp without getting badly soiled with mud.

The soil here in Virginia is of such a kind that it heaves badly in the fall when frost appears, so that rains at this season produce mud very easily, especially when roads are traveled as they necessarily must be where an army is in quarters. There is little of interest that I can write you at this time. Our regiment has not drilled any since we moved to this camp. There is so much duty to do that it is difficult to get men enough together to make the drill agreeable. A part of the old soldiers in the brigade have re-enlisted and have gone home on 35 days furloughs. So you see that it makes more duty for those that remain, since we hold the same length of picket line that we did while all were present.[6]

The regiment is in a very healthy condition and has been so for some time past. Our quarters are much better than they were last winter. The boys have all improved on them, more or less; and besides, they have, in their various marches and visits through the different regiments, had an opportunity of finding out and judging which kind of tents are best adapted to a soldier's needs. I was fortunate enough to procure a sufficient quantity of boards, of which to build my tent.

My house is about 12 feet long, 17 feet wide and 4 feet high. In the front end is the door and chimney and about ½ of the room inside of the tent is taken up by the bed, which is made of poles about 2 inches in diameter. These poles raised about 3 feet from the ground. The poles are covered with straw, which we got off of a plantation about ½ miles from camp. The bedclothes are thus summed up. There are 3 of us, 3 woolen blankets, 3 overcoats and 2 rubber blankets. We make pillows of our pantaloons, which we place upon our knapsacks. There is a table made of rough boards standing in a part of the room not occupied by the bed. There is one shelf and several nails stuck up to places and hang things on. Our dishes are all either tin, iron, or steel, so that even if the housewife is not so careful she never breaks the dishes, though they fall a thousand and one times a day. Our food this winter is good and wholesome, and we have no reason to complain. Draw bread nearly every day.[7]

It will be impossible for me to procure a furlough this winter, so that you will have to wait until another winter when I trust, if alive, I can return home and remain as long as I choose to stay. I received a letter from Father a few days ago. Several of the family had been sick. Caleb and Ada had had the sore throat, but had nearly recovered. Harmon was confined to the house, he having caught the ache. Charley is at home and expects to stay until March, when I understand he is agoing West again where he intends marrying and, I suppose, settle down. If you go home, you will of course learn all the news and I hope your next letter will contain all the news from about home. I remain your affectionate brother.

Wm. Remmel

Camp of the 121st Regiment
Near Hazel River, Va.
January 22nd, 1864
My Dear Parents,

Having a little leisure time this evening, I concluded to improve it by writing you a few lines. I shall not make a long letter of it, for I have nothing of particular interest to write.

Yesterday I had the privilege and pleasure of chatting with Moses Bliss. I tell you we had a lively old chat together. Called up many of past scenes in the army, such as marches, battles, all kinds of hardships, and ended with the disposing of a half a pie, which we boys had bought. Moses looks rugged and healthy and he told that he enjoyed fine health. His severe sickness and the hardships endured in the army have made a deep impression on Moses' countenance and makes him look much older than he otherwise would had he remained at home. Moses was wounded at Mine Run, while over the Rapidan the last time. His wound was in the arm, but was not very severe. He is now right again. His time is out next September when, if he lives, he intends to go home, not to return to the war again, for he told me he had seen fighting enough to satisfy him.[8]

The weather here now is quite warm and pleasant, though the nights are quite cold. The snow has all disappeared and through the day it is quite muddy underfoot. All are just now looking quite anxious for the Paymaster, for it is already past the usual time for paying off this army; but I think that he will yet come after they get the full amount of money to pay the whole army.[9]

As I shall not be able to procure a furlough I should like very much to have Charley to come down here to make me a visit, but he says in his letter that it will not be convenient for him to do so. So I suppose it is no use asking him again. If you send me a box or any articles this winter, just write me immediately whatever it maybe, so that I can be on the watch for it.

Albert Jennings told me a few days ago that his father had written him that you were agoing to send some articles in a box of Albert's from his father. Is this true? But I will write no more at this time, so good night to you all. May this find you all well again.

From your far off son,
Wm. Remmel

Camp of the 121st Regiment
Near Hazel River, Va.
February 1st, 1864
My Dear Parents,

I once more take pen in hand to write a few lines to you. I would have written you before, but I had written Charley twice and given him all the news, so I thought that it would be unnecessary to write you.

There is but little news from this army at present, of a military character. Everything is quiet at the front. Heavy firing was heard across the Rapidan a few days ago, within the rebel lines. It has since been ascertained that a body of rebel troops had taken their arms and were agoing home to fight no more, but they were stopped by the military authorities. Many deserters are flocking into our lines daily and were it not for the river, which divides the 2 armies, I am sure that we would have a good part of Lee's army within our lines before spring. I think that the rebel armies will not fight as desperate next spring as they have done heretofore and we all think that, with our armies properly reinforced, this rebellion must and will be crushed next summer; may our hopes be fully realized.[10]

The weather here for the past few days has been very pleasant indeed, but since yesterday it has been clouded and some rainy overhead. Our regiment is in a very healthy condition, but few have been sick this winter, but one man is in the hospital at present. Our camp is kept very clean and tidy and has to be kept so. A clean camp is very essential to good health. We do not live as well as last winter, but we have enough to eat. We draw bread nearly everyday, but potatoes and onions are issued but once a week. Beef, such as it is, is twice a week.

Moses Bliss came to see me a few days ago. He was well, but looked quite thin in the face. I spoke of him in Charley's letter. Egbert Spencer, whose father lives near the Wiley tollgate, was over to our regt. yesterday. He gave me quite a history of old Salisbury and what was agoing on there. He said that he saw Charley and Harmon and that they were well. He said that Charley looked a little older and was rather more sober looking than he used to be. I guess that these old soldiers have pretty lively times when they get home, with their large bounties.[11]

You want to know what you shall send me. I do not want to trouble you with sending me anything, for I can get along well enough with the victuals the government furnishes and it will be quite an expense to get a box here. But if you want to send me something, I can name a few articles; as follows: a little butter, a few sausages, if you have them; some fried cakes, or such cakes as will keep; apple, berry, or other kind of pies; a few crust shorts; some dried apples; a few berries, if you can spare them. This is about all. Do not go to any trouble to get these things, if it is not convenient. It will be just as well if you do not send me anything. Hoping this will reach you, I will close. I send my love to all the children.

From your affect[ionate] son,
William Remmel

Camp of the 121st Regiment
Near Hazel River, Va.
February 6th, 1864
My Dear Brother [Augustus],

Your short message, which you sent me in Charles' letter, was duly received a few days ago and, having a little leisure time, I thought I would answer it today.

Nothing of importance has transpired in the military line in this army for several weeks, as you will know. Several thousand of the old veterans in this army have re-enlisted and gone home on 30 and 35 days furlough.

There are many rumors constantly afloat, with reference to the future movements of the Potomac Army. Some claim to have it on good authority that the army is to be consolidated into 3 corps, each corps containing 50,000 men, making a total of 150,000 men in this army in the coming spring. Others prophecy and have heard, as they say, from reliable quarters that the greater part of the army will be sent (Southwest) to participate in the coming great struggle in East Tennessee. However reliable and trustworthy these reports may be we place little value or worth upon them, and are willing to wait the issue and know for ourselves.

We also hear a great deal about our corps, the 6th, relieving the 8th Corps, which is performing garrison duty, &c around Washington, Baltimore, and many other intermediate places. This looks rather more sane or, rather, more true. For 1 division has already been attached from the corps to a garrison along our northern military frontier and many other regiments have re-enlisted and gone home, and it is understood that they are not coming back into this army for the present. I would like well enough to be relieved of my present position and perform garrison duty the remainder of my term of service, but I do not expect it. Neither do any of my comrades, but enough of this.

The weather, which for the last few days has been quite cold and somewhat rainy, has now moderated down considerable and today the sun shone brilliantly through the whole of its majestic travels. Our wood and water is very convenient, this together with our beautiful quarters causes us to place strong attachments on our temporary winter quarters.

We do not fare as well as we could wish at present, but I suppose it is difficult to transport so many vegetable provisions to the army upon but a single railroad from Washington to the army. I am willing to deprive myself of potatoes and onions &c, if they cannot be well procured.

The soldiers are all in excellent spirits and possess buoyant hopes of the future. We are all looking and, we think, with consistency to a speedy close of this struggle, if the spring campaign is carried on with skill and determination. We all fully weigh the task which is before us, and the great sacrifices of both life and property we will have to make in the coming great struggle for freedom and right, but we are determined to win and conquer. We must in so glorious a struggle. The soldiers are all united in this and now we want the people at home to be united and either come or induce others to come and fill the thinned ranks of our brave legions, who have endured so much but are willing to endure more.

I saw Edgar Spencer last Sunday. He had just returned from home. He said that he saw Charley and some others of the family. He looked well and was finely dressed. He has re-enlisted. We are all pretty short of money. The Paymaster has not been around as we expected. There is no special news from the regiment, so will bring this to a close.

Believe your affectionate brother,
W. Remmel

I wrote this last evening. This morning we have received orders to leave camp with 3 days rations. I know not where we are agoing.

Camp of the 121st Regiment
Near Hazel River, Va.
February 11th, 1864
My Dear Parents,

Your letter of the 5th instant was received 2 evenings ago, and now I sit me down to answer it. I was pleased to hear from home once more and happy to hear that you were all well again. I too am well, so we have no reason to feel bad or sorrow over our present circumstances. I received a letter from Louisa the other evening. She and William were all well and seemed to enjoy themselves.

You have probably all, ere this, heard of the fighting on the Rapidan between our troops and a part of Lee's army last Saturday, February 6th. Our loss is reported quite severe. Our corps, the 6th, did not move out of camp, but was in readiness to move. On the morning of the 6th we rose early and prepared to march. We drew rations for 3 days and were to go in light marching order, as it is called, that is take such articles as would be necessary to keep comfortable during that time. Our regiment waited all day Saturday expecting to move, but we received no orders and therefore did not go. The cannonading commenced about noon of Saturday and continued all the remainder of the day. No musketry was to be heard at our camp, until about 5 O'clock (P.M.), at which time sharp musketry firing could be distinguished from that time until dark. And after, one continuous roar of musketry could be heard at our camp. Long after dark the flashes could be seen very distinctly.[12]

We learn that the movement was made in order to keep Lee's army in our front, while General Butler was to move upon Richmond and, if possible, capture it. But it appears that Butler was unsuccessful and has returned to Norfolk again. It is to be regretted that Butler could not accomplish his object, for had he captured Richmond our prisoners could have been released and what a happy affair that would have been.

I heard from John McDougal the other evening. John is well, but says he don't like Heavy Artillery and think he will try to get into Cavalry or Light Artillery. He writes that, had he possessed a good home, he would not have reenlisted, but he had no place to stay and so concluded to take the bounty and become a soldier again. Such boys are to be pitied, for they are too much overlooked.[13]

I received those stamps and am very thankful for them. You say that you are going to send me a box. I hope that it will come through all right. I think that it will, if the box is well nailed and bands placed around the box. Some boxes that have come to the regiment have been badly handled and many things taken out, but not unless the box were broken by handling them on the cars or on the wagons.

The weather is quite cold today and a good fire feels very comfortable. The Captain of our company, together with one of the men, is agoing home tomorrow to recruit for the regiment. I hope that the Captain will be successful in getting a goodly number. But enough for this time, for I must mail this letter, so goodbye.[14]

From your son,
Wm. Remmel

I send my love to all the family. We expect to draw our pay this week.

Camp of the 121st
Near Hazel River, Va.
February 13th, 1864
Dear Brother [Augustus],

I once more seat myself for the purpose of committing a few lines upon paper to you. As this is our only intercourse with each other, I take great pleasure in thus communing with you, and suppose that it affords you equally as much pleasure to drop an occasional line to me.

I have nothing of importance to write you at this time. The army, which one week ago today was marching and fighting, is now again in its quarters and everything wears a look of stillness and quiet.

The weather, the greater part of the time, is mild and pleasant, though the nights are somewhat cold. We have had no snow since the 1st part of January, and may possibly not see anymore this winter. It seems strange enough to be where hardly any snow is to be seen through the long winter months, when most of one's life has been spent among the northern mountains of snow and ice.

The boys in the regiment are enjoying themselves pretty well this winter. The duty is pretty hard, when we consider that we are soldiers; but if we had no more to do at home than what we are adoing here, no complaint would be made. But it is natural for a soldier to find fault when there is much to do, for he knows that if he does but little he will yet get as much pay as another that labors diligently all day. This is not altogether the case, but in many instances it is so.

Our regiment drills but little. Dress parade is all the drill that we have, and that is but a short performance, and rather have it than not. Our regiment has considerable picket duty to perform. About 50 men are detailed every 3 days on picket and 20 camp guard each day, making a total of 70 men that are on duty everyday. The pickets stay out 3 days, while the camp guard come off duty in 2 hours.

Our regiment reports about 400 men in the regiment for duty. When we came out we were 1,040 strong. Since that time we have received about 200 recruits. So you will see from these figures that there has been quite a falling off, in about 18 months, in the strength of the Regt.[15]

We are tolerable well this winter, though not as good as last winter. Draw bread everyday, beans and onions about twice a week, beef 2 per week. We have had no potatoes for some time and it is said that the government can't buy enough to supply the army. On the whole we have no reason to complain of our food, for it is good and wholesome.

I saw Edgar Spencer a few days after he got back to the army and he gave me all the news from around home. I am looking quite wishfully for the box that our people have sent me, for I suppose that it is pretty well on the way by this time. If it come through direct, I will receive it next week. Today is Saturday. As soon as I receive it, I will write and inform you how things are, &c.

I will write no more for the time, so goodbye and accept my kindest wishes, &c. Give my love to all the family.

From your affectionate brother,
W. Remmel

Camp of the 121st Regiment
Near Hazel River, Va.
February 18, 1864
My Dear Parents,

It is with much delight that I take this opportunity of dropping a few lines to you. I am happy and thankful to you for being able to acknowledge that the box, which you sent me the 9th instant, with its many luxuries and necessary articles, was safely received this evening. The box I do not think had been opened, for it was yet firmly nailed. I opened it immediately after I got it into my tent. I am very glad to tell you that everything is in good condition. The pies were a little smashed, but it does not hurt them. I fried some of mother's sausages for supper and, I assure you, my tent mate and I smacked our lips after eating the delicious meat. The cakes too are very nice and, in fact, everything is just right. There is not a happier soldier in the Army of the Potomac tonight than I am. The stockings are just what I want, and so are the handkerchiefs. The writing paper got wet, but I think I can dry it all right. One of my tent mates got a box too tonight and, on the whole, I guess we will live pretty well for a few weeks. The boys in my company are all very fond of sauerkraut and they are anxious to get a taste of the pure article. I guess I can accommodate them with the real Dutch dish. I wish that I could repay you for all the little luxuries you have so kindly sent me and the great trouble you have been to, besides the expense it has incurred. But it is impossible for me at present to give anything more than my true heartfelt thanks for all these beautiful gifts, that none but kind and loving parents could prepare and send so far. Should I ever return to your fireside, as I trust that I will, I shall try and reward you in a manner worthy a true and affect[ionate] son.

The weather at present is bitter cold. It seems as though it was almost as cold as in [New] York State and, if we had snow as North, it would be quite as severe some of the time. But this kind of weather lasts but a few days and after that it is warm and pleasant again.

The army is not yet paid off, except the old soldiers who have re-enlisted. It is generally thought that we will not be paid until next month, when we will draw 4 months pay. Since it has run along so far, we had rather wait another month and draw 2 months more of Greenbacks.

There is some talk of this regiment being allowed to re-enlist for 3 years longer. I do not think there is anything in it. If there is, $1,000 will be quite an inducement. We will know more about it in a few days. You need not trouble yourself about me, for I do not think of serving longer than the remainder of my term, which is about 18 months. There is nothing new from this army that I know of. Everything is quiet on the Rapidan. Nothing has been heard in that direction for 8 or 10 days. Not having much news to write this evening I will bring this letter to a close, so goodbye.[16]

From your affect[ionate] son,
Wm. Remmel

I send my love to all.
I sent Charley my likeness. Has he received it yet?

Camp of the 121st Regiment
Near Hazel River, Va.
February 21st, 1864
My Dear Brother [Augustus],

I have been looking for a letter from you for several days past, but have not received any of yet, and, thinking that perhaps you were waiting to hear from me first before writing, I take this opportunity of dropping you a few lines. My health is yet good and am robust and hearty in every respect and trust that these lines will find you in as favorable circumstances, physically speaking. I take pleasure in letting you know that I have received the Express box that Father sent me the 9th instant. Everything came through uninjured and I assure you that all a Mother's thoughts were sent in that one box, for everything that was eatable was sent me, besides numerous other articles that a soldier needs. On the whole it is a valuable present and will give me a rare opportunity of feasting for several days to come. But I am not alone in receiving prizes of this kind. My tent mate has also received one with many luxuries. I never lived better to home or anywhere else than I am living now.

Today is Sunday and our brigade has been out on review and so, of course, our regiment had to appear. The review was a very fine one indeed. Several ladies from the North were present, they having come down to visit their husbands, brothers, and friends, and to get some idea of the Army probably in many instances. It is a rare sight, indeed, in the army to see groups of ladies standing about in camp, or parading our corduroy sidewalks, which are so prominent in most camps in the army. These sidewalks are made of small round poles and are very acceptable in muddy weather. It is quite a novelty to us soldiers to behold our opposite sex in our camps. Yet it revives a feeling of tenderness and love to look upon them in their innocence and patriotic devotion to the soldiers. One of the men in our company had his wife arrive here last night and our Lieutenant has given up his tent to the use of the husband and wife. I trust that they will enjoy their limited visit satisfactorily, for probably she will not be able to make a very lengthy visit.[17]

The boys have been paid off and money is quite flush, though many of the boys are indebted to the sutler their full 2 months pay, $26.[18]

I have not heard from Louisa or William in some time, but expect to hear from Fort Wayne before many days. Charley will probably leave for the West sometime next month and I believe he intends to invest his money in real estate. I hope he will be successful in making his purchase.

Today I was favored with a visit by an old acquaintance, Jerome Walter. I recognized his countenance immediately, but could not call him by name until I had talked with him awhile. He belongs to the 1st NY Independent Battery in our (6th) corps. Jerome is a veteran soldier. He has re-enlisted for 3 years longer. He did not know that I belonged in this regiment, until he was told so by Caleb while visiting at Devereaux. I will not try to write more at this time, so goodbye.[19]

From your brother,
Wm. Remmel

Answer this soon.

Camp of the 121st Regiment
Near Hazel River, Va.
March 1st, 1864
My Dear Parents,

You probably have been wondering why I have not written you sooner and this is the answer I have to make. Our corps has been out 5 days on a reconnaissance and got back night-before-last. Being weary and tired from our hard travels, I have waited until today ere I wrote to you.

I will give you a short history of our march into the enemy's country. Last Friday evening, one week ago tonight, our pickets, that is the 6th Corps pickets, were relieved by men from the 3rd Corps, and in the course of the night we received orders to be ready to march at 7 O'clock (A.M.) next morning. Saturday morning we rose earlier than usual and prepared for the march. 8 O'clock found us under way. The morning was warm and clear and everything bid fair to go off right, in the weather line. We marched that day about 15 miles and stopped for the night. The day was a beautiful and pleasant one, but it proved to be a fatiguing day for us soldiers. The weather had been dry and windy for several days and the roads were very dusty. When we halted that night a dirtier lot of fellows than we were, I never saw. We were, one and all, a complete smudge from head to foot. There being a creek nearby, the boys soon began to rush for it and in a very little time its banks were lined with soldiers anxious to wash off the thick dust gathered on the road. We were all very tired and sleepy, besides a pretty hungry, but the boys were in good spirits and took the fatigue as a matter of necessity and all went off well. It being near sunset when we halted.[20]

An hour after found the men, the most of them, snugly wrapped up by the fire for the night. But it was not my fortune to go to sleep early that night, for I had scarcely laid down ere one of my teeth began to ache terribly and it was not till near midnight that I closed my eyes for sleep. A soldier, when he feels pain, has but to bear it until it is over. There is no mother or sister to call to in the army, so the soldier contents himself by keeping his feelings to himself. But I must not dwell here.

Next morning early found us on the move again and by noon we found ourselves on the north bank of Robertson's River. Here we halted and formed a line of battle and here we remained until we moved to our camp. Sunday night a heavy body of cavalry crossed the river and marched direct for the enemy's encampments. Monday and Tuesday we could hear cannonading at a very great distance and we have since learned by the papers that the cavalry had a fight with the rebels. I do not think that there was a gun fired at a rebel while we were gone, in the corps. The object of our going with the cavalry was to reinforce and assist them in case that they were pressed too much by the rebels.[21]

Tuesday it began to rain and night set in with a snowstorm, which lasted about 2 hours. As we had no tents with us, we had to make shanties of rails and boards and cover them with straw. We passed the night quite comfortable and next morning started for camp, which we reached after dark, having traveled over 25 miles through the deep mud. This, I suppose, is the beginning of our spring work. No more of importance in camp, so goodbye. I will write again soon.

From your son,
Wm. Remmel

Camp of the 121st Regiment
Near Hazel River, Va.
March 2nd, 1864
Kind Brother [Charley],

I have been looking quite wishfully for a letter from you, but thus far have watched in vain. Knowing that you have a good deal of business to devote your time and attention to, I predict that it is with difficulty that you find time to write to your many friends when you feel so disposed, for your continual confinement must cause much weariness and indisposition. You will think [it] strange, perhaps, when I tell you that just now we are almost snowbound in camp. All day yesterday it was windy and cold and toward night it began to snow and by 9 O'clock P.M. the snow lay nearly 8 inches deep. This is remarkable depth of snow for this so called sunny state and one would almost infer that Virginia ranked, or should rank, with some of the polar regions in rigor of climate at certain time of the year. But today is warm and genial rays of that moving orb (the sun) has evaporated a part of the cold, but beautiful, winter robe already and another 48 hours will sweep all this fleece covering from us, not perhaps to return in many months.

Tonight our regiment is being paid off and the boys are jovial and happy, for it is the soldier's holiday. Many of the boys get short before Uncle Sam chooses to pay his legal tender to his thousands of nephews and then there is some want experienced by the men, by not being able to buy the many knicknacks always supplied in camp. It is actually necessary that the soldier should have at least a few dollars in money at all times, but most of soldiers become too free with this money and it lasts but a short time and perhaps injures the body more than it strengthens the system.[22]

Card playing for money is the most prevalent evil in the army among the common soldiers. Thousands are divested of their hard earned wages as often as they are paid off, by those sharkers who at home were beggars and scoundrels and who have come here to carry on their games on a larger scale. The simple game of bluff will bring thousands of our brave soldiers back to civil life, to home and family, with the stain of robbery by gambling upon their characters. Gambling is much more prevalent than drinking in the army, for a soldier can have but little access to liquor. It would be to the honor of the nation, and the everlasting benefit of the soldier, if this accursed card playing was entirely swept away by prohibition.

Military affairs are about at a standstill. Everything is quiet at the front. Important military changes are taking place among the generals in this army and another reorganization will take place, it is thought. It is generally supposed that the army will be consolidated into 3 corps, with accomplished and fire tried veterans at their heads. The boys are quite jubilant over the nomination of General Grant as commander of all the armies and none cherish a doubt of his entire success, if he is let alone by the political generals at Washington and newspaper dictators abroad.[23]

But I will not attempt to fill this sheet, as I have already perhaps written what will not be interesting to you to read. I am yet healthy in body and mind and trust that this letter will find yourself and Louisa in that same desirable state. Hoping to hear from you soon, I remain your affectionate brother. Accept my kindest wishes for your welfare and believe me your loving soldier brother.

Wm. Remmel

Camp of the 121st Regiment
Near Hazel River, Va.
March 6th, 1864
My Dear Brother [Caleb],

Yours of the 2nd instant was received last evening and was exceedingly happy to hear once more from you. Am glad to hear that you are yet well and contented in your distant home. I must confess that you have made a remarkable improvement in penmanship, as well as in composing and spelling within the last few months. And, if you progress as rapidly the next year as for the few months past, you will not have your equal in the family in a little while. Only strive to persevere in all you undertake. Make an effort to make your mark in the world and you will succeed. Let progress be your motto in whatever you are engaged and your life will be crowned with success.

But to another subject. Ere this you have, no doubt, heard of the recent movements in the army. Awhile ago, if you remember, there was a reconnaissance made by a part of this army on the Rapidan, and a somewhat similar movement was executed by another part of the army about 1 week ago. One week ago Friday night orders were received at our headquarters to be ready to move early next morning. The order was given to the companies at roll call next morning and we all made arrangements accordingly. We prepared ourselves in light marching order with 4 days rations in haversacks and 2 in wagons. Eight O'clock found us on the road to the front. Our brigade, which lays apart from the rest of the corps, soon joined it and the whole corps was soon under motion. The day was sultry and dry, and the dust flew very disagreeably over us during the whole day. We marched that day about 15 miles and halted for the night, weary, dirty, and sleepy.[24]

We bivouacked that night upon the cold, damp, ground in a thick cluster of scrub pines. That night I experienced some pain from the teeth ache, and slept but a part of the night. Next morning we rose early, rather stiff and sore, prepared and swallowed breakfast and soon were on the tramp again. At about noon brought up on the north bank of Robertson's River. Here we formed line of battle and posted a strong picket line. We were about 25 miles from camp. I shall not have time to relate particulars. Our corps laid here until Wednesday supporting the cavalry, who were out in front on a raid, until they returned, when we retraced our steps toward camp, which we reached that evening after dark, nearly worn out with fatigue and hunger. We were out 5 days and had quite a severe siege of it, although we did not encounter a rebel.

It stormed all day Tuesday and ended with a light fall of snow. As we had no shelter tents along with us, we had to manage as best we could. We built houses of rails and boards and covered with straw, which we got from a large haystack. Wednesday morning, when we started for home, it was exceedingly muddy and the tramp of 25 miles that we had through the deep mud that day was not of the pleasantest.

We are now all right again in our comfortable quarters, where we hope to stay until we break up for the campaign, which will soon come. All is quiet in camp. We have but little drill, other than the all day knapsack drill while on the march. The weather is delightful. The birds sing sweet songs of returning spring and all nature is clothed with beauty.

I send you enclosed a small Ambrotype of myself, which I fancy you will like. I received a letter from father last night. Our people are all well. No more this time, so goodbye.

William Remmel

Camp of the 121st Regiment
Near Hazel River, Va.
March 10th, 1864
Dear Parents,

Your kind letter was duly received and was glad to hear that you were yet all well. I was pleased to hear that Caleb had got a good situation, as he certainly is getting large wages. Charley, you say, has started for the West. I hope that he may be successful in investing his money profitably in some real estate land.

I am gratified to know that your circumstances are much easier and better than they used to be. Of course, as the family becomes smaller, the expenses become less and, of course, the lighter the expenses are the sooner father will be able to support the family upon his small farm. Father writes me that he intends placing most of my money upon interest. Now I would like very well to have a little money to start with in some kind of business when I return from the war. But, if by the use of the money I have sent home, father can avoid working in that filthy old tannery during the long dreary nights, when all people should be at rest, I would thankfully let you have it. I mean give it and that I shall have to spare while I am a soldier.

Since your place is paid for and the children all able to earn their living, and some of them something besides, I do not see the necessity of father wearing out his health and life by toiling in that way any longer. It is as bad and worse to be compelled to work all night the year round, at the kind of work you have to do, as it is to be a slave here in Virginia. Now I beg of you, as your interested and affectionate son, who is looking and caring for the welfare and happiness of his dear and much beloved parents, to leave off thinking that to get along in this world you will have to look to that old tannery for a living. I wish you would think of this father.

I am on guard today. It has rained hard the great part of the day and it is quite disagreeable out. Everything has been very quiet since we returned from the march about 1 week ago. We are fast getting ready for the spring campaign by drawing such articles of clothing as we need and supplying our cartridge boxes with a proper amount of ammunition.

I have received a letter from Louisa and also from Augustus. At the time of writing, they were both well. I received a rather queer letter from Allan Jennings tonight. I thought Allan Jennings was studying for a doctor, but he informed me that he had been teaching school this winter and did not know what he was agoing to employ his time in the coming summer. He is troubled again with one of his uneasy spells, I guess, and wants to get in some new business. He writes that he is making maple sugar and syrup and wants to know whether he could make anything by bringing a quantity of cans of each of these articles, and also some butter, to the army and selling them. It seems strange to me that a young doctor should ask such questions, or turn his attentions to such matters, in which he would not earn his victuals. But I must close. The postage stamps I received. Goodbye.[25]

From your beloved son,
Wm. Remmel

Camp of the 121st Regiment
Near Hazel River, Va.
March 18, 1864
Dear Brother [Caleb],

Your kind letter was received this evening and I concluded to reply right away. There is nothing new here, although tonight we received orders to draw 3 days rations and be ready to move at anytime, but I heard a little while ago that the order had been countermanded and we would not be likely to go at all. This may be true and may be not true. We will know more about it in time.

I received a letter from our people last night. They are all well and getting along, I guess, all right. Father thought that I had no money, so he sent me $5, but, as I happen to have enough, I shall send it back again. For I do not need it just now.

Everything is very quiet in the army. Nothing but the dull monotony of everyday life attracts our eyes wherever we may look. Here may be seen a regiment or perhaps a company on drill, while somewhere else groups of blue jackets are having an exciting game of ball and still further on a long train of supply wagons are slowly winding their way toward the government depot for the everyday food of soldiers.[26]

We do not expect to remain much longer in our comfortable winter tents, for we have got a great work before us as soon as the weather will allow it to be carried through. It is the bloody work of destroying Lee's army, which will cause an ocean [of] blood to be spilled on both sides. We all are aware of this and we know that thousands will have to lay down their lives in the next battle to be fought, yet this does not make us falter only for a moment, for we are bound to win and win we will. Let the cost be what it may. Those that have and will fall will forever be gloriously remembered, while the survivors will carry with them a bright record through life and will have the honor of saying that they helped put down the southern traitors and restore peace and prosperity to our glorious republic.

The soldiers are getting anxious to return to civil life and, as long as we know that there will have to be more fighting, we think that the sooner the shock is commenced the quicker it will be completed. So it makes little difference how soon it is brought about, when everything is got ready.

I am glad that my Ambrotype suits you. I wish you would send me, if convenient, a photograph of yourself and I will pay the cost. I am highly pleased with your writing. You have made a marked improvement and can well afford to pay $4.50 tuition. It grieves me that I cannot hold a steady hand, which makes it impossible for me to write plain and smooth, but since I cannot do it I will have to do as well as I can.

Albert Jennings is yet in the regiment. He is robust and healthy. Hardly a boy from Salisbury that I know remains in the regiment. They are either killed, to the hospital, or discharged.[27]

I heard from Charley a few evenings ago. He was then in Fort Wayne with William and Louisa, but was agoing to Wisconsin in a few days to buy a farm, come back and marry, and then settle down. I hope that his plans will work all right. How does the draft take with the people where you live? Write me soon.

Goodbye,
W. Remmel

Camp of the 121st Regiment
Near Hazel River, Va.
March 30, 1864
Dear Parents,

Your kind letter was duly received, but as I had written you 2 or 3 days before I have waited until today before I replied. Last Thursday evening our company was paid off and the next morning I sent enclosed to you $25. If the letter has gone through direct, you ere this have received it. I hope to hear soon whether you have or not. If you have not received it write me as soon as this reaches you, but I am quite sure that it is all right. A few days before, I sent in return the $5 you sent me. Have you received it?[28]

There is nothing new from this army of a military character that I have heard of, I mean of a fighting character. We are agoing to have a large army this spring to operate against Richmond. I understand that we are agoing to be reinforced by 75,000 men and that they are coming at the rate of 4,000 per day. Transportation is short upon the railroad and they cannot come faster. If this is true, we will not be ready to move in sometime yet.

It is also reported that Burnside will come down the Shenandoah Valley with 50,000 men. With such an army, and with such a general as Grant, I do not see what will save the rebels when once we get started. The army is in splendid condition and it will fight equally as well as at any previous time. The boys do not think that we can be whipped with Grant to lead them and such an army as we will have when the time comes for the work.[29]

We have had terrible rainy weather, together with a severe snowstorm, within the past week and the roads are terrible bad. Hazel River, near where we are encamped, raised 8 or 10 feet last night and two of the bridges across the stream went down in the night. The water is going down fast and by tomorrow the river will be all right again.

My health is excellent. I never felt better than now. Our regiment is in a fine physical condition; but very few are sick at present. Mrs. Watson's son, I have forgotten his name, has returned to the regiment. He has been away over a year and has escaped much danger and hardship. He looks strong and healthy and feels well, he tells me.[30]

I hope that you will be able to get a situation for Augustus in Bennett's store, of which you wrote in your letter. I think that it would be a good place for him and hope that you will be able to get him in the store.[31]

I received a letter from William the other day. He and Louisa were well and they were getting along finely. William has a good position. They had not heard from Charley in several days, but as soon as he had bought a farm was coming back to marry. I have no more to write, so will close and wait for more news to write.

I remain your affectionate son,
William Remmel

I send you another small Ambrotype.

Camp of the 121st Regiment
Near Hazel River, Va.
April 2nd, 1864
Dear Brother [Augustus],

Having nothing of particular note to attract the dullness of evening camp life, the thought struck me had I not better write a letter to Augustus, or commence one at least, to finish tomorrow for it cannot go out until tomorrow night. And acting on the impulse of the moment I have commenced the task, intending to close the same by daylight.

I am, as usual, in good health and light spirits and this fortunate and indispensable blessing is shared by nearly all in the regiment. True to my word, I have waited until today (Sunday) to finish this message. Today is the holy Sabbath, yet little is this glorious day appreciated by the soldiers. You may think strange, but it is nevertheless true, that I was not a little surprised this morning upon asking what day of the week it was, I was answered *Sunday*. You have reason to infer from this that I am living rather a heathenish life and am unjustifiably irreverent to the laws of the Creator. This is true, but our life in the camp or out of it is of such a character as to almost dispel all thoughts of the holy Sabbath. Our duty upon the Sabbath day is equally as great as upon the other days. Therefore, with no Christian influences as at home and no chaplains (for we have none) to preach to us, we have nothing to indicate to us that it is the day of rest, only as we trace the day from one week to the other.[32]

Today it is quite pleasant out, though there is a high wind. For the past 2 weeks, the greater part of the time, the weather has been terribly boisterous. Snow and rain has fell alternately in great quantities. We can yet behold strong traces of the former upon the Blue Ridge, where it remains in great quantities, looking black and cold upon the genial valley at its feet. The rain fell in such storms that it raised the river near which we lay upwards of 10 feet within 12 hours and, unfortunately, carried off 2 bridges for transporting provisions to the troops. The bridges will not be rebuilt, for it is too near spring. All the travel now passes over the government pontoon bridge, which spans the river and [is] formed of boats.

Active operations will soon be recommenced in earnest and we look for decisive blows on our part, and we hope not to be disappointed. The struggle will be a bloody one, without doubt, but if we are successful the struggle will soon have to close favorable to our army. The survivors will then be enabled to return to the bosom of their friends and dear ones, with a record that will be bright as Christianity and as imperishable as virtue.

Father wrote me in his last letter that he had applied at Bennett's store (Little Falls) for a situation for you and thinks that he will be successful. Should you go there the coming summer, I warn you again of evil society and fast young men, for they are a curse to the world and bring dishonor upon themselves and their friends. My health remains good and trust this finds you as well. Hoping to hear from you soon.

I remain your affectionate soldier brother,
Wm. Remmel

Camp of the 121st Regiment
Near Hazel River, Va.
April 11th, 1864
Dear Parents,

Having aplenty of leisure time, I thought I would take this opportunity of dropping you a few lines. I am well, as I have always been able to write you. We have experienced some rather disagreeable and strong weather for the past 3 weeks. It has stormed here nearly the whole time for near twenty days. It commenced first with a heavy fall of snow, which laid two or three days, when it commenced raining and we have had rain the greater part of the time since. The high water in the river has carried off many of the bridges between here and Alexandria, so that we have had no mail since Saturday.[33]

Our brigade is between 2 rivers, separated from the rest of the army altogether. Besides the government bridge across the Hazel River, across which we procure supplies, there have been 2 others built by the men of the brigade—which cost considerable labor. These both have gone down stream by the freshet and the government bridge built of boats had to be taken up, the water raised so high. I think, however, that our rainy weather is about over and fair weather will follow. So long as it keeps raining nothing can be done in the military line of any importance. Should the weather clear off and the roads become dry, the army, I think, will move within 2 weeks if not sooner.

General Meade had issued an order that all sutlers and citizens should leave the army by the 16th of this month and that the officers should pack such articles as they will not need and send them to Alexandria, for safe keeping, until the army settles down again next fall. Only 5 days are left for this order to be carried out and, if the sutlers are then yet in the army, their goods are used for the hospitals.[34]

This shows plainly that, as soon as the weather will permit, a forward movement will be made. The soldiers do not seem to care how soon the time arrives for the bloody work which is before us. It has got to be done and the sooner it is commenced, the quicker it will be through with. We all feel confident that we can whip the rebels with the large army that we have this spring and, should we do this, I am sure that the heavy fighting will be over with and the rebellion will soon be crushed. May God prosper us in the mighty campaign and all will be well.

I sent you $25 along the last days of March. If you have received it, write me soon. I sent it in a letter. I also sent back the $5, which you sent me in a letter. Let me know in your next whether this money has been received.

I remain, very affectionately,
Your son,
Wm. Remmel

Camp of the 121st Regiment
Near Hazel River, Va.
April 16, 1864
Dear Parents,

Your welcomed letter has been duly received. It perhaps was unwise in me sending you that amount of money in a letter, but, as I had never lost any money before, I thought I would send the $25 in the same manner—there being only two bills, a $20 and $5. But I have not given it up yet, it may yet come through all right. The letter may have been miscarried. It might not have been plainly directed. If the letter is lost, I fear the theft was committed in the army ere it reached the railroad. The mail passes through several hands before it reaches the railroad station and it would be a very easy matter to extract the money from any letter that contained any.

There is nothing new from this army that I have learned. Mighty preparations are being made to commence the campaign as soon as the weather will allow a safe movement to commence. The sutlers and citizens are all out of the army, or ordered to be out by the 16th, which is today. The surplus clothing that would not be needed by the soldiers has been sent to Alexandria, for safe keeping, until the men need it again next fall. Most of our time is now taken up with drills and target practice.

Everything to place the army on good footing for a great battle is being done. Everything needless to our army is put entirely out of the way. Officers, such as Colonels and Majors, that need to have 3 or 4 large tents on the march to stop in now have but one and that small. Line officers, such as Captains and Lieutenants, carry their own tents, as we soldiers have to. This system of cutting down baggage to what is actually needed is one grand order that ought to have been enforced before. It will make our wagon train so much smaller and render our army more safe on a retreat, should it be at anytime necessary; which we hope it will not be.

We all have great confidence in General Grant and a loving opinion of Meade, the hero of Gettysburg. With two such generals and with Sedgwick, our 6th Corps commander, Hancock and Warren and scores of other equally as brave, our cause cannot fail. For certainly a better army than the old Army of the Potomac, for fighting qualities, cannot be found; and the men, when they go into action, push forward for the old flag (the stars and stripes).

The weather has been quite pleasant for the past few days, but last evening it commenced raining and it is yet continuing. It is now M. I think as you write with regard to Augustus remaining with Van Vorst at Ephratah. Should he stay there until the end of the year, he will not perhaps be able to procure a situation such as he ought to have; and if he leaves now, he could not live out to advantage somewhere where he would be learning more. I would see about it.[35]

I am glad to hear that Caleb has got a good place and where he gets enough to eat, which with boys is the main feature. Harmon, I suppose, is having a fine time making molasses. I wonder if he can eat as much as I used to, on Bennett's farm, 8 or 10 years ago. Ada, I suppose, helps mother. She must be quite a young lady by this time. How I would like to see her once more and kiss her rosy cheek. Long as that time may seem, I hope and trust it will soon come, when I can greet you all with smiles and kisses, never to go to battle again. May the time soon come when the armed hordes of our land shall lay down their weapons of death and destruction, returning to the peaceful pursuit of northern industry and enterprise. Goodbye.

I remain, very affectionately,
Your son,
Wm. Remmel

Camp of the 121st Regiment
Near Hazel River, Va.
April 23rd, 1864
Dear Brother [Caleb],

Your last letter was received a few evenings since, but being pretty busy a most of the time for the past two or three days I have delayed answering it a little longer than I ought to have done. Everything is yet pretty quiet in this army. Reviews and drills are the order of the day, which is a strong indication that there is active and terrible work before us. Our corps (6th) had review last Monday and it was a grand affair. Generals Grant and Meade were present, together with a row of other generals. The review, it is said, was highly gratifying to the commanding general, who complimented General Sedgwick upon the fine appearance and splendid discipline of the troops.[36]

The time is mostly taken up by the regiment in drills and inspections. We have had some practice in target firing, which was highly interesting to us, for we are all anxious to become good marksmen, as that is a very essential part of a soldier's trade. For you very well know that one fatal shot is worth more than a score of the old cartridges on hand, and give the men an opportunity to habituate themselves to firing.

The weather is delightful just now. The air is mild and warm and the sun, as it reflects its brilliant rays upon the genial earth, makes all nature appear lovely. The roads are in a splendid condition for moving an army and I do not think that we will have to wait long to behold a forward movement.

There are rumors in camp that Lee is preparing for an advance. The sooner he does this the quicker we will dispose of him, but of this there is no hopes. Lee knows well who he has to deal with, to venture such an undertaking. This army was never in a better condition for a campaign than the present spring. The soldiers seem to all comprehend the magnitude of the struggle and are prepared for the worst, but all seem to feel confident that victory will perch upon our banners, which we trust ere many months bring peace to our distracted and long afflicted country.

I heard from home a few evenings ago. Our people were all well at the time of writing. I sent father $30 a few weeks ago, and he has not received it. It is probably lost. I have also heard from William, Louisa, and Charley. They were all well at the time of writing. Charley and his lovely wife are safely settled in their new home and are getting along finely, judging from Charley's and Annie's letters. Anna writes a beautiful letter and possesses rather more than ordinary intelligence, judging from her composition.[37]

Austin Ferrell is over to our regiment. I had quite a talk with him. Austin has re-enlisted and has been to home on a 35 days furlough. He looks very natural, is lively and foolish as ever. He gave me a handkerchief that mother sent by him. Mother's name is upon it and I think very much of it. Nathan Wood is on his way to the regiment.[38]

You say that you sent me a quantity of sugar by a soldier in the 77th New York. I am very sorry that you sent it, for I do not expect to ever hear from it. I do not know where the 77th is quartered. I shall, however, appreciate the great kindness just as deeply.[39]

But I must not dwell longer at this time. I will bid you a welcome good night, which will burst upon us too soon.

I remain, very affectionately,
Your brother,
William Remmel

Camp of the 121st Regiment
Near Hazel River, Va.
April 30th, 1864
Dear Parents,

Your kind letter was received last evening and, not knowing that I shall have a better time to answer it, I sit me down to reply this morning. I hardly expected, when I wrote you last, that I would yet be here in my winter quarters. This army is yet in quarters, but there is every prospect of breaking camp within the next 48 hours. It is reported that Gregg's division of cavalry are crossing the Rappahannock at Kelly's Ford below the Rappahannock Station and that Burnside, with 40,000 men, is coming down the Shenandoah Valley and is already approaching close to the rebels. I think that there will be a great battle fought within the next 10 days.[40]

The sick of our regiment are all ordered away this morning for Washington. The weather is delightful. We have had no rain to speak of for several days. The roads are dry and firm, and heavy loads can be drawn without effecting them.

Our brigade has a good deal of drilling to do this spring. We have to drill 5 days out of a week, 2 drills per day, besides come out every pleasant afternoon on dress parade with everything polished. These drills are fitting us for hard marches, of which we expect to have aplenty.

The boys are feeling well and they do not care how soon we break camp. They have got just so much fighting to do and they think that the sooner it is commenced, the sooner it will be through with; and I share in their feeling, but I want to have everything in readiness before we start in order to make a victory sure.

When we move we shall look forward and not back, for we do not expect to be compelled to turn back this spring, with Grant to lead us on and Meade to guide our fortunes. And we pray that it will be God's Will to give us strength to crush the rebels, who are trying to enslave four millions of human beings to save their own necks from labor and to lead the lives of Lords and Masters.

I am very sorry that the money did not reach you. I think that it was taken out by someone who takes charge of letters between here and the Station Master. I shall not send it in a letter, if I can avoid it.

Austin Ferrell was to our regiment the other day. He gave me the handkerchief that mother sent me. It is a very nice one and I think a great deal of it. Austin said that he had a very pleasant visit at home and that you treated him very kindly, with boiled eggs and other little luxuries.

I received a letter from Augustus a few days ago. He was well and said that he stayed in the store more than he had done before he talked with Mr. Van Vorst. I think, as you do, that Augustus is getting too little pay for the times. I hope that you will do something about it. Augustus could do better to go into a larger establishment, where he would have more and get larger wages.

I am glad to hear that Caleb has got a good place to work and get aplenty to eat. Tell me in your next letter where he works, so that I can write him a letter occasionally. I was very glad to receive a letter from Harmon and I hope that he will write me often, and Ada too. I shall always be glad to hear from them and I will try to write to them when I can. I suppose they have to read my letter to you. I am afraid that they cannot read my letters very well, for I write very poorly.

I hear from Charley once in awhile. Anna, his wife, wrote a very interesting letter to me. She has lost a brother William in this war. He was killed at the battle of Chickamauga. But must bring this letter to a close. If it is God's Will, I hope to be able to write to you of the great battle, which will soon take place; but, if I should fall, my prayer is that I may meet you in Heaven.[41]

From your affectionate son,
W. Remmel

Accept my love for yourselves and the children.

Emory Hospital Ward
Washington, D.C.
May 22nd, 1864
My Dear Parents,

God has spared my life to write you a few lines once more. I am now well cared for in a Washington hospital. I arrived here from Fredericksburg this morning and, so far, have been kindly cared for. It is difficult for me to write at all, on account of the wound in my little finger and being quite nervous. My arm is getting on nicely. I think that my finger will be stiff and may have to be taken off.[42]

You need not be surprised if, in a few days, you should meet me at your door in old Salisbury. Most of the soldiers that are able to write are on their furloughs (in length according to the injury of the wounds). I think I can get a 30-day furlough. I will know about it in a few days. I will get a new suit of clothes as soon as I can and am going to try to get my 2 months pay tomorrow, and then I will be all right.[43]

I will write no more this time. Do not write me until you hear from me again, for I know not what may turn up. I bid you a kind good night and hope I shall see you before many days.

From your affectionate son,
Wm. Remmel

Emory Hospital Ward (M)
Washington, D.C.
May 22, 1864
Dear Brother,

Having arrived in Washington today I thought I would drop you a few lines, though I can scarcely write on account of my wounded finger and arm. I am happy to say that my wounds are doing well. I may lose my little finger, for it is badly smashed and is stiff. The arm, I think, will in time be all right.[44]

I am writing now on the supposition that Louisa received the letter I wrote her while at Fredericksburg, which I trust she has received. If not, I will say that I was wounded May 10th, while our division was charging the rebels' rifle pits. We lost heavily. I fell before I reached the rifle pits. I have been lying in Fredericksburg most of the time since. We are well cared for here and no anxiety need be felt, by either yourself or Louisa, because of my wounds.[45]

They are sending many of the soldiers home and I hope to go on a furlough in a few days. Will get a new suit first and make an effort to draw my pay. Do not write to me until you hear from me again, for if I do not stay here the letter will be lost. It is getting late and I must close this. Please excuse the horrible scribbling, for I can do no better at present. I hope to write my next from home.[46]

I remain your affectionate brother,
W. Remmel

I send my love. Good night.

Emory Hospital Ward (M) Section (4)
Washington, D.C.
July 21st, 1864
Dear Parents,

I once more seat myself to write you a short letter. I am well, with the exception of a little stiffness in my right hand finger. The finger which was stiffest I do not think will ever be entirely well again. The men in the hospital were examined this morning, to find out those that were able to go to their regiments. The doctor said I was not fit to go yet, but I think that I will go in 2 or 3 weeks. My arms are both perfectly healed. A great many are leaving for their regiments this morning.

The weather is very warm. No rain has fallen here for several weeks, of any consequence. The fields are scorched by the dry weather and the roads are completely covered with a heavy coat of dust.

When I returned to Washington, from home, I was detained 2 days in Philadelphia on account of the raid made by the rebels upon the railroad between Baltimore and Philadelphia. While in Philadelphia I was treated with great kindness by the people there. There was great excitement in the city during my stay. Men were everywhere dashing to the Telegraph Office to hear the news. Little boys, like Harmon, had their drums out drumming together recruits for 100 days. The rebels came within 6 miles of the city of Washington. I did not get here until after the rebels had left for the Potomac River. The 6th Corps, to which I belong, was sent from the army to meet the rebels, but when the rebels found that they had the old soldiers of the army to fight they skedaddled away. I think that by this time the government ought to learn a lesson from these raids.[47]

How is the weather about home? And are the crops looking better than when I was at home? Have you commenced haying yet?

The day that I left home I stopped in Little Falls and had 9 photographs taken. The artist told me that they would be finished in 2 days (on Wednesday). I told Charley to tell Case to bring them up to you when they were done. Did he do so? I do not know whether they were well taken or not, or whether they were natural. Tell me in your next letter how they are, whether you have received them. If not, you ask Charley Wood about it. If they are all right send one to each of the boys and one to Louisa, and the others do with what you choose.[48]

I went to the Paymaster's yesterday to try to get my pay, but could not get it. The payrolls were with the regiment and as soon as they come back I can get the money. I have bought me a watch since I have come back. It cost me $10 and a jewelry man told me in the city yesterday that it was worth $30. The fellow was hard up for money and sold it for half what it was worth.

But I am pretty short of news to write, so will not attempt to fill this sheet. As soon as I leave for my regiment, I will let you know. I do not expect to remain here very long. When you write, direct to Emory Hospital, Ward (M), Section (4), Washington, DC. Hoping to hear from you soon, I bid you goodbye.

From your affectionate son,
Wm. Remmel

I send my love to all the friends.
I hope I shall hear from Harmon and Ada soon.

U.S. Christian Commission
Branch Office, 500 H Street
Washington, D.C.
August 3rd, 1864
Dear Sister [Louisa],

Your very interesting letter was duly received and, after a few days delay, I now seat myself to reply. Your letter, like that written by myself to you, was of more than ordinary interest. For, unlike many previous letters, a much longer time had intervened since either of us had heard from each other. But thanks to that kind Providence, who doeth all things well, He has, in His wisdom and goodness, returned me again to health without any serious detriment to my future usefulness to the army and, I trust, practical good after the war is over if spared my life.

I was gratified to learn that William had risen to such a lucrative position as that you say he occupies, for according to present appearances, without a large salary, families in cities cannot sustain themselves and mingle in the society of city circles even though they be not of the Aristocratic. Be this as it may, it is with satisfaction that I look upon his present position. I earnestly hope that this success will continue till easier times approach our present unhappy and distracted country.

You are evidently getting quite discouraged and, perhaps, a little out of humor over our country's affairs. I do not know that this is strange, though it is wrong thus to think while there is a spark of hope for the country. It is true that the loss of life has been fearful and sad to contemplate, but is no time now to falter. After a protracted war of nearly 4 years, it is becoming plainly evident that the rebels are pushing their last men to the rescue. With 500,000 more men, I venture to say, the rebels themselves will admit that they will be pushed to the wall. True, Grant has not yet accomplished all he anticipated, but is not discouraged. Neither do I think that the men are discouraged and demoralized, but will go as far as it is prudent to advance and stand as long as they have officers to stand with them. So far as my confidence in General Grant is concerned, I must say, I believe him an able general and my faith still remains unshaken. For he remains undaunted in his purpose and while his plans with the Potomac army have not been fully realized, other parts have, I venture to say, been carried out with perfect satisfaction.

No fault can be found with the progress of units (Southwest) under Sherman and it maybe that the capture of Atlanta, which we do not doubt will be accomplished, will open the road for Grant to move with success against Petersburg and Richmond. But I must not dwell here longer, but keep up courage. The time will come affairs will look brighter. All that is needed is unity of action in support of the government on the part of the North. All will be well.[49]

My wounds are healed, as I have written you once before, but I am getting more use of my hand than at that time. In my present condition I am liable to be sent away to distribution camp, at Alexandria, to be examined for my regiment. And yet, it is not impossible that I may remain some time. But, go where I may, I shall try and do my duty wherever I am.[50]

The fare at this hospital is very good, though not as good as in many other hospitals. Yet we have no reason to complain. The weather has been extremely warm here since I have returned and but one shower has been received during the time. The hospital is situated in an open field, with not a single shade tree under which to recline in a scorching day. There are about 500 patients in the Hospital, but most of them are able to be out and walk to the table to eat. There are many of the men that have limbs off and it is no uncommon sight to see men walking on crutches with a leg off.[51]

I have received 2 letters from home since I wrote you. Father's cold is entirely cured and mother is feeling much better than when I left.

While at Little Falls, on my way here, I had 9 photographs taken. I could not wait for them and, therefore, left them to be finished and for our folks to call for them. If they were well taken, you will have one sent to you by our folks. But it is getting late and this sheet will admit no more. I must, therefore, close. Please write me as soon as you receive this.

From your affectionate brother,
William Remmel

Emory Hospital Ward (M) Section (4)
Washington, D.C.
August 4th, 1864
Dear Brother [Augustus],

Your letter was received a few days since and the same day a letter from Louisa was also received. I am sorry to learn that you had been so unwell since returning from your visit home, but I hope ere this you have fully recovered. Your photograph was thankfully received by me. I feel much pleased with it. It looks very natural. I hope by the time this reaches you, you will have received one of myself from our people. While on my way here from home I stopped at Little Falls long enough to have several photographs taken, but could not have them finished within the time that I remained there. I ordered them sent by the stage driver to the street when they were finished.

I received a letter from home today, saying that the pictures had been received. Our family were well at the time of writing. They complained much of the weather and gave a discouraging description of the crops. There had been a heavy fire in the North woods, which, it appears, has destroyed and run over a great deal of timber. The letter stated that there was much excitement over the recent call for 500,000 men and that many of the young men were making their disappearance very mysteriously. If so, it is entirely disgraceful to the parties that are guilty. They ought to be ferreted out and brought to bear this burden with the rest.

Louisa writes that discouraging prospects are entertained of the crops. She says their garden, which they took so much pains with through the spring, is totally destroyed and that the dry weather yet continues. If rain comes soon to drench the scorching earth throughout the West, I fear from the account given that hard times are near the door of many a poor man's house. But hard as the times may be the coming winter, there is provision enough to spare, if the rich will only open their granaries and give to the needy, as true Union men should. Louisa says William is chief clerk in the railroad house now and is getting $40 per month. Pretty good wages, but no more than enough to support the two, Louisa writes.[52]

I have not heard from Charley or Anna since I have returned. I am looking for a letter anxiously every mail and, probably, will be gratified ere long with one. Their crops, I learn, are much if not entirely destroyed by the drought.

But, I fancy you wish to hear a word of myself. I am enjoying excellent health and, for myself, I could ask for no better times than I have had since I have returned from my furlough. My wounds, as I have written you before, are healed and, with the exception of one finger which is stiff, I am as well as I shall ever be, which will be equal to previous bodily health, although my finger will be missed by me very often no doubt. The fare is as good as can be expected. The food is good and wholesome and enough of it.[53]

We have experienced very warm weather here for the past few days, though today it has been very cool. I have had some very interesting walks through the city of Washington and, in my travels, have seen some very useful and instructive sights. Yesterday I was to the city to draw my pay and while there took a walk through the Smithsonian Institute, where almost every species of bird and animal could be seen; not alive, but stuffed in their skins and natural size. I also took a stroll through the Patent Office a few days before, where every kind of patent can be seen. I also saw the uniform worn by Washington, his sword, and many other things belonging to him. But I must close this letter and write more next time.[54]

I remain, very truly, your brother,
Wm. Remmel

Emory Hospital
Washington, D.C.
August 6th, 1864
Dear Parents,

Ada's letter was duly received and I now seat myself to reply. I am still remaining in this hospital, which I had expected to leave long ere this. I am unable to say how long I shall remain here, yet I think not long. My health is good and our fare is as good as could be expected, perhaps, for a hospital. We have better food now than in the spring. I will give a list of the articles of food that we have for breakfast, dinner, and supper. Breakfast: cold meat, 2 slices of bread and cup of coffee. Dinner: plate of meat soup (or beans), piece of meat, 1 piece of bread, cup of water. Supper: 2 slices of bread and plate of applesauce and cup of tea; Fridays have codfish. Once a week have 2 eggs and butter enough to spread 2 pieces of bread. This constitutes our fare through the week. There are about 500 men in the hospital. It will accommodate more if necessary.

The weather is still very warm here, though this morning it is somewhat cooler, for a light shower this morning cooled air. There is much complaint among the farmers in Maryland over the dry weather, which is destroying all the rebels do not take from them. I fear that the crops this year will be very light all through the country, from present indications.

Louisa writes that the dry weather yet continues where she lives, the same that she wrote you a few days before. She writes that William is getting $40 per month and is Chief Clerk in the Office. So I should think they ought to get along even if everything is very high, for the family is small. I answered the letter and told her to be patient and all would yet be well.

I have written one letter to Charley since I returned, but have not heard from him yet. I am looking for one everyday. You probably know how he is since I left home. His crops will probably be light this year.

Augustus wrote me a letter a few days ago. He said he had not felt well since he had returned from his visit home, but hoped to recover soon. He sent me his photograph, which is very natural. Please send him one of mine, if you have not done so yet.

I have also received a letter from Caleb. He is well and says they have finished their haying and their other work is not going to be very hard. Their hops are very light and potatoes will be nothing unless rain comes soon.

I was in the city Thursday to draw my pay for the months of May and June, which amounted to $22, taken out the money that it cost to go home, $18.72. I do not know that I shall send you any of this now, but wait until I receive more for the months of July and August.

I have had some very interesting walks through the city of Washington, but the city is not very pleasant and not much business done in it. The Capital, Treasury, Post Office, and Patent Office are very large marble buildings and form noble spectacles for strangers, and adds much to the look of the city. There is also a large school called Smithsonian Institute, where all kind of animals, birds, snakes, and many other things maybe seen. They are not alive, of course, but the skins are stuffed and they appear lifelike. The city contains several hospitals and many are situated outside the city. Emory Hospital is about ½ mile from the Capital. We can look upon the city very plainly. The president's house is also a splendid white marble building, with a beautiful grove and walk around it.[55]

It is reported that the rebels are again coming across the Potomac in heavy force. About 3,000 cavalry started for Maryland this morning and more will be ready soon. Should I leave here within a few days, I will write when I leave.[56]

As there is no more room for any further remarks, I will close for the present. I send my love to all.

From your affectionate son,
William Remmel

Soldier's Rest
Washington, D.C.
August 14, 1864
Dear Parents,

I thought I would write you a few lines ere I started for my regiment, which I expect to be able in a day or so, maybe tonight. I left Emory Hospital last Thursday, today is Sunday. From the hospital I was sent to distribution camp, about 5 miles from here, where the soldiers all have to go before they return to their regiments. The soldiers of the different corps are put together in squads there and sent off to their respective corps. There are about 500 men of my corps here.[57]

We are agoing to leave in about 1 hour for Harper's Ferry, a place about 70 miles from here, on the Potomac River. You have probably read of the place. The 6th Corps, you remember was sent to Washington at the time the rebels made their march on Washington and Baltimore. And after the rebels retreated across the Potomac River, the 6th Corps followed up as far as the river and since laid in camp in the vicinity of Harper's Ferry, Maryland.

I am well and in good spirits. So you need not worry about me. I will write you often after I arrive to my regiment. When you write me, direct to the 121st Regiment, Co. I, Washington, DC. I hope this letter will find you all well, as it does me.

From your affectionate son,
William

I send much love to all.

Camp near Sandy Hook, Va.
August 17, 1864
Dear Sister [Louisa],

I am now seated, while penning these lines, on the bank of the beautiful and picturesque Potomac, not more than 5 miles from the renowned village of Harper's Ferry. You, of course, will be somewhat surprised at this announcement, for my last letter was written at the hospital; but a soldier's home is at best a moving habitation, roving through the country without any permanent place of rendezvous. You remember I wrote a few weeks ago that there was a prospect of my leaving for my regiment in a few weeks, if not days, and I was not wrong in this judging. Last Thursday, which was the 11th, a squad of men thought to be fit for their regiments, I included among the number, was sent to distribution camp about 5 miles from Washington; there to be sent to our respective corps, wherever they might be. I remained in this camp one day only, when a squad of 300 of the 6th Corps were sent off to Washington; there to take transportation for Harper's Ferry, where the corps was supposed to be encamped or at least the nearest depot to the corps from the cars.[58]

After remaining in Washington 24 hours we were loaded in a train of cattle cars and just at the edge of evening we took our departure and many of us, no doubt, [took our] last look of Washington, the nation's capital. The train being of an inferior class, the speed was provokingly slow all of the way. The ride nevertheless was an interesting and romantic one. From Washington to the Relay House, a depot 9 miles southwest of Baltimore, scenes appeared quite natural, since I have traveled the road 4 times. It being a clear moonlight night, the eye could take a view of everything within some distance of the road. From the last named point, the Harper's Ferry Road form a junction. As I had never traveled over this road, I kept my eye perched for anything that might chance to fall within the scope.

The road is terrible crooked for the first 20 miles and passes through a deep ravine, with high hills and projecting rocks bounding its sides, for several miles at a time no symptom of civilization. In the midst of this apparent wilderness our engine gave out and we were left without locomotion. The engineer informed us that we would have to content ourselves until another Horse could be brought to our assistance. It being midnight, the boys all laid down upon the car platforms and we were soon all sound asleep, and but a few awake, until the shrill whistle of cars told us that we were once more under way.

After riding some miles further, we emerged into an open country with beautiful farmhouses and golden fields of corn together with large stacks of wheat and other grains. We passed through this kind of country for many miles when, at last, about 11 O'clock (A.M.) hauled up at Harper's Ferry. This town, of which so many have read so much, is situated on the south side of the Potomac River. It was once a beautiful town, but the war has made havoc here as everywhere and now it is mostly a wreck of ruins.

Upon inquiry it was ascertained that the 6th Corps, with other troops, was in hot pursuit of the rebels and not less than 40 miles from the Ferry. Our squad being without arms it was not prudent to follow up after them and, finally, after some marching and counter-marching we have settled down, not knowing how long, near Sandy Hook below Harper's Ferry.

We are having a gala time yet, foraging, fishing, and swimming. Here as I sit writing I behold boys fording the Potomac, to give our southern host a visit in Virginia, and, could I wait long enough, I would see them return with everything that is good. Do not worry about me just now, I beg of you, for all is going well. When you write, direct to the regiment as of old. Hoping this will find you and William well, I bid you goodbye.

Yours affect[ionately],
William

Camp near Knoxville, Va.
August 20th, 1864
Dear Parents,

I am at present encamped about 4 miles from Harper's Ferry. Have not yet arrived at my regiment. A squad of about 250 men of us arrived from Washington at Harper's Ferry last Sunday, the 14th instant. Upon inquiring it was ascertained that the 6th Corps, to which most of us belong, had a few days before started up the Shenandoah Valley after the rebel raiders that had destroyed so much of Maryland and Pennsylvania a few weeks before.

We were told that they had got so far from the Ferry that it would not be safe for us, without arms, to undertake to overtake them. We were, consequently, taken to a place about 4 miles below the village of Harper's Ferry and there ordered to go into camp until further notice. We are all yet stopping here and many more are daily joining us. There are now about 600 of us in all.

We are having a fine time of it, I assure you. All draw their rations of the government and enough of them, but we are not content with that so long as we can get better of the farmers around. Corn, apples, and peaches are just about right now and we help ourselves to what we want of them. I have went out several times for corn and apples and each time brought back a fine lot.

The officers placed us between the Potomac River and the Chesapeake and Ohio Canal, which runs along her, thinking to keep us from leaving camp, but this has done no good. For when we wish to go out we strip ourselves and wade through the canal, or swim, according to where we wish to go. We have no duty to do and, on the whole, the boys had rather stop here than go to the regiment. There is no prospect of remaining here much longer, for the troops are falling back toward Harper's Ferry. I think as soon as arms can be procured for us, we will all be sent away to the corps. So long as we are here we intend to enjoy ourselves, for certainly we have everything good to eat and nothing to do.[59]

We have been looking for Mosby and his guerrillas for the past few nights, but he has not made his appearance yet. As most of us have no guns, it would not be very strange if such a thing should happen.

The weather has been very pleasant for the past few days. Some very refreshing showers have fallen several times and the air is very cool and refreshing. Crops are looking fine here. The wheat is all in stacks and much of it is already thrashed. Corn is an excellent crop and apples and peaches are very plenty. The trees are hanging full of them in every orchard that the soldiers have not disturbed.

By the way, I will say that we have more or less milk everyday, enough at least for our coffee. There are lots of cows here all through the day and, though there are about 10 times as many milkers as cows, each one gets a little; sometimes as much as 2 quarts and often not more than ½ gallon.

I have received no letters since I left the hospital and do not expect to until I arrive at my regiment, which I think will be soon. I have wrote all of interest this time and so close this.

From your affectionate son,
Wm.

I send my love.

Camp of the 121st Regiment
Near Bolivar Heights, Va.
August 24, 1864
Dear Parents,

I arrived at my regiment this morning and, therefore, thought I would drop you a line informing you of my whereabouts.

I was much pleased to see the boys, those that are left, for many of them are gone. There are 18 men in my company, including myself, and 178 in the regiment. Our Lieutenant Colonel came back to the regiment last night. He has been a prisoner since the 6th of May and was exchanged recently at Charleston, South Carolina.[60]

There has been some fighting here for several days, though none that has been very severe. My regiment had 2 men killed and 6 wounded a few days since. One man in my company was killed on the skirmish line. I do not know whether there will be much fighting here or not. It is reported that the rebels have got a heavy force here and that they will attempt to cross the Potomac River into Maryland and Pennsylvania again. We have got a large force here and think that the rebels will get enough of it, if they should attempt to give us battle. We have 3 corps of infantry and one of cavalry here, so that you see we are not entirely deficient of men.[61]

The weather is very warm at present, but we have had some very refreshing showers of rain for the past week. The boys are all feeling well and have had some very gay times in the Shenandoah Valley. They say that they have lived most of the time on the farmers, killing hogs and sheep and taking such stuff as they could find.

They have also had hard marching, chasing the rebels and then falling back again. They say that the fighting is much easier than the marching. Nathan Wood and Nathaniel Lamphere are both in the regiment, though I have not talked with either of them yet.

I had expected that there would be several letters in the regiment for me, but none have yet arrived. There probably will be several in a few days, as soon as they can be sent from the hospital to the regiment. When you write, direct to the regt: Company I, 121st N.Y. Vols. I will find out who I can get to read German letters and then father can write me. I will write you again in a few days and let you know. I hope Harmon and Ada won't get angry because I don't write them, for they hear from me when I write you. I will write them both when I get a little settled.

There is quite heavy firing in our front just now, from artillery and infantry, and there may be a battle soon. I will, therefore, stop writing and wait for a better opportunity. Hoping to hear from you soon.

I remain,
Your affectionate son,
Wm. Remmel

Camp of the 121st Regiment
Near Charlestown, Va.
August 31st, 1864
Dear Parents,

I have not yet received a letter from you; but this does not stop my writing to you, [n]or will it while I am able to write you. I do not understand why letters do not reach me, but I suppose most of them are directed to the hospital and, therefore, will take longer to get here. Have received but one letter since I have returned to the regiment, which was from Augustus, written the 17th instant of this month and directed to Emory Hospital, which delayed it several days. Augustus writes that he has been sick with the fever, but it is now nearly well again.

The regiment has been in no battle since I have returned to it. We have been encamped very near the rebels for the last week. There has been more or less fighting nearly the whole time since I returned to the regiment. For 3 days there was fighting within ½ mile of our camp, but, so used to firing and fighting have our boys become that they did not mind it at all, though liable at any moment to be called on to go into the midst of danger and death.

Two days ago I thought surely our corps would have a fight with the rebels. We had marched the day before about 5 miles up the Shenandoah Valley, following up the rebels. The cavalry had, this day, followed up the rebels pretty sharply. And next morning the rebels rushed their main force, infantry, cavalry, and artillery, upon our cavalry. The cavalry fought well, but could not stand against the whole rebel army and, therefore, had to retreat shortly. They fought about 7 miles of ground over, when in the afternoon about 4 O'clock the cavalry reached our infantry. Orders were now given for us to pack up and be ready to move upon the rebels, should they attempt to come any further. This we done very quickly and everything soon was ready for a battle. We waited anxiously for sometime, expecting to receive the order to move forward, but we soon had our tents pitched for another night's repose.[62]

There has been no firing since of any amount and it is generally thought here that the greater part of the rebel army is falling back upon Richmond to drive General Grant from his position in front of Petersburg and the Weldon Railroad. It is also reported that one corps from here is going down to Grant. It may be that the 6th Corps may have to go back to Petersburg again.

Nathan Wood, Nathaniel Lamphere, and Merton Tanner are the boys living around home that are now with the regiment. Merton has been sick for a few days past, but is now well again. Nathaniel Lamphere is feeling well. His arm is yet stiff, though not very bad. Nathan is not very well at present. I have had quite a conversation with him. He appears to feel sorry for what he has done and means to live a better life in the future.

The war is making terrible havoc here in the valley. Barns, houses, wheat stacks, fences, and everything else of any use to the people or rebels is being destroyed. I most every night witness bright lights along our lines, caused from a burning building or some wheat stacks set afire by our soldiers. I hardly know what the people will live on the next year in this quarter, for everything is taken away from them.

If you wish to write me German letters you can do so, for I can get them read by some of the Germans in my regt. Dengler, who used to read them, was killed or taken prisoner the night I was wounded. Please send me 50 cents worth of stamps in your next. It is getting late and, not having more room for news, I will close for this time. Hope this will find you all well. Good night.[63]

From your son,
Wm.

Camp of the 121st Regiment
Near Berryville, Va.
September 5th, 1864
Dear Brother [Augustus],

Your letter was recorded some days since. It was delayed somewhat in consequence of being sent to Emory Hospital, whereas I was on my way to my regiment. It, therefore, had to re-mailed at the hospital and sent on, which took some little time to reach me.

Was glad to learn that you had fully recovered from your illness, which must have been very severe for a time. Hope that you will not have a relapse of the disease and, therefore, you must be very cautious of yourself to not catch cold or expose yourself needlessly to the weather. I feel grateful in being able to write you of my usual good health, which I have been so abundantly blessed with from early childhood up.

If I remember right, I wrote you a letter while lying in the vicinity of Harper's Ferry. After moving back and forth in the vicinity of the Ferry for several days after my letter to you, I, with a squad of men from the 6th Corps, was sent to my regiment, which I reached the next day. The boys were glad to see me and, I assure you, [I] was none the less happy to behold them.

There were more boys left than I anticipated ere I arrived. There are now nearly 200 muskets in the regiment and men are constantly arriving from the hospital, having recovered from their wound or illness. We are also expecting several hundred recruits within a few weeks for the regiment, which will make a pretty good-sized regiment of the 121st once more.[64]

We have been confronting the rebels ever since my return to the regiment, but, lucky for the 6th Corps, it has not yet become engaged with them. There has been more or less skirmishing and fighting while I have been back. This army moved into its present position 2 days ago. The army broke camp at daylight Saturday morning near Charlestown, a poor village about 12 miles from Harper's Ferry and well known as the place where John Brown was executed after the insurrection at the latter place in the fall of '59, and moved to the front about 8 miles, which distance we made by 9 O'clock (A.M.).

The whole army is still in the same vicinity and was yesterday busily engaged in entrenching itself. Our brigade was hard at work putting up breastworks with rails and this morning there is a detail out covering the same with dirt. On the night of the same day that we arrived here, there was quite a fight between a portion of our troops and the enemy. The result of which I have not learned; but certain it is that they did not drive our troops, for the firing gradually receded as the contest continued. It raged until late in the evening, when it slowly became situated.

It has been generally thought that the greater part of the rebel forces had retreated from the valley and were falling back on Richmond, but reconnaissances made prove this supposition to be false. It is known that the rebel Gen. Early is still confronting us with a heavy force, variously estimated from 30,000 to 50,000, and is strongly entrenched, determined to dispute our further advance. I do not pretend to know much of our military movements, but it is my opinion that a battle will, ere this reaches you, have been fought. Though it may be delayed longer. Since the rebels have been defeated at Atlanta it will be well to try to crush or at least hold them here, so as not to allow their main armies to be reinforced, thereby making our victories more complete.[65]

Not having received letters from anyone but yourself, I am unable to tell you anything of any of the family. N. Lamphere, N. Wood, and M. Tanner are back to the regiment, doing duty again. The boys are foraging very much upon the people taking everything in the eatable line and often more, I think, saying the least. The boys will not want while in the valley. Hoping that in my next I shall be able to write of a brilliant victory, I will close.

From you affect[ionate] brother,
Wm. Remmel

Camp of the 121st Regiment
Near Berryville, Shenandoah Valley, Va.
September 17, 1864
Dear Parents,

Your letter was received night before last and yesterday I had it read by one of the Germans in my regiment. I was very glad to receive a German letter again and if I could only read them as well as I can understand the writing I should be very much pleased, but it is very pleasant as it is, and I hope that you will write more often.

I am gratified to hear that your crops are so much better than was expected last July, when everything looked so gloomy and bad and, perhaps, you will have enough to live on next winter. Provisions of all kinds, I learn, are very high at present. Should your potatoes do well they will help to support the family and hope you will have hay and straw enough to keep your stock through the winter months.[66]

Was glad to hear that Harmon was getting better and he will probably soon be well again. Augustus writes me that he is well again. Caleb also writes that he is well.

I was very much surprised by a letter from Charley and Anna stating that Charley had enlisted for 1 year, having received a bounty, or would receive one, of $410. I was very sorry to hear this, for Charley is not situated as well as one year ago to go as a soldier. For then he was a single man, having nobody to care for, while now a dear wife will be left behind to mourn after him and a large farm upon his hands, which he has to entrust to another keeping. But if Charley has gone it is no use now to sorrow over his absence. And all that we can do that is right now is to hope and pray that God will spare him amid the dangers that he will have to pass through and the many hardships he will be compelled to endure, so that in one short year he will be permitted to return home to his dear wife and many friends, a brave and honored soldier who helped to save this glorious country.[67]

There are now two brothers out of our family in the army fighting, as I know I have been, for a government and country that I love and [for] which I am willing to battle another year. I am willing to battle another year for when, if I live, I hope to see this bloody war closed and an honorable peace declared. How happy you would be if you could see Charley and William return home together within the next 12 months, even if I should carry with me 2 more scars than now are upon my limbs. And although we will not go home together, I hope, if it is God's Will, we will all meet again at the dear home I love so much.

Now father, you wished me to consider calmly and candidly what I would do if I were in your stead, with regard to consenting to let either Augustus or Caleb go to war. Now father, I will tell you plainly what I would do were I at home and knew what I do now about the war. I would reason with them in this way. I have now 2 sons in the army and I do not know that they will ever return, although I trust that they will. Did every family in the whole North do half as well, our army would be larger today than it is. I think much of my country and will not see it destroyed, but for the present I have contributed my share of soldiers and stood my share of the burden of the war.

No father, I would advise the boys not to go. I will write them so and you can tell them what I think. I have been a soldier now very nearly 25 months and I think I know something of what it is to be one. The large bounties all look very nice and the bright side appears for a moment. But there is a dark side to it and no one knows so much of it until he finds himself deprived of the comforts of home and amid the deadly shells and bullets of the rebels.

The postage have been received. My health remains good. There is no prospect of a battle at present, yet tomorrow may see us in bloody conflict with the rebels. It is impossible to tell what will take place. I hope this will reach you soon.

From your son,
W. R.

Camp of the 121st
Near Harrisonburg, Shenandoah Valley, Va.
September 27, 1864
Dear Parents,

I suppose you have been in deep anxiety about me since you first learned of the battle of Winchester and, afterwards, that of Strasburg. In each of which we whipped the rebel army under Early. I passed, through the providence of God, through each of these battles without injury, though running some narrow chances often. At the battle of Winchester a shell burst in front of me or, rather, near my back, for I was looking away from the rebels and one of the pieces passed through my knapsack in which several articles were torn, cut my coat and shirt and then stopped after bruising the skin a little. I felt much pain at first and told the Adjutant of our regiment that I was wounded. I had him look where it struck and he could see no blood. I, therefore, concluded to stop till the battle was over at any rate. The pain, however, soon ceased and I was able to stay with the boys. At the battle of Strasburg our regiment lost but 2 men wounded, for we did not get engaged with the rebels and consequently were further off. At Winchester our loss was also very light, though we fought nearly all day. We lost 2 killed and 12 wounded, making in both battles 2 killed and 14 wounded.[68]

Other regiments lost much heavier. The rebels were never so completely thrashed as they have been this last time and, though we have followed them up day and night and tried to have them stop and fight us since the battle of Strasburg, we can get no fight out of them. The rebels will not stand. We have captured nearly all of their artillery, 5 pieces were taken at Winchester and 21 at Strasburg, making in all 26 pieces of cannon captured that we know and it is reported that the cavalry have taken 12 more pieces making in all 36 cannon. The prisoners taken will number 4,000 and their killed and wounded as many more, making in one week a loss of 8,000 men and 26 pieces of artillery, perhaps 36 pieces, much ammunition taken and some wagons captured and others destroyed. I do not believe that any of the rebel armies were ever so completely routed as in these 2 battles.[69]

After the battle of Strasburg we followed the rebels all night, marching nearly 15 miles. Wagons were left burning on the road by the rebels and the next morning many prisoners were taken on the road by us. Our rations having all given out, we had to wait until the train reached us before we could follow them further. After drawing rations in the morning, we started after them the next day again in the afternoon and overtook them the next day. We tried to make them stand and fight us, but they would not do it for they had no artillery left with which to keep us back and the men could not stand. The rebels had become so demoralized that our batteries were run out upon the skirmish line and would fire into their wagon train while they were retreating. The rebels could do nothing, only fall back to prevent their whole army from being taken. We followed the rebels in this way until Sunday, when they had got so far ahead of us that we could not catch them, and we halted for we were getting too far from our supplies.

Our army is at what is called Harrisonburg, a pretty little village about 80 miles from Harper's Ferry. Our supplies all have to come by wagon from Harper's Ferry, so you see that it is a difficult matter to supply the army with food. I do not know whether we will move on further or not. Probably we will as soon as we get a new supply of rations, which will be today.

We have passed through a very pretty country and one that is very rich. The rebel army has taken most of the grain raised, but there is much left for our army, and I guess that after we get through there will not be much left. Our army is feeling well. I never saw the boys feel better than now.[70]

I do not know how soon this will reach you, it may be more than one week. You can have a pair of boots made for me and send them in about 3 weeks, and also a couple of pair of socks. Have the boots good kipskin, not very large leg, and size No. 9. Some of they boys around home were hurt in the battles. My health is good and am feeling well.

I would like to write more but have no room, neither time. Hope to be able to write to you again soon.

From your affect[ionate] son,
Wm. Remmel

Camp of the 121st Regiment
Near Middletown, Shenandoah Valley, Va.
October 15, 1864
Dear Parents,

I was very greatly surprised the other day to receive a letter directed to Caleb Remmel, Co. I, 121st. Upon reading it, found that Caleb too had enlisted for this regiment and the company to which I belong. The letter was written by Augustus, who was then at home. I was very sorry to hear this, for there are many objections to Caleb coming to the army, but there is no use mourning over what has been done now. Yet I cannot help feeling bad for, had I known that Caleb was coming to the army, should have written him not to come to this regiment in any event. For the thought of a brother in the same company does not make me feel well, especially when I think of the battles that we may both have to be engaged in the future. It would not be pleasant, but rather sorrowful, for either of us to see the other in so much danger and liable at any moment to be killed or wounded, but will not dwell on this unpleasant subject.[71]

Caleb has not arrived yet, but probably will be here very soon, perhaps today or tomorrow. He would now be here, but our corps was ordered away from here the other day and had marched nearly all day toward Alexandria when an order came for us to return to this place, which we did yesterday. Upon hearing that the corps had left this department, Caleb, with many others, was sent back to Harper's Ferry. They will now be ordered back.[72]

I shall do all that I can to make it pleasant for him, when he gets here, and shall try as much as I can to have him do right, to always do his duty. Do not worry about his getting in bad company, for the orders here are very strict. If a soldier does not conduct himself right, he is severely punished.

I hope that you, dear mother, will not allow yourself to sorrow and trouble over us here in the army, for it will not better the matter nor make our position any safer here and certainly will make it more unpleasant and sad at home. Your health is very feeble, as you know. And should you make yourself sad and constantly keep thinking about our being killed or wounded, when as you well know that I have lived nearly 26 months in the army and though wounded once am yet alive and well, God only knows what would be the consequences.

There is a possibility of some of us never returning, but let us look on the bright side of life and especially this war. For it cannot, nor will it, last many months longer. There will be some hard fighting yet, but this fall I honestly believe will close the hard fighting. If Abraham Lincoln is re-elected for president for another 4 years, the rebels will certainly surrender, for they will plainly see that they cannot hold out so long. Should McClellan be elected, which I sincerely hope not, then surely the war will close, for the Copperheads will let the rebels go if they choose to, or give them back their slaves and high offices and tell them to come back; but enough of this.[73]

Was sorry to learn, from Augustus' letter, that father had been so dangerously ill. I thought it very strange that I had received no letters from him. This explains it, but he (Augustus) stated that he was getting better slowly, so that I feel hopeful that he will get along.

Our family has always been so free from sickness that it seems strange to us that we are sometimes afflicted. I hope that father will soon be well again. He must try to work soon.

The death of Mrs. Bliss is a very sad affair and how bad that Moses could not see her before she died. Each family has its afflictions and ours is of the number, but we ought to be thankful that its no worse. Charley has written me a letter. He is in Cairo, Illinois, in the 42nd Wisconsin Regiment, Co. F. He was well at the time of writing.[74]

The boots and socks you may send by Adams Express Company when you get them ready. No more this time.

From your affect[ionate] son,
Wm. Remmel

I have sent $20 by Doctor Holt, of my regiment, to deposit with Mr. Galpin that keeps the store depot at Little Falls and in care of Case the stage driver, to deliver to you. Send for it by him and you will get it. It will be there very soon, perhaps when this letter reaches you.[75]

Camp of the 121st Regiment
Near Middletown, Shenandoah Valley, Va.
October 16th, 1864
Dear Sister [Louisa],

Your last letter was duly received and read with such interest. Was sorry to hear that William was in feeble health and that you too were feeling so bad. Hope that, when this reaches you, you will both be well again.

William's task must be very severe and exhausting and quite unpleasant for you, not being able to associate together sufficiently to make it pleasant. But it will be best for both of you to be contented and try to stride by the unpleasant circumstances as best you can, for brighter days are, I trust, in store for you. It will, at least, be best to think so and look on the bright side of life.

William's salary is certainly a very respectable one and, though it may not be more than will sustain you at present, it will I trust increase as he (William) becomes better known as his knowledge of the different branches of business becomes fully acquired. I see no reason why William cannot, in time, command as high a salary as the best accountant in the city.

I am grieved to inform you, if you have not already heard of it, that Caleb has enlisted for this regiment in the same company to which I belong. I say that I am grieved over this, not so much because he has enlisted, as because he has come to this regiment. I never could consent to have a brother in the same regiment with me, were it in my power to prevent it. There are too many unhappy hours in a soldier's life to make this at all pleasant. The thought of 2 brothers in the same company in a battle makes me feel sad. But it is no use now to make this matter worse, but we must content ourselves as best we can and try to do the duty of the hour with the true heroism of soldiers battling in a righteous cause.

Caleb will probably be to the regiment very soon. Augustus has already written him and directed it to Company I, 121st. I had no previous notice of his coming; upon opening the letter the mystery was solved. Caleb is on the road somewhere between here and Harper's Ferry. Perhaps he will be here today or tomorrow. He would now be here but our corps was, the other day, ordered to Petersburg and we had already marched nearly one day toward Alexandria when the order was countermanded and we returned to this place, Middletown. This order made the authorities at Winchester send all the men for the 6th Corps back to Harper's Ferry, from which place they will now be returned.

I shall do all in my power to make it pleasant for Caleb and endeavor to guard, as much as possible, his moral habits against vice and the temptations of the camp. I cannot see how it was that Caleb was passed by the surgeon. It was certainly a fraudulent surgeon that approved him for a soldier, with his crippled hand.[76]

Augustus also wrote that father had been severely sick with the lung fever, but was slowly recovering. Father had been sick about 2 weeks at the time of writing. It will be a very severe blow upon the family, together with the other many unhappy circumstances attending them of late.

Augustus was sent for, for a few days, to help to do the work upon the place until father could get around. I hope that father will soon be well again. Mother, I fear, will be taken down with all her anxiety for us all. Should we lose her, I know not what the family would come to. It would no longer be a happy home. God forbid that such a loss should befall us now.

Charley has written me one letter since he has become a soldier. He was then at Cairo, Illinois, in the 42nd Wisconsin Regiment, Company F. He was well and he knew not where he was going. Hope he will write you very soon and give you particulars.

There is nothing of importance going on here that I know of. I learned, however, this morning that 4 pieces [of] Artillery had been very recently captured from Mosby. The operations here have, thus far, been entirely successful. What the future plans will be, it is difficult to say. My health, at present, is excellent and hope this letter will find you and W[illia]m both well again. No more at present.[77]

From your affectionate brother,
Wm. Remmel

Camp of the 121st Regiment
Middletown, Shenandoah Valley, Va.
Evening of October 16th, 1864
Dear Parents,

I drop you these lines this evening in another letter, for the one this afternoon is already in the mailbag and cannot get it. I write you to inform you that brother Caleb has just arrived to the regiment with about 20 others.[78]

Caleb is looking well and, so far, has stood soldiering first rate. He has now been in the service just 1 month. He was glad to learn, from Augustus' letter, that his bounty had been received by you. He sends much love to you all and hopes that mother will not worry about him. He has told me much news, which I was glad to hear. Nick Governour and Allan Jennings came part of the way with him. They are in the 19th Corps, which is lying but a little distance from here. Caleb brought gun, cartridge box, knapsack, and everything with him. I think he will stand it well, for he is strong and healthy.[79]

And now, dear parents, I hope that you will try and bear up in your troubles and not get discouraged. For it is God's Will, and in Him we must put all our trust, we will all 3 return safely in one year to our dear home.

I suppose you know that the soldiers vote this fall and, as I am a voter, I shall put in my vote this year. I shall send it directed to father. Father will please take the letter to Mr. William Dutton and he will tell him how to put it in at the polls on Election Day. The ticket will be in a large envelope with Soldier's Vote printed on the outside. Be sure and put it in on Election Day. If you cannot go yourself, ask Mr. Dutton how to manage.[80]

I hope, father, you will write me as soon as you get able to do so. With these lines, I bid you a kind good night.

Your son,
Wm. Remmel

Epilogue

The Remmel family last heard from William in his second letter of October 16, 1864. Three days later, he and his regiment participated in the battle of Cedar Creek, part of Maj. Gen. Philip Sheridan's campaign to drive Confederate forces under Lt. Gen. Jubal Early out of the Shenandoah Valley. Sheridan achieved initial success in this campaign, with consecutive victories at Winchester and Fisher's Hill, and believed he controlled the valley; Early, however, pressed the issue. Surprised on October 19 by an early-morning attack against their position along Cedar Creek, the Yankees suffered heavy casualties in the first phase of fighting and teetered on the brink of a rout reminiscent of First Manassas. Two Union corps, the 8th and 19th, gave way against an incessant wave of Rebel infantry under Maj. Gen. John B. Gordon. A determined stand by several units of the 6th Corps, along with Early's failure to fully exploit the gains won by Gordon's troops, combined to stanch the retreat and stabilize the Union line.[1]

As the initial attack intensified, the 121st New York, along with the rest of the 2nd Brigade, moved out of their camps at daylight and prepared a hasty defense against the anticipated Confederate onslaught. They took up position on the Hite Road, about 400 yards behind their camps, with a gap of 200–300 yards from an unidentified body of Federals on their left. Shortly after establishing this position, they were ordered "to move to the rear by the right of battalions." Before this movement could be fully realized, however, they were ordered to re-form along the road with the 121st placed behind "a slight crest" about 100 yards from the road, with its right flank "refused." The brigade held these positions for thirty minutes under "heavy fire"—made all the more vulnerable due to the withdrawal of the unidentified troops on their left—until ordered to follow the general retreat already under way to their right. As the last of the morning fog burned away the enemy discovered and struck the gap on the brigade's left flank, advancing to within 200 yards of their line and obliging them to "move rapidly to the rear" another 1,500 yards. Hard pressed by Gordon's veterans, the brigade withdrew "still farther" around midday; detailed as skirmishers, the 121st New York and the 2nd Connecticut Heavy Artillery covered the brigade's withdrawal, with instructions to "retire slowly, from crest to crest, holding the enemy in check if he advanced." The retreat continued for approximately one mile, when the brigade faced about and formed new lines of battle in a patch of woods, with the New Yorkers positioned on the far left of the second line. Between 3 and 4 P.M. the first line "pressed forward" under "a galling fire" to a crest 150 yards from the second line, where a "heavy volley" checked its advance. The second line, commanded by Lt. Col. Egbert Olcott of the 121st, quickly advanced in support and helped drive the enemy 400–500 yards. After a thirty-minute pause to allow the 3rd Division to re-form, the renewed charge quickly drove the enemy from the field "in confusion," pushing them across Cedar Creek, so that by sundown the Federals reoccupied their original camps.[2]

The sacrifice of the 6th Corps, along with Sheridan's dramatic leadership, allowed the Union forces to reverse the tide of battle; by the end of the day the boys in blue had turned a near disaster into a decisive Union victory and set the stage for the eventual conclusion of the Valley campaign. The cost, however, proved quite dear. The Union suffered an estimated 5,665 casualties in the battle, out of an effective force of 30,000; the 121st New York lost a total of 57 men, with Sgt. William Remmel listed among the regiment's missing.[3]

For more than forty years the Remmel family attempted to learn more about William's fate, but precise details proved elusive. They assumed that William—wounded and captured during the regiment's desperate rearguard action prior to the successful Union counterattack—died as one of the unknown at Andersonville Prison. Ada Remmel Benson, the younger sister to whom William addressed much fraternal advice and concern, spearheaded the family's search for many of those years. From her home in West Winfield, New York, she contacted several "old soldiers" of the regiment. Despite her persistence, her efforts produced no definitive answers. The men responded promptly and politely, but their replies illustrate the confusion and varied perspectives that occur in combat. Although well-meaning in their attempt to provide comfort, the veterans' letters are ultimately devoid of the specific details sought by the family. To a man, however, William's comrades remembered him as a brave and responsible soldier, among the best in the regiment. At least three veterans, including his former company commander, indicate that William ranked as acting sergeant major for the regiment at the time of his disappearance—a further indication of his leadership and ability.[4]

Several of the veterans suggest that Remmel died on the field rather than in a prison camp, but this opinion probably represents a polite effort to comfort the family with the belief that their loved one died quickly rather than suffering the slow, debilitating death that awaited inmates of a prison camp. The limited amount of documentation on this subject does seem, however, to confirm the family's long-held belief that William died in captivity.[5] Two undated accounts of a conversation with a veteran named Frank Mumford specifically place Remmel at Andersonville during the late autumn of 1864. Both accounts summarize a conversation between Mumford and Louisa Remmel Empie that occurred several years after the war. According to these accounts, Mumford told Louisa that he spoke to "Billie" Remmel at Andersonville on December 16, 1864, and noticed that Remmel suffered from wounds to the head and arm, with gangrene evident in the arm. It is, therefore, likely that Remmel died sometime that winter as a result of this infection. The lack of sufficient medical facilities and the deplorable sanitary conditions prevalent in Civil War prison camps make this scenario rather likely.[6]

The question of where William's death occurred, however, remains partially unanswered due to additional circumstances of war. The autumn of 1864 witnessed a sharp decline in Andersonville's population as Confederate authorities transferred thousands of Union captives to camps at Charleston, South Carolina, Millen, Georgia, and elsewhere to prevent their liberation by troops under Maj. Gen. William Tecumseh Sherman. Mumford finally began his journey homeward from Andersonville in November with a brief transfer to Millen, followed by parole at Savannah near the end of the month and a long-awaited trip northward in early December. Because Mumford departed from Andersonville prior to December, his meeting with Remmel, which he recalled as having occurred on December 16, would have had to occur no later than the second week of November—possibly at Millen.[7]

The rest of the Remmel family survived the war years. Gottlieb and Henrietta continued to live just west of Stratford, in the village of Devereaux. In an effort to make peace with their loss, the family held a memorial service in the fall of 1865; the service included such popular melancholy songs as "Sleeping for the Flag" and "Who Will Care for Mother Now?" Ada identified the latter piece as "Brother William's favorite song." In the decades after the war the Remmels received a small government pension as the parents of a Civil War casualty. Gottlieb died in Devereaux on January 17, 1892, at the age of seventy-nine; Henrietta died in Newport, Arkansas, on June 22, 1896, at the age of eighty-two. They are buried in the family plot in Stratford Cemetery in Salisbury.[8]

Charley returned from California sometime in 1863, married Annie, and purchased a farm in Walworth, Wisconsin. On September 2, 1864, he enlisted in Company F of the 42nd Wisconsin Infantry. This regiment performed garrison and post duty at Fort Defiance in Cairo, Illinois, as well as provost duty by detachments at various points in the state; other than the occasional presence of small bands of guerrillas, disease proved to be the most persistent threat faced by the 42nd. Charley mustered out with his regiment on June 20, 1865, with the rank of corporal and returned to his homestead in southern Wisconsin. On May 4, 1866, Annie gave birth to a son named Willie—presumably named in honor of William Remmel and the brother Annie lost at Chickamauga. Annie apparently died sometime prior to 1870, but an exact date and burial location are not known. On November 24, 1870, Charley married Mary Samantha Bliss, with whom he had two more children: George Edson Remmel, born in Walworth, and Ada Elizabeth Remmel, born in Geyserville, California. Charley died on November 19, 1890, at the age of fifty and is buried in Healdsburg Cemetery in Geyserville.[9]

Louisa, who taught school prior to her marriage to William Empie, initially remained in Fort Wayne after the war. She and William had one daughter, Ada Louise Empie, known in the family as "Lula." During their years in Fort Wayne, Louisa and her husband established a successful pharmacy and general merchandise store in partnership with Caleb and Augustus, but they soon looked for other business opportunities. In 1873 they settled in Newport, invested extensively in the lumber business, and became civic leaders. Soon thereafter, several other members of the Remmel family also settled in Newport. Louisa died on July 30, 1904, at the age of sixty-three and is buried in Lindenwood Cemetery in Fort Wayne.[10]

Augustus wrote and received more letters than any of Remmel's other siblings. He also read many of the letters received by their parents. Although he and Caleb both sought parental permission to enlist in the summer of 1864, no service record exists for Augustus; the recurrent eye ailment mentioned in several of the letters may have prevented his enlistment. In 1876 Augustus joined the family in Newport and, beginning in January 1882, served as postmaster. When the second devastating fire in two years swept through the small community later that year, his leadership of the town's volunteer fire company helped save one million feet of lumber. This resource helped provide many of the town's residents and merchants with temporary shelter until the damage could be repaired. Augustus remained a bachelor throughout his brief life; he developed a serious illness in 1883 and died in Newport on April 12 of that year, at the age of thirty-five; he is buried in Fort Wayne.[11]

Caleb, who enlisted as a sixteen-year-old private in Company I against his older brother's express wishes, survived his military service. The day after the battle of Cedar Creek he searched the field for signs of William but found none. Remaining with the regiment until the end of the war, Caleb fought at Newtown, Hatcher's Run, Fort Fisher, and the capture of Petersburg. On April 2, 1865, he received a slight wound to the head—"just over the right ear"—during the regiment's assault on the Petersburg trenches. He received medical treatment at Point of Rocks and City Point hospitals in Virginia and at Ira Harris General Hospital in Albany, New York. Hospitalized through most of June, he received an honorable discharge upon his release. During his convalescence, Caleb wrote his parents of his unsuccessful search for William. This letter, included in the William Remmel Papers at the University of Arkansas, represents the family's first known effort to discover specific details about William's fate.[12]

After the war Caleb initially returned to his parents' home. Soon thereafter he moved to Walworth, probably due to the presence of Charley; eventually, however, he moved to Fort Wayne, where he invested in the family business interests and worked as a railroad engineer. On December 11, 1878, he married Gertrude L. Goodwin—a kindergarten teacher—at her parents' residence in Stratford. The couple had two sons, Augustus C. and Harmon G. Remmel. Disabled by numbness on the right side of his head as well as sciatic rheumatism and unspecified spinal trouble, all of which limited his ability to work, Caleb applied for a federal veteran's pension in September 1886; he received four dollars per month. Caleb died on August 13, 1887, shortly before his thirty-ninth birthday, and is buried in Lindenwood Cemetery.[13]

Ada also joined the family in Newport in the years after the war. She became the town's first female postmaster when she succeeded Augustus in May 1883, and she served at that post for almost five years. Following her marriage to Rev. John George Benson, a Methodist Episcopal minister, Ada moved back to the Mohawk Valley. She and her husband produced no children together but did raise Benson's son from his first marriage. Her efforts to locate information about "dear William" continued into the early twentieth century, but his fate remained unresolved; the replies she received constitute a significant portion of the search correspondence in the William Remmel Papers. After Benson's retirement from the ministry around 1921, he and Ada moved to Little Rock to be near her brother Harmon. She died on April 29, 1946, at the age of ninety-three, and is buried next to her parents in the family plot in Salisbury.[14]

Harmon grew into the educated and prosperous man envisioned by his older brother. He attended Fairfield Academy, where he also taught school for one term, but soon moved to Fort Wayne and engaged in business. In 1876 Harmon joined his siblings in Newport. On March 13, 1878, he married Laura Lee Stafford, the daughter of a former Confederate colonel; this marriage produced no children. Laura Lee Remmel died on October 19, 1913. On October 6, 1915, Harmon married Elizabeth I. Cameron, with whom he had a son, Harmon Jr., and adopted a daughter, Elizabeth Cameron Remmel. Harmon remained a highly successful businessman in Newport and championed the causes of industrialization and modernization in his adopted state; in recognition of this leadership the state named its first hydroelectric facility, "Remmel Dam" in Hot Springs, in his honor.[15]

In 1894 Harmon moved to Little Rock to manage the Mutual Life Insurance Company's agency in Arkansas, the Indian Territory, and Texas. In addition to his success in business, he served as a leading force in political and civic concerns and became a prominent figure in the Republican Party at the turn of the century. In his capacity as chairman of the Arkansas Republicans, Harmon opposed the growth and influence of the Ku Klux Klan as well as the regressive administration of Gov. Jeff Davis (a political demagogue of the early twentieth century). In addition, he served as a confidante to such nationally prominent Republican figures as Marcus Hanna and Presidents William McKinley, Theodore Roosevelt, and William Howard Taft. He died of a stroke in Hot Springs at the age of seventy-five on October 14, 1927, and is buried in Oakland Cemetery in Little Rock.[16]

As a final tangible link to their lost loved one, the Remmel family preserved William's wartime letters for more than 120 years. In March 1986, Harmon Remmel Jr. donated them to the Special Collections Department of Mullins Library at the University of Arkansas, where they remain.[17]

Notes

Abbreviations

OR	*The War of the Rebellion: A Compilation of the Official Records of the Union and Confederate Armies.* 128 vols. Washington, D.C., 1881–1901. Unless otherwise noted, all references are to series 1 and part 1 of the specified volume.
OR Supplement	Janet B. Hewett, ed. *Supplement to the Official Records of the Union and Confederate Armies. Part 2: Record of Events.* Vols. 42–47. Wilmington, N.C.: Broadfoot, 1997.
Remmel Papers	William Remmel Papers, Special Collections, University of Arkansas Libraries, Fayetteville.
Service Records	Records of Volunteer Union Soldiers Who Served during the Civil War. National Archives and Records Administration. Washington, D.C.

Introduction

1. Henrietta Remmel and her children arrived at the port of New York on January 25, 1851, less than a month before William's eighth birthday. Charles was born in 1840. Louisa Christiana was born in 1841. William was born February 22, 1843. Augustus was born in 1847. Caleb was born in 1848. Harmon was born in 1852. Ada was born in 1853. Remmel Family Genealogical Files, in possession of Harmon Remmel Jr., used by permission [hereafter cited as Remmel Family Genealogical Files]; William Remmel to Parents, August 31, 1862, Remmel Papers, folder 1; Harmon L. Remmel Jr., "Harmon L. Remmel," *The Stream of History* 29, no. 2 (1992): 2–3.

2. Remmel to Parents, February 9 to July 6, 1862, Remmel Papers, folder 1, items 1–4; Remmel to Parents, September 8 to November 19, 1861, Remmel Papers, folder 13, items 2–6; Tod Waterbury, of Herkimer County Historical Society, to Robert Bender, November 9, 1999 (confirmation of Remmel's enrollment at Fairfield Academy during the 1861–62 school year), in possession of the editor. For a history of Fairfield Academy see Thomas C. O'Donnell, *Tip of the Hill: An Informal History of Fairfield Academy and Medical College* (Boonville, N.Y.: Black River Books, 1953).

3. Alphonzo Casler enlisted at Salisbury as an eighteen-year-old private in Com-

pany H of the 121st New York Infantry on August 14, 1862. He received a fifty-dollar bounty on March 31, 1863. Service Records, microcopy 551, rolls 23 and 116; Louis N. Chapin, *To Sacrifice, to Suffer, and If Need Be, to Die: A History of the Thirty-fourth New York Regiment* (1903; reprint, Little Falls, N.Y.: Captain Henry Galpin Civil War Round Table, 1998), 9–60; Isaac Hall, *History of the Ninety-seventh Regiment New York Volunteers ("Conkling Rifles") in the War for the Union* (1890; reprint, Baltimore: Butternut and Blue, 1991), 3–99; Isaac O. Best, *History of the 121st New York State Infantry* (1921; reprint, Baltimore: Butternut and Blue, 1996), 1–4; Roy P. Basler, ed., *The Collected Works of Abraham Lincoln,* vol. 5 (New Brunswick, N.J.: Rutgers University Press, 1953), 293–94, 296–97; Frederick H. Dyer, *A Compendium of the War of the Rebellion,* vol. 3 (New York: Thomas Yoseloff, 1959), 1452; O'Donnell, *Tip of the Hill,* 193–201; David P. Krutz, *Distant Drums: Herkimer County, New York, in the War of the Rebellion* (Utica, N.Y.: North Country Books, 1997), 3, 5–7, 14–16; James M. McPherson, *Battle Cry of Freedom: The Civil War Era* (New York: Oxford University Press, 1988), 491.

4. The service record of Richard Franchot dates his commission as colonel of the 121st New York on August 30, 1862 (with rank to date from August 23, 1862), while Best cites July 19, 1862. Both sources cite September 25, 1862, as the date of his resignation. Service Records, microcopy 551, roll 48; Certificate of Promotion, April 12, 1863, Remmel Papers, folder 18; Service Records, microcopy 551, roll 116; Best, *History of the 121st,* iv–vii, 1–4, 22–25, 28, 34, 54, 66–67, 230–32; Salvatore G. Cilella Jr., "The 121st New York State Infantry Regiment, 1862–1865" (M.A. thesis: State University of New York College at Oneonta at Its Cooperstown Graduate Programs, 1972), 26–32.

5. Maj. Gen. Philip Sheridan commanded the Army of the Shenandoah as part of the Middle Military Division. It consisted of the 6th Corps from the Army of the Potomac, the 19th Corps from the Department of the Gulf, the 8th Corps from the Army of West Virginia, and three cavalry divisions and artillery support, numbering in total approximately forty thousand men at the beginning of August 1864. Service Records, microcopy 551, roll 116; David S. Heidler and Jeanne T. Heidler, "Army of the Shenandoah, U.S.A.," in *Encyclopedia of the American Civil War,* ed. Heidler and Heidler (Santa Barbara, Calif.: ABC-Clio, 2000), 103–4. For a discussion of Sheridan's 1864 Shenandoah Valley campaign see Jeffry D. Wert, *From Winchester to Cedar Creek: The Shenandoah Campaign of 1864* (New York: Simon and Schuster, 1989); Thomas A. Lewis, *The Guns of Cedar Creek* (New York: Harper and Row, 1988); John L. Heatwole, *The Burning: Sheridan in the Shenandoah Valley* (Charlottesville, Va.: Rockbridge, 1998).

6. Remmel Papers, Finding Aid description of collection and folders 14 and 15; Remmel, "Harmon L. Remmel," 4.

Chapter 1

1. The 121st New York originally mustered 946 enlisted men and 30 officers. Best, *History of the 121st,* iv–vii, 2–3, 5–9; *OR Supplement,* 46:457; Dyer, *Compendium,* 3:1452; James M. Greiner, Janet L. Coryell, and James R. Smither, eds., *A Surgeon's Civil War: The Letters and Diary of Daniel M. Holt, M.D.* (Kent, Ohio: Kent State University Press,

1994), 28; Stephen W. Sears, *George B. McClellan: The Young Napoleon* (New York: Ticknor and Fields, 1988), 168–222; Bruce Catton, *Mr. Lincoln's Army* (New York: Doubleday, 1951), 49–51; McPherson, *Battle Cry of Freedom,* 533.

2. William Remmel to Parents, September 14, 1862, Remmel Papers; Best, *History of the 121st,* 22–25, 34, 54, 66–67; Ezra J. Warner, *Generals in Blue: Lives of the Union Commanders* (Baton Rouge: Louisiana State University Press, 1964), 519–20; Stephen E. Ambrose, *Upton and the Army* (Baton Rouge: Louisiana State University Press, 1964), 15–17, 20–21; James M. Greiner, *Subdued by the Sword: A Line Officer in the 121st New York Volunteers* (Albany: State University of New York, 2003), 15–17.

3. Remmel to Parents, September 14, 1862, Remmel Papers, folder 1; Best, *History of the 121st,* x, 28–29, 32–34; Bell Irvin Wiley, *The Life of Billy Yank: The Common Soldier of the Union* (1952; reprint, Baton Rouge: Louisiana State University Press, 1997), 30–36.

4. In 1860 New York City ranked as the largest city in the nation, with a population of 813,669. The population of the entire metropolitan area exceeded one million. Ira Rosenwaike, *Population History of New York City* (Syracuse: Syracuse University Press, 1972), 42, 55–56, 63; United States Census Bureau, *Eighth Census (1860): Population, Manufactures, Mobility and Miscellaneous* (Washington, D.C.: Government Printing Office, 1864), 609.

5. George K. Rogers, a resident of Salisbury, died at the age of forty-three on February 4, 1870, and is buried in Dibble-Tuttle Cemetery in Salisbury. "Mr. Kimble" may refer to Chester Kimball of Salisbury, who died in 1892 at the age of eighty-two and is buried in Stratford Cemetery in Salisbury, or to G. H. Kimball, a mechanic who lived in Stratford. Best, *History of the 121st,* 6–7; Dibble-Tuttle Cemetery Records, Herkimer County Historical Society; Stratford Cemetery Records, Herkimer County Historical Society; *Gazetteer and Business Directory of Montgomery and Fulton Counties, New York, 1869–1870* (Syracuse: Hamilton Child, 1870), 277–79.

6. These movements by Union and Confederate troops occurred at the beginning of the Antietam campaign. *OR,* 19:814–15; *OR Supplement,* 46:457, 504.

7. During the battle of South Mountain the 6th Corps attacked A. P. Hill's position at Crampton's Gap. The 121st New York came under artillery fire while moving into position. The regiment, which was not put into direct action, was ordered to lie behind the protective cover of a hill. Remmel observed the battle from this vantage. Col. Joseph J. Bartlett commanded the brigade to which the 121st belonged. The 121st suffered no casualties in the battle. *OR,* 19:374–82, 388–90; Best, *History of the 121st,* 15–21; Stephen W. Sears, *A Landscape Turned Red: The Battle of Antietam* (New York: Ticknor and Fields, 1983), 145–50.

8. Fort Lincoln, located in Hyattsville, Maryland, formed a portion of the defenses around Washington, D.C. The regiment named the fort in the president's honor after receiving Lincoln's praise during a review of troops. Best, *History of the 121st,* 7; Cilella, "The 121st New York," 27–29.

9. Members of the Remmel family mentioned in this letter include younger brothers Augustus, Caleb, and Harmon, younger sister Ada, and older sister Louisa and her husband, William Empie. Remmel, "Harmon L. Remmel," 2.

10. Alphonzo Casler of Company H received a furlough at Camp Schuyler in September, which lasted until October 1. In Casler's service record his first name is spelled "Alphonzo." Remmel occasionally spells it "Alphonso." Remmel's spelling has been retained in his letters, but all editorial references to Casler spell his name with a "z." Service Records, microcopy 551, roll 23.

11. Maj. Gen. Henry W. Slocum commanded the 2nd Brigade of the 1st Division, which formed part of the left wing of Maj. Gen. William B. Franklin's 6th Corps during the Maryland campaign of 1862. The area Remmel calls "Hampton Gap" is actually named Crampton's Gap, which figured prominently in the battle of South Mountain on September 14, 1862. Franklin's inability to properly follow up his hard-won success of September 14 helped to ensure the Confederate capture of the arsenal at Harpers Ferry by Stonewall Jackson. The 121st New York was not engaged in this action. *OR,* 19:374–82; Best, *History of the 121st,* 15–21; Anne Hartwell Britton and Thomas J. Reed, eds., *To My Beloved Wife and Boy at Home: The Letters and Diaries of Orderly Sergeant John F. L. Hartwell* (Madison, N.J.: Fairleigh Dickinson University Press, 1997), 25–27; Greiner, Coryell, and Smither, *A Surgeon's Civil War,* 18–25; Warner, *Generals in Blue,* 451–53; Sears, *A Landscape Turned Red,* 145–50.

12. On September 20, 1862, Col. James A. Suiter of the 34th New York Infantry reported 32 killed, 109 wounded, and 9 missing at the battle of Antietam. The regimental history of the 34th cites 43 killed and 74 wounded and does not include a figure for those missing. Survivors of the 34th New York visited the 121st New York soon after the battle of Antietam and shared their experiences. Although not engaged at Antietam, the 121st New York—along with part of the 5th Corps—helped to capture four batteries covering the Confederate retreat. *OR,* 19:315–16, 380–81; Chapin, *To Sacrifice, to Suffer,* 61–70; Best, *History of the 121st,* 22–27; Britton and Reed, *To My Beloved Wife,* 23–26; Cilella, "The 121st New York," 27–29.

13. For a description of the position of Union troops at Crampton's Gap prior to the arrival of the 121st New York see Sears, *A Landscape Turned Red,* 145–49.

14. The 121st New York arrived at Bakersville, Maryland, on September 23, 1862, and remained there until October 30, when it joined in McClellan's belated pursuit of Lee's army. *OR Supplement,* 46:457, 504; Greiner, Coryell, and Smither, *A Surgeon's Civil War,* 26–38.

15. Camp Schuyler was named for Henry J. Schuyler, who leased out a tract of land in the township of German Flats, New York, at the rate of ten dollars per acre for use as an army training ground. Best, *History of the 121st,* 2–3.

16. No service record for a Captain Thompson of the 97th New York Infantry could be located. At the battle of Antietam the 97th New York participated in the struggle for the Miller Cornfield, where it lost 23 killed and 62 wounded out of 196 effectives. Hall, *History of the Ninety-seventh,* 91–99.

17. "Anna" cannot be identified, due to the absence of a surname. William's older brother, Charles, married a woman named Anna in the spring of 1864, but at the time of this letter William did not know Charles's location or whether he was alive. The woman referred to here, therefore, is most likely an acquaintance of William's and not the same

woman who later married Charles. Casler is marked as "present" on the company muster roll of October 31, 1862, and on all rolls thereafter until his death. Service Records, microcopy 551, roll 23.

18. Allan Jennings enlisted at Stratford as a twenty-one-year-old private on August 21, 1862, in Company H of the 121st New York Infantry. He received a discharge for disability at Frederick, Maryland, on May 11, 1863. Charles Tompkins enlisted at Little Falls as a private at the age of twenty-two on August 13, 1862, in Company H of the 121st New York Infantry. Wounded at Salem Church, he transferred to the 55th Company, 2nd Battalion, of the Veteran Reserve Corps on November 13, 1863, and served in Philadelphia. He mustered out on August 23, 1865. Jake Prame enlisted at Salisbury as a thirty-four-year-old private in Company A of the 121st New York Infantry on July 30, 1862. He received an honorable discharge on November 8, 1862, after the accidental discharge of his musket caused a severe wound to his left hand. He died on January 20, 1874, twenty-nine days after turning forty-six years old, and is buried in Dibble-Tuttle Cemetery in Salisbury. Dr. Holt treated Prame's injured hand, which required amputation. Service Records, microcopy 551, rolls 71, 141, and 113; Service Records, microcopy 636, rolls 39 and 40; Greiner, Coryell, and Smither, *A Surgeon's Civil War*, 36–37; Dibble-Tuttle Cemetery Records, Herkimer County Historical Society.

19. Austin B. Ferrell of Stratford enlisted as a thirty-year-old private in Company D of the 97th New York Infantry on December 18, 1861, and reenlisted on January 5, 1864. He was wounded at Gettysburg on July 1, 1863, and at Laurel Hill on May 12, 1864. He transferred as a private to Company F of the 24th Regiment in the Veteran Reserve Corps on February 15, 1865, and was discharged at Washington, D.C., on July 29, 1865. John McDougal enlisted in Stratford as a twenty-one-year-old private in Company K of the 34th New York Infantry on October 16, 1861. He mustered out with his regiment on June 30, 1863, at Albany, New York. He served subsequently as a corporal in Company C of the 16th New York Heavy Artillery. He received an honorable discharge on June 30, 1865. After the war McDougal married a woman named Rosina, with whom he had two children, and lived in Salisbury Center, where he farmed, operated a lumber mill, and was a partner with Daniel Wagner in a tanning and currier business. He is buried in Fairview Cemetery in Salisbury. Service Records, microcopy 636, rolls 13 and 14, and microcopy 551, rolls 45 and 92; Chapin, *To Sacrifice, to Suffer*, 137; *Gazetteer and Business Directory of Herkimer County, New York, 1869–1870* (Syracuse: Hamilton Child, 1869); Hall, *History of the Ninety-seventh*, 386.

20. John S. Kidder joined the 121st New York Infantry as the thirty-two-year-old captain of Company I on August 18, 1862, and remained with the regiment throughout the war. He received promotion to major on March 14, 1865, to date from January 24, and to lieutenant colonel on May 18, 1865, to date from April 27. Wounded in action on May 10, 1864, during the regiment's charge at the battle of Spotsylvania Courthouse, Kidder mustered out with the regiment on June 25, 1865. Best places Kidder's promotion to major on May 22, 1865. Service Records, microcopy 551, roll 76; Best, *History of the 121st*, 5, 232–3.

21. The regiment remained in camp at Bakersville until October 31. During this

time, Franchot resigned and helped gain the appointment of Upton as his successor. The regiment moved to White Plains for ten days, then to Catlett's Station and Stafford Courthouse. Best, *History of the 121st,* 27–29, 31; *OR Supplement,* 46:504.

22. Merton Tanner enlisted as a nineteen-year-old private on August 13, 1862, in Company H of the 121st New York Infantry. He mustered out while at Mower Hospital in Philadelphia on May 17, 1865, where he convalesced from a wound sustained on October 19, 1864, at the battle of Cedar Creek. Norman P. Goodwin enlisted at Salisbury on July 11, 1862, as a twenty-nine-year-old private in Company A of the 121st New York Infantry. He transferred to the Veteran Reserve Corps at an unspecified date. Nathan Wood enlisted at Salisbury as a twenty-one-year-old private on August 12, 1862, in Company D of the 121st New York Infantry. He mustered out with the regiment on June 25, 1865, at Halls Hill, Virginia. Charles Jenkins enlisted at New York City on April 7, 1864, as a twenty-six-year-old private in the 82nd New York Infantry but received no company assignment. Service Records, microcopy 551, rolls 138, 54, 155, and 71.

23. While at Bakersville in October, the regiment suffered much from disease. Best credits the removal of the regiment's sick to Maj. Egbert Olcott, who had charge of the regiment while Upton was absent on other business, but Upton apparently approved of the move upon his return. Upton quickly earned the regiment's respect and admiration due to his discipline, leadership, and character. His selection as colonel of the 121st New York did, however, produce criticism from at least one officer. Dr. Holt believed that favoritism played a role in Upton's promotion, as a means by which Gen. Henry Slocum's brother—Dr. John Slocum, then serving as assistant surgeon of the 122nd New York Infantry—could be promoted to regimental surgeon of the 121st. This opinion, however, is entirely without merit. Endowed with intelligence, bravery, and a strict sense of discipline, Emory Upton quickly emerged as one of the rising young stars of the Union army. By the end of the conflict he earned the rank of brevet major general of both volunteers and regulars. After the war he served as superintendent of the United States Military Academy at West Point and as commander of the Presidio in San Francisco. Upton also repeatedly advocated in favor of reforms within the post–Civil War army. Suffering from mental duress, he committed suicide in March 1881. Service Records, microcopy 551, roll 143; Best, *History of the 121st,* 26–29, 54–55, 230–34, 250; Greiner, Coryell, and Smither, *A Surgeon's Civil War,* 30, 50, 107; Ambrose, *Upton and the Army,* 3, 20–21; Cilella, "The 121st New York," 27–40; Greiner, *Subdued by the Sword,* 18–19; Warner, *Generals in Blue,* 519–20.

24. Best and Dr. Holt both describe this storm as a snowstorm rather than hail. Dr. Holt also mentions the recent presence of frost and ice. The storm forced the regiment to spend the next two weeks performing drill and parade at Stafford Courthouse. George B. McClellan began to move the Union army out of Maryland toward the Rappahannock River on October 26, 1862, in slow pursuit of the Confederates. Best, *History of the 121st,* 32–33; Greiner, Coryell, and Smither, *A Surgeon's Civil War,* 43; Daniel E. Sutherland, *Fredericksburg and Chancellorsville: The Dare Mark Campaign* (Baton Rouge: Louisiana State University Press, 1998), 6–12; Francis Augustin O'Reilly, *The Fredericks-*

burg Campaign: Winter War on the Rappahannock (Baton Rouge: Louisiana State University Press, 2003), 12–14; George C. Rable, *Fredericksburg! Fredericksburg!* (Chapel Hill: University of North Carolina Press, 2002), 8–9, 11, 43–44.

25. The "united movement" is a reference to the consolidation of Union forces at Fredericksburg. *OR Supplement,* 46:457, 504; Best, *History of the 121st,* 39–57; Greiner, Coryell, and Smither, *A Surgeon's Civil War,* 45; Sears, *A Landscape Turned Red,* 84–85; Kathleen A. Ernst, *Too Afraid to Cry: Maryland Civilians in the Antietam Campaign* (Mechanicsburg, Pa.: Stackpole Books, 1999), 5–9; Sutherland, *Fredericksburg and Chancellorsville,* 6–13; O'Reilly, *The Fredericksburg Campaign,* 12–14, 24–27; Rable, *Fredericksburg,* 56–59.

26. Lt. Delevan Bates and Capt. John Kidder, both of Company I, were away from the regiment due to illness. Bates mustered into Company I at the age of twenty-two on August 18, 1862, with the rank of second lieutenant. Promoted to first lieutenant on May 4, 1863, he resigned on March 15, 1864, to accept a promotion as colonel of the 30th United States Colored Troops. Severely wounded during the July 30, 1864, battle of "The Crater" at Petersburg, Bates was awarded the Medal of Honor. He married Lana A. Green on January 1, 1870, and settled in Aurora, New York, engaged in banking, and raised three daughters. He died on December 19, 1918, and is buried in the Aurora Cemetery. Service Records, microcopy 551, rolls 7 and 76; Best, *History of the 121st,* 237; Cilella, "The 121st New York," 27–29.

27. No military service file was located for DeLoss Perkins. After the war, Perkins owned a farm and lived in Stratford. *Gazetteer and Business Directory of Herkimer County, New York, 1869–1870.*

28. Moses Bliss served with Company B of the 44th New York Infantry. He frequently wrote letters to the *Herkimer County Journal* during his service. Wounded at Mine Run in November 1863 and briefly captured at Spotsylvania in 1864, Bliss reenlisted on March 2, 1864. Jerome Satterlee (sometimes spelled Satterly) enlisted at Albany, New York, on August 20, 1861, as a twenty-three-year-old private in Company B of the 44th New York Infantry. He was promoted to corporal on May 11, 1863. Taken prisoner at the battle of Gaines Mills on June 27, 1862, he remained absent as a paroled prisoner through December. Frequently absent thereafter due to illness, he transferred as a corporal on February 15, 1864, to the 116th Company of the 2nd Battalion in the Veteran Reserve Corps. After the war he lived in Stratford and worked as a carpenter and millwright. Service Records, microcopy 551, rolls 11 and 123; Service Records, microcopy 636, rolls 35 and 36; *OR Supplement,* 43:694–95; *Gazetteer and Business Directory of Herkimer County, New York, 1869–1870;* Krutz, *Distant Drums,* 20–21, 39, 187–88, 229.

29. During the Fredericksburg campaign Maj. Gen. William B. Franklin commanded the Left Grand Division, Maj. Gen. William F. "Baldy" Smith commanded the 6th Corps, Brig. Gen. William T. H. Brooks commanded the 1st Division, and Brig. Gen. Joseph J. Bartlett commanded the 2nd Brigade. Sutherland, *Fredericksburg and Chancellorsville,* 14; Warner, *Generals in Blue,* 23–24, 47, 159–60, 462–64; O'Reilly, *The Fredericksburg Campaign,* 24; Rable, *Fredericksburg,* 60.

30. Louisa Remmel Empie, William Remmel's older sister, is the recipient of this letter. Remmel addressed his younger sister, Ada, through letters to their parents.

31. "William" is William Empie, who married William Remmel's older sister, Louisa, on March 6, 1862. See note 17 above regarding "Anna," here called "Annie." The village of Ephratah is in Fulton County, New York, southeast of Stratford. Remmel, "Harmon L. Remmel," 2–4; James I. Robertson Jr., *Soldiers Blue and Gray* (Columbia: University of South Carolina Press, 1988), 108–9; *Gazetteer and Business Directory of Montgomery and Fulton Counties, New York, 1869–1870*, 228–33.

32. Despite losing the element of surprise by mid-November, Burnside insisted on painstaking preparations before ordering the assault on Fredericksburg. Drills and rumors about possible movements filled the time for the Army of the Potomac as it massed on Stafford Heights opposite Fredericksburg. Best, *History of the 121st*, 27–29; Greiner, Coryell, and Smither, *A Surgeon's Civil War*, 28, 107; Britton and Reed, *To My Beloved Wife*, 34; Ambrose, *Upton and the Army*, 20–21; Sutherland, *Fredericksburg and Chancellorsville*, 14–29; Rable, *Fredericksburg*, 57–58.

33. "Dear William" refers to Remmel's brother-in-law, William Empie. Remmel, "Harmon L. Remmel," 2–4.

34. The Union army had 12,653 casualties at Fredericksburg, including 1,284 killed, 9,600 wounded, and 1,769 missing. The Confederate army had an estimated 4,576 casualties. *OR*, 21:545–49; Best, *History of the 121st*, 50; Sutherland, *Fredericksburg and Chancellorsville*, 28–68; O'Reilly, *The Fredericksburg Campaign*, 498–99; Rable, *Fredericksburg*, 66–73.

35. The 121st New York sustained sixteen casualties at Fredericksburg, with four killed and twelve wounded. *OR*, 21:140, 522–24, 526–27; Best, *History of the 121st*, 43–6, 50, 230; Britton and Reed, *To My Beloved Wife*, 34–36.

36. On December 15, 1862, Burnside ordered a withdrawal back across the Rappahannock River. The withdrawal took the Confederates by surprise and caused some criticism of Lee in the South as being a lost opportunity to inflict further damage on the Federals. Sutherland, *Fredericksburg and Chancellorsville*, 63–66; O'Reilly, *The Fredericksburg Campaign*, 443–44, 447; Rable, *Fredericksburg*, 281–83.

37. Northern morale declined after the details of Fredericksburg became known. Sutherland, *Fredericksburg and Chancellorsville*, 68, 86–88; Rable, *Fredericksburg*, 282, 394–96; McPherson, *Battle Cry of Freedom*, 571–75.

38. The Finding Aid for the Remmel Papers mistakenly dates this letter as December 21, 1862. Remmel to Parents, December 21, 1862, Remmel Papers, folder 2.

39. Albert N. Jennings enlisted at Little Falls, New York, as a twenty-four-year-old private in Company H of the 121st New York Infantry on August 13, 1862. His service record lists him as absent due to illness since May 6, 1864. He mustered out with the regiment on June 25, 1865, at Halls Hill, Virginia. After the war he lived in the Fulton County village of Brockett's Bridge, near the town of Manheim, and worked as a carpenter and joiner. Service Records, microcopy 551, roll 71; *Gazetteer and Business Directory of Herkimer County, New York, 1869–1870*.

Chapter 2

1. Alphonzo Casler is listed as a corporal on the company muster rolls beginning in January and February 1863. He was killed in action on May 3, 1863, at the battle of Salem Church. William Remmel to Parents, May 5, 1863, Remmel Papers, folder 3; Service Records, microcopy 551, roll 23.

2. Certificate of Promotion, April 12, 1863, Remmel Papers, folder 18; Remmel to Augustus, June 20, 1863, Remmel Papers, folder 4; Service Records, microcopy 551, roll 116.

3. For additional commentary on the battle of Fredericksburg, see Best, *History of the 121st,* 39–50; Britton and Reed, *To My Beloved Wife,* 36; Sutherland, *Fredericksburg and Chancellorsville,* 70–77, 86–88.

4. Andrew A. Smith enlisted at Little Falls on May 1, 1861, as a twenty-nine-year-old private in Company K of the 34th New York Infantry. He was killed in action on December 13, 1862, at the battle of Fredericksburg. "Jack" may be Remmel's friend John McDougal, who also served in Company K of the 34th New York. Service Records, microcopy 551, rolls 130 and 92; Chapin, *To Sacrifice, to Suffer,* 82–84, 137, 145.

5. John S. Hyatt lived in Stratford and died in 1887 at the age of eighty-three. His first wife, Lucretia Hyatt, died in 1858 at the age of fifty-four. His second wife, Lucinda H. Hyatt, lived from 1828 to 1910. They are all buried in Stratford Cemetery in Salisbury. Stratford Cemetery Records, Herkimer County Historical Society.

6. Capt. John Kidder commanded Company I of the 121st New York Infantry during Remmel's entire term of service. The opinion expressed here, albeit negative, appears to have been temporary. It is Remmel's only negative comment in relation to Captain Kidder and comes at a relatively early phase in regiment's service, when soldiers and officers were still adapting to military life. Kidder's service record suggests nothing less than skill and efficiency. Service Records, microcopy 551, roll 76.

7. Fueled by the monotony of marches and frustration over insufficient supplies, desertions rose throughout the Union army during the winter of 1862–63. A similar increase occurred the following winter. Dr. Holt mentions several episodes of desertion in the regiment, including nineteen cases on January 18, 1863. Best, *History of the 121st,* 53; Greiner, Coryell, and Smither, *A Surgeon's Civil War,* 50, 59, 69; Rable, *Fredericksburg,* 409–26; Robertson, *Soldiers Blue and Gray,* 74–77, 135; Wiley, *Billy Yank,* 204–7.

8. Joseph Hooker succeeded Ambrose Burnside as commander of the Army of the Potomac on January 25, 1863. *OR,* 21:82, 752–55, 1004–5; Warner, *Generals in Blue,* 57–58, 233–35.

9. Dr. Holt's letter of February 17, 1863, records the regiment's recent receipt of pay for the period through January 1, 1863. On February 14, 1863, Sergeant Hartwell of Company C anticipated pay for the past two months and twenty-four days. Greiner, Coryell, and Smither, *A Surgeon's Civil War,* 76–78; Britton and Reed, *To My Beloved Wife,* 49.

10. Henry M. Galpin of Little Falls initially enlisted as a private in Company B of

the 44th New York Infantry in 1861. Promoted to first sergeant, he was wounded at the battle of Gaines Mills on June 27, 1862. In the summer of 1862 he served as a recruiting officer in Little Falls. Galpin mustered in as captain of Company A of the 121st New York Infantry on July 31, 1862. He was promoted to major on March 23, 1864, to rank from January 26, 1864. He received an honorable discharge on December 21, 1864, due to wounds received at the battle of Cedar Creek. He also earned the brevet rank of lieutenant colonel. Widely regarded as a skilled and courageous officer, Galpin earned the respect of the entire regiment. After the war he was a partner in the Little Falls mercantile firm of Wheeler and Galpin. His brother, Samuel J. Galpin, operated a hardware store in Little Falls and often arranged for soldiers to send money home via his store. William M. Dutton lived in Stratford and was a partner in the Hyde, Dutton, and Company leather tannery of Stratford. Service Records, microcopy 551, roll 50; Best, *History of the 121st,* 4, 232–33; Greiner, Coryell, and Smither, *A Surgeon's Civil War,* 181; Britton and Reed, *To My Beloved Wife,* 78, 85; *Gazetteer and Business Directory of Montgomery and Fulton Counties, New York, 1869–1870,* 277–79; *Gazetteer and Business Directory of Herkimer County, New York, 1869–1870;* Krutz, *Distant Drums,* 39, 49, 319.

11. Remmel is referring to his older brother, Charles, whose name William usually spells "Charley." Born in Germany on February 7, 1840, Charley moved to California sometime around 1859. As William's speculation suggests, the family heard little or nothing from him for a considerable period of time and did not know if he was alive. Charley returned to New York sometime prior to October 1863, but moved to Walworth, Wisconsin, by early November. While in Wisconsin he purchased a farm and married a woman named Anna. See note 59 below. Remmel Family Genealogical Files, "Charles R. Remmel"; Remmel, "Harmon L. Remmel," 4. See William's letter of October 9, 1863, which refers to Charley being at home in Herkimer County, New York.

12. Lucinda cannot be identified, due to the absence of her surname. She and Augustus may have been engaged at this time, but Augustus never married.

13. The 121st New York arrived at White Oak Church in November 1862 and did not break camp until late April 1863, at the start of the Chancellorsville campaign. Poor weather in early April prevented an earlier general movement by the Union army, although departure was frequently rumored and numerous marching orders were rescinded. *OR Supplement,* 46:457, 504–5; Greiner, Coryell, and Smither, *A Surgeon's Civil War,* 67, 69–70, 81, 86, 89–92.

14. Eliphelet Shaver was born in 1838 to Henry and Malinda Shaver of Salisbury. He died in 1863 and is buried in Stratford Cemetery in Salisbury. Stratford Cemetery Records, Herkimer County Historical Society.

15. No charge of desertion or any other offense is noted in Nathan Wood's service record. Service Records, microcopy 551, roll 155.

16. Charles Northrup joined the 97th New York Infantry on October 2, 1861, and received a commission as major on March 10, 1862, to date from December 16, 1861. Wounded in the knee at the battle of the Wilderness on May 6, 1864, he resigned his commission on December 15, 1864, due to disability. He received a brevet promotion of lieutenant colonel of both New York and United States volunteers. Alphonzo Casler is

listed present on the company muster roll for March and April 1863. Service Records, microcopy 551, rolls 105, 23, 11, and 138; Hall, *History of the Ninety-seventh,* 345.

17. "Mr. Carry" could not be identified, but he was apparently Caleb's employer.

18. Alphonzo Casler is listed as a corporal beginning with the company muster roll for January and February 1863. Service Records, microcopy 551, roll 23.

19. The 6th Corps, under Gen. John Sedgwick, broke camp on April 27 and crossed the Rappahannock on April 29 along with the 1st and 3rd Corps under the command of John Reynolds and Daniel Sickles. The 6th was ordered to guard the crossing and threaten the enemy holding the heights beyond the city. *OR,* 25:557–62; Best, *History of the 121st,* 58–59; *OR Supplement,* 46:458, 504.

20. The official report cites 276 total casualties out of 453 effectives for the 121st New York at Salem Church, including 3 officers and 45 men killed, 3 officers and 170 men wounded, and 2 officers and 47 men captured or missing. Best cites a total of 278 casualties, including 7 officers and 113 men killed or mortally wounded and 3 officers and 155 men wounded. The discrepancy primarily concerns the fates of the mortally wounded and missing, many of whom never returned and which Best, therefore, counted among the killed. Company I lost 8 men killed and 18 wounded. *OR,* 25:189, 557–62, 566–70, 579–83, 589–90; *OR Supplement,* 46:505; Ernest B. Furgurson, *Chancellorsville 1863: The Souls of the Brave* (New York: Knopf, 1992), 274–80, 364; Stephen W. Sears, *Chancellorsville* (Boston: Houghton Mifflin, 1996), 378–86, 485; Sutherland, *Fredericksburg and Chancellorsville,* 160–70; Ambrose, *Upton and the Army,* 21–22; Best, *History of the 121st,* 58–83, 230.

21. Capt. Thomas S. Arnold joined Company C of the 121st New York Infantry on August 13, 1862, as a thirty-year-old first lieutenant. He was promoted to regimental adjutant on October 16, 1862, with rank to date from October 13. Following the resignation of Capt. John Ramsey, Arnold was promoted to captain of Company H on December 18, 1862, with rank to date from October 19, 1862. He died on May 18, 1863, from wounds received at the battle of Salem Church. Hartwell also reported prematurely of Arnold's death. 1st Lt. Ulysses F. Doubleday, also of Company H, died on the field. Gen. William T. H. Brooks commanded the 2nd Division of the 6th Corps at this time. The following Herkimer County residents numbered among the 121st's casualties at Salem Church: Merton Tanner, Nathaniel Lamphere, Jenks Perkins, Charles Tompkins, Oliver C. Gransbury, and Alphonzo Casler. Pvt. Oliver C. Gransbury of Salisbury and Company A, referred to by Remmel as "C. Gransberry," was killed in action. Nathaniel Lamphere enlisted at Little Falls as a twenty-three-year-old corporal in Company H on August 13, 1862. Wounded at Salem Church, he returned to the regiment and was eventually killed in action on April 6, 1865, at the battle of Saylor's Creek. Jenks Perkins enlisted at Salisbury as a twenty-one-year-old private in Company H on July 29, 1862. He died June 1, 1863, from wounds received at Salem Church. *OR,* 25:191, 557–62, 566–70, 579–83, 589–90; Service Records, microcopy 551, rolls 3, 38, 138, 80, 110, 141, 55, and 23; *OR Supplement,* 46:457, 499, 405–505; Britton and Reed, *To My Beloved Wife,* 92; Greiner, Coryell, and Smither, *A Surgeon's Civil War,* 95; Best, *History of the 121st,* 42, 59, 236–37; Warner, *Generals in Blue,* 47; Krutz, *Distant Drums,* 117–18, 123.

22. For discussion of the performance of Generals Hooker and Lee and of the Union army's 11th Corps at the battle of Chancellorsville see Sutherland, *Fredericksburg and Chancellorsville,* 183–94; Sears, *Chancellorsville,* 431–43.

23. John H. and Mary M. Casler owned a farm in Salisbury. In addition to Alphonzo, the Caslers raised a daughter named Lauretta and a son named Milo. The Caslers moved to Kalamazoo, Michigan, in 1868. Mary Casler died there in 1886. John Casler applied for a federal pension in 1889, as the parent of a Civil War casualty, and a small collection of letters from Alphonzo to his family exists in the files of those applications. Service Records, microcopy 551, roll 23; Krutz, *Distant Drums,* 120.

24. Neither Hartwell nor Dr. Holt mentions this slight change of the regiment's camp. *OR Supplement,* 46:457.

25. This is Remmel's first mention of his promotion to sergeant, but his certificate of promotion was signed on April 20, 1863, to date from April 12. Certificate of Promotion, April 12, 1863, Remmel Papers, folder 18.

26. The identity of Mariah Remmel and her relationship to William Remmel could not be determined.

27. The identity of Remmel's roommate at Fairfield Academy is not known. William mentions having his photograph taken on at least three occasions during the war. The only known photograph of him is in the Remmel Papers, folder 19.

28. Based on Remmel's description of this photograph and the proximity to his promotion, this is may be the photograph located in the Remmel Papers. That photograph, included in this publication, shows Remmel wearing the chevrons of a sergeant; it appears to have been made in the field by an itinerant photographer. Remmel Papers, folder 19.

29. After the battle of Chancellorsville, the original enlistments began to expire for many two-year regiments. When these regiments mustered out of the service, the 121st New York received many of their three-year recruits as transfers. Regiments from whom the 121st received replacements included the 16th, 18th, 27th, 31st, and 32nd New York Infantry. Service Records, microcopy 551, rolls 141 and 80; Best, *History of the 121st,* 76–8.

30. Until June 14 it was not entirely evident what move the Confederates were making, which made the move across the river necessary. At this time, Gen. Ulysses S. Grant was fully engaged in operations against Vicksburg, Mississippi. *OR,* 27:29–33; Best, *History of the 121st,* 84–5; Stephen W. Sears, *Gettysburg* (Boston: Houghton Mifflin, 2003), 58.

31. While at Fairfax Courthouse, Virginia, the 121st New York learned of light skirmishing in Maryland from Confederate cavalry prisoners. The regiment, with the rest of the First Division, relieved the troops of Howe's 2nd Division on June 7, 1863, which took up a new position across the Rappahannock River. The 2nd Brigade took the lead position for the division and began to prepare rifle entrenchments. Brig. Gen. Albion Parris Howe graduated eighth in the 1841 class at West Point and served on the frontier and in the Mexican War. Appointed a brigadier general of volunteers to rank from June 11, 1862, he commanded the 2nd Division of the 6th Corps during the battle of

Fredericksburg the previous December and retained command through the Chancellorsville and Gettysburg campaigns. Howe was primarily an artillery officer, and his performance in command of infantry troops apparently did not impress his superiors. Reassigned to command of the Artillery Depot and the Office of the Inspector of Artillery in the fall of 1863, Howe later received the standard end-of-war brevets through the rank of major general for both the regular and volunteer services. *OR Supplement,* 46:457, 505; Best, *History of the 121st,* 86; Britton and Reed, *To My Beloved Wife,* 98–100; Warner, *Generals in Blue,* 239–40.

32. Emerson Northrup enlisted at Salisbury as a nineteen-year-old second lieutenant in Company K of the 34th New York Infantry on May 1, 1861. On November 22, 1861, he succeeded to the rank of first lieutenant, following the resignation of Henry B. Chamberlain. Following the promotion of Capt. John Beverly to major on July 1, 1862, Northrup became captain of Company K. Wounded in the leg at White Oak Swamp on June 30, 1862, he returned to the regiment in time to participate in the battle of Antietam. He mustered out with the regiment at Albany, New York, on June 30, 1863. After the war he studied medicine and practiced that profession for several years in Kansas City, Missouri. In 1899 he moved to Los Angeles, California. Even from this distance, Northrup remained an active member of the 34th New York's regimental association. Service Records, microcopy 551, roll 105; Chapin, *To Sacrifice, to Suffer,* 94–97.

33. The 121st New York was ordered to abandon its position in the forts. The regiment moved to Fairfax Station, remained one day, and moved out on June 18. They followed a trail of abandoned and burning campsites produced by the more forward elements of the Union army, which indicated a general movement. *OR,* 27:37–50; Best, *History of the 121st,* 85; *OR Supplement,* 46:457, 460, 468, 505; Sears, *Gettysburg,* 60, 74–106.

34. For a discussion of total war and soldier attitudes toward that development see Mark Grimsley, *The Hard Hand of War: Union Military Policy toward Southern Civilians, 1861–1865* (New York: Cambridge University Press, 1995), 171–86; McPherson, *Battle Cry of Freedom,* 392, 396–415, 422–23, 586–88, 591–93.

35. After the battle of Chancellorsville, distrust for Hooker's ability to command the army ran high among the general officers. John Sedgwick expressed the opinion that Hooker was drunk. Hooker repeatedly accused Sedgwick of deliberate sloth and blamed him for the defeat. On June 27, 1863, Hooker asked to be relieved of command, and George G. Meade took command of the Army of the Potomac the following day. *OR,* 27:60–61; Best, *History of the 121st,* 83, 88–9; Britton and Reed, *To My Beloved Wife,* 104–5; Sutherland, *Fredericksburg and Chancellorsville,* 191; Sears, *Chancellorsville,* 18–29; 434–38, 449, 504–6; Richard Elliott Winslow III, *General John Sedgwick: The Story of a Union Corps Commander* (Novato, Calif.: Presidio Press, 1982), 76, 85–86.

36. The 121st New York embarked on the Gettysburg campaign from its encampment near Fairfax Courthouse after shipping all non-essential baggage to Washington, D.C. *OR,* 27:53–54; Best, *History of the 121st,* 85–86.

37. Maj. Gen. Julius Stahel commanded the Union cavalry in the Washington, D.C., defenses in the spring of 1863, but he was relieved of command on June 27, 1863, and reassigned to command of the cavalry in the Department of the Susquehanna. Maj. Gen.

Alfred Pleasanton commanded the Cavalry Corps of the Army of the Potomac during the Gettysburg campaign. *OR*, 27:51–52, 58–60; Sears, *Gettysburg*, 130; Warner, *Generals in Blue*, 469–70.

38. Such fraternal advice about school, ethics, morals, and general behavior often had a lasting effect on the lives and belief systems of the children and younger siblings of Civil War soldiers. James Marten, *The Children's Civil War* (Chapel Hill: University of North Carolina Press, 1998), 87–93.

39. The regiment camped near Germantown, Maryland, on June 30, 1863, and marched continuously thereafter toward Gettysburg, Pennsylvania. When they arrived on the field at Gettysburg on July 2 they crossed Pipe Creek, moved off the Baltimore Pike in sight of Cemetery Hill, and took up position at the rear of Little Round Top. Because they were not actively engaged, the regiment suffered only two wounded during the battle. Moses Bliss and the 44th New York served under Col. Strong Vincent in the 3rd Brigade, 1st Division, 5th Corps, and helped to defend the Union position on Little Round Top. *OR*, 25:663–67, 671–73; *OR Supplement*, 46:457, 468, 505, 43:689; Service Records, microcopy 551, roll 11; Best, *History of the 121st*, 87–91, 230; Britton and Reed, *To My Beloved Wife*, 106–7; Greiner, Coryell, and Smither, *A Surgeon's Civil War*, 116–21; Sears, *Gettysburg*, 464–65.

40. Charles Wheelock joined the 97th New York Infantry on September 30, 1861, and mustered in as colonel at the age of forty-nine on February 7, 1862. Although wounded on December 13, 1862, at the battle of Fredericksburg, Wheelock led his regiment through the battle of Gettysburg, where he was briefly captured near the close of action on July 1, 1863. Dismissed from the service on August 20, 1863, due to a mistaken charge of fraud, Wheelock was restored to full rank and command on September 12, 1863, after an investigation cleared him of all charges. He received a brevet promotion to brigadier general on August 9, 1864. He died of disease on January 21, 1865. John P. Spofford joined the 97th New York Infantry as lieutenant colonel on September 5, 1861. Captured along with Wheelock on the first day at Gettysburg, Spofford later rejoined the regiment. He succeeded Wheelock as colonel of the 97th on January 31, 1865, with rank from the date of Wheelock's death. Although wounded at the battle of Hatcher's Run on February 7, 1865, Spofford remained with the regiment until it mustered out on July 18, 1865. Francis (Frank) Murphy joined Company G of the 97th New York Infantry in the town of Herkimer on September 4, 1861, as a first lieutenant. Murphy was wounded on July 30, 1862, at the battle of Second Bull Run and was captured on July 1, 1863, at Gettysburg. On August 18, 1863, he transferred to the 2nd Battalion of the Veteran Reserve Corps. Fred Munson enlisted at Salisbury as a twenty-six-year-old corporal in Company D of the 97th New York Infantry. Promoted to sergeant in April 1863, Munson was killed in action at Gettysburg on July 1, 1863. James H. Styles (sometimes spelled Stiles) enlisted as a twenty-four-year-old first sergeant in Company D of the 97th New York Infantry on September 18, 1861. He was promoted to second lieutenant on August 30, 1862, and was killed in action at Gettysburg on July 1, 1863. Austin B. Ferrell enlisted at Stratford as a thirty-year-old private in Company D of the 97th New York Infantry on December 18, 1861. Wounded at Gettysburg on July 1, 1863, he returned to the regi-

ment in December. Wounded on May 12, 1864, at the battle of Laurel Hill, he returned to the regiment in June but received another wound on June 8, 1864. On February 15, 1865, he transferred to Company F of the 24th Regiment of the Veteran Reserve Corps. He was discharged in Washington, D.C., on July 29, 1865. *OR,* 27:309–10; Service Records, microcopy 551, rolls 150, 133, 102, 101, 135, 45; Service Records, microcopy 636, rolls 13 and 14, 29 and 30; *OR Supplement,* 45:623–25; Hall, *History of the Ninety-seventh,* 345, 352, 386, 392.

41. On July 5 the 6th Corps' 1st Division took the lead position in the post-Gettysburg pursuit. Sedgwick attempted a flanking movement over South Mountain in order to cut off Lee's retreat, but he was unable to catch a sufficient portion of the Confederate army to prevent it from crossing back into Virginia. Skirmishing occurred throughout the pursuit. *OR,* 27:78–95, 113–19, 663–67, 671–73; Best, *History of the 121st,* 90–92; *OR Supplement,* 2:46, 505; Winslow, *General John Sedgwick,* 107–13; Sears, *Gettysburg,* 355, 465, 479, 488–89, 495–96; Jeffry D. Wert, *Gettysburg: Day Three* (New York: Simon and Schuster, 2001), 253–54, 300–301.

42. On July 12, 1863, Companies E and I of the 121st successfully attacked a Confederate force near Funkstown, Maryland. This action, however, only served as a diversion to allow the retreat of the main body of the Confederate army. *OR,* 27:663–64, 671–73; *OR Supplement,* 46:484, 505; Best, *History of the 121st,* 90–92; Britton and Reed, *To My Beloved Wife,* 111–12; Greiner, Coryell, and Smither, *A Surgeon's Civil War,* 121–24, 130–31.

43. From August 8–10, 1863, the 121st New York conducted a scouting expedition in the area of White Plains and Middleburg, Virginia, in pursuit of Confederate guerrillas under Col. John S. Mosby. *OR Supplement,* 46:505; Britton and Reed, *To My Beloved Wife,* 120–21; Greiner, Coryell, and Smither, *A Surgeon's Civil War,* 132–35; Best, *History of the 121st,* 95–96.

44. Mosby captured a wagon train on August 11, 1863, near Annandale in Fairfax County, Virginia. New Baltimore and Warrenton are both in Fauquier County, Virginia. *OR,* 29:68–70; Best, *History of the 121st,* 95–96; John E. Clark Jr., *Railroads in the Civil War: The Impact of Management on Victory and Defeat* (Baton Rouge: Louisiana State University, 2001), 22–23; Jeffry D. Wert, *Mosby's Rangers* (New York: Simon and Schuster, 1990), 114–27.

45. Upton took command of the 2nd Brigade after Gen. Joseph J. Bartlett's promotion to command of the 1st Division. Upton's temporary rank became permanent in the spring of 1864, in recognition of his achievement at Spotsylvania. Ambrose, *Upton and the Army,* 23–24; Warner, *Generals in Blue,* 23–24, 519–20; Wert, *Mosby's Rangers,* 116–19.

46. Egbert Olcott, of Cherry Valley, enlisted at Albany as a twenty-four-year-old private in Company C of the 44th New York Infantry on September 9, 1861. Promoted to second lieutenant, he transferred in November to Company B of the 25th New York Infantry, where he ranked as a first lieutenant from December 12, 1861. He served as major in the 121st New York from August 23, 1862, until his promotion to lieutenant colonel on April 10, 1863, and to colonel on April 18, 1865. Except for an absence after he was

wounded and captured at the battle of the Wilderness, Olcott commanded the 121st from the time of Upton's promotion to brigadier general until being mustered out with the regiment on June 25, 1865. Dr. Holt accompanied Upton's wing during the operation against Mosby and considered the raid "a total failure." Service Records, microcopy 551, roll 106; Greiner, Coryell, and Smither, *A Surgeon's Civil War*, 132–36; Britton and Reed, *To My Beloved Wife*, 120–21.

47. Upton secured the services of local Negro guides during this mission. Hartwell indicates that three such contrabands served as guides, while Dr. Holt mentions only one specific Negro guide in relation to Upton's wing. Best, *History of the 121st*, 95–96; Britton and Reed, *To My Beloved Wife*, 120–21: Greiner, Coryell, and Smither, *A Surgeon's Civil War*, 133.

48. Theodore Sternberg mustered in as first lieutenant for Company E of the 121st New York Infantry on August 18, 1862. He served as regimental quartermaster from January 5, 1863, to June 25, 1865, when he mustered out with the regiment. Service Records, microcopy 551, roll 135. Best, *History of the 121st*, 4, 55, 232–33, 234.

49. Dr. Holt states that only one man and two women were captured and that most of the civilians were released. Greiner, Coryell, and Smither, *A Surgeon's Civil War*, 133; Britton and Reed, *To My Beloved Wife*, 120–21.

50. Hartwell indicates that a draft took place in the area of Little Falls. Dr. Holt expressed support for the Conscription Act of 1863. Britton and Reed, *To My Beloved Wife*, 124; Greiner, Coryell, and Smither, *A Surgeon's Civil War*, 138; McPherson, *Battle Cry of Freedom*, 600–611.

51. Mosby attacked General Bartlett's headquarters on September 4, 1863, while the 121st New York was camped near New Baltimore. Hartwell dates the attack on the morning of September 5 and cites nine wounded and the loss of the brigade headquarters flag. J. E. B. Stuart reported no Confederate casualties. *OR*, 29:102–3; *OR Supplement*, 46:457, 469, 505; Best, *History of the 121st*, 93–96; Britton and Reed, *To My Beloved Wife*, 123–24.

52. Furloughs were difficult to obtain, especially for enlisted men, due to the extensive furloughs granted to veterans who reenlisted after the expiration of their original two-year enlistments. Robertson, *Soldiers Blue and Gray*, 79–80.

53. Maj. Gen. William S. Rosecrans occupied Chattanooga on September 9, 1863. He withdrew into Chattanooga following the disastrous defeat at the battle of Chickamauga. Morris Island, including Fort Wagner, fell on September 7, 1863. The city of Charleston, however, did not surrender until February 17, 1865. James Lee McDonough, *Chattanooga: A Death Grip on the Confederacy* (Knoxville: University of Tennessee Press, 1984), 41–42; McPherson, *Battle Cry of Freedom*, 670; Shelby Foote, *The Civil War: A Narrative*, vol. 2, *Fredericksburg to Meridian* (New York: Random House, 1963), 696–702.

54. The regiment received conscripted replacements after Gettysburg. Best, *History of the 121st*, 93; Krutz, *Distant Drums*, 165–70; McPherson, *Battle Cry of Freedom*, 600–611.

55. Northern Democrats opposed to the war were called "Copperheads," in reference

to the venomous snake. McPherson, *Battle Cry of Freedom,* 684; Mark Mayo Boatner III, *Dictionary of the Civil War* (New York: David McKay Company, 1987), 175; Frank L. Klement, *Dark Lanterns: Secret Political Societies, Conspiracies, and Treason Trials in the Civil War* (Baton Rouge: Louisiana State University Press, 1984), 1–6; Foote, *Fredericksburg to Meridian,* 696–702.

56. The 96th Pennsylvania Infantry served as pickets on the night of the unsuccessful raid by Mosby's men against Bartlett's headquarters. Best, *History of the 121st,* 94.

57. The 6th Corps relieved the 2nd Corps on the picket line on October 5, positioned alongside the 1st Corps. Having retired behind the Rapidan River until the beginning of October, Lee moved out on October 5, 1863, in an attempt to get between the Army of the Potomac and Washington, D.C. The 121st New York crossed the river at Germania Ford and pushed toward Centreville, near Bull Run. Although officially prohibited, the practice of pickets meeting between the lines for conversation and small trades or exchanges was quite common throughout the war. *OR Supplement,* 46:457, 469, 505; Britton and Reed, *To My Beloved Wife,* 136; Greiner, Coryell, and Smither, *A Surgeon's Civil War,* 141; Robertson, *Soldiers Blue and Gray,* 139–44.

58. The execution of Pvt. Joseph Connelly of the 4th New Jersey Infantry occurred on October 9, 1863, after his conviction on the charge of desertion. Britton and Reed, *To My Beloved Wife,* 136; Greiner, Coryell, and Smither, *A Surgeon's Civil War,* 143.

59. Samuel Miller enlisted as a thirty-year-old sergeant in Company B of the 121st New York Infantry on August 23, 1862. Miller served as second lieutenant for Companies C and H from February 20 until May 13, 1863, when he resigned his commission. After he resigned, Miller served as the regimental sutler for the remainder of the war. "Charley" refers to William's older brother, Charles, who had recently returned to New York from California. Service Records, microcopy 551, roll 97; Best, *History of the 121st,* 49–50, 234, 237; J. Matthew Gallman, *The North Fights the Civil War: The Home Front* (Chicago: Ivan R. Dee, 1994), 80; Wiley, *Billy Yank,* 156; Remmel, "Harmon L. Remmel," 4.

60. The 6th Corps moved toward Culpeper Courthouse to counteract Lee's move, crossed the river at Rappahannock Station, and joined the main body of the Army of the Potomac. The enemy made no attack. The 6th Corps was then sent back over the river, toward Brandy Station, and drew up in line of battle. The cavalry engaged the enemy, while the infantry was sent back toward Centreville. Best, *History of the 121st,* 96–99; *OR Supplement,* 46:457, 469–70, 505–6.

61. Hartwell and Dr. Holt shared Remmel's belief about the possibility of a Confederate invasion of Maryland. Lee considered offensive movements in the fall of 1863 but decided against the idea after the transfer of Longstreet's corps to the Army of Tennessee in late August and early September. The opportunity was reconsidered after Bragg's victory at Chickamauga forced a reduction in the Army of the Potomac via the transfer of the Union's 11th and 12th Corps to reinforce Rosecrans at Chattanooga. After a defeat at Bristoe Station, however, Lee decided to withdraw toward the Rappahannock. After the Federals captured a bridgehead on November 7, Lee withdrew toward the Rapidan

and settled in for the winter. Best, *History of the 121st,* 96–99; Britton and Reed, *To My Beloved Wife,* 139; Greiner, Coryell, and Smither, *A Surgeon's Civil War,* 144; Emory M. Thomas, *Robert E. Lee: A Biography* (New York: Norton, 1995), 309–11.

62. Remmel mistakenly cites September 5, 1863, as the date for this movement, which actually took place on October 5. *OR Supplement,* 46:457, 505; Britton and Reed, *To My Beloved Wife,* 136; Greiner, Coryell, and Smither, *A Surgeon's Civil War,* 141–42.

63. Hugh Judson Kilpatrick rose relatively quickly through the ranks of the Union cavalry service, but he also developed a reputation for political machinations and impetuous command decisions that often placed his troops at unnecessary risk. *OR,* 29: 378–83; Samuel J. Martin, *Kill-Cavalry: The Life of Union General Hugh Judson Kilpatrick* (Mechanicsburg, Pa.: Stackpole Books, 2000), 136–37; Warner, *Generals in Blue,* 266–67.

64. The 121st New York followed Lee and on October 22, 1863, arrived at Warrenton, where it remained for two weeks while it repaired railroad track and bridges. *OR Supplement,* 46:458–59, 470; Best, *History of the 121st,* 99.

65. Charles Remmel moved to Walworth, Wisconsin, sometime around early November 1863. Dorothy Diehl Pruett, comp., *Landowner's Index and Patron's Business Directory, Compiled from Combination Atlas Map of Walworth County, Wisconsin,* vol. 2 (1873; reprint, Philadelphia: Duval and Hunter, 1974), 34; Remmel, "Harmon L. Remmel," 4.

66. Louisa and William Empie moved to Fort Wayne, Indiana, in 1864 and established a successful pharmaceutical and mercantile business. Remmel, "Harmon L. Remmel," 4–5.

67. Hiram Cady enlisted at Little Falls as a thirty-one-year-old private in Company A of the 152nd New York Infantry on September 5, 1862. Promoted to corporal on April 15, 1865, he mustered out with his regiment on June 13, 1865. After the war he lived and farmed in Stratford. In October 1863 the 152nd belonged to the 1st Brigade, 2nd Division, 2nd Corps, Army of the Potomac. Service Records, microcopy 551, rolls 20 and 11; Henry Roback, *The Veteran Volunteers of Herkimer and Orange Counties in the War of the Rebellion* (Utica, N.Y.: L. C. Childs, 1888), 172; Dyer, *Compendium,* 3:1462; *Gazetteer and Business Directory of Herkimer County, New York, 1869–1870.*

68. Due to its proximity to Washington, D.C., Warrenton lay in the path of several campaigns. Britton and Reed, *To My Beloved Wife,* 142–43; Best, *History of the 121st,* 93, 99; Greiner, Coryell, and Smither, *A Surgeon's Civil War,* 144, 149–53.

69. On October 26, 1863, Mosby and a force of fifty men attacked a wagon train between New Baltimore and Warrenton and carried away forty or fifty wagons, 145 horses and mules, and thirty prisoners. Increased Union pickets and patrols around Gainesville and Warrenton in the fall of 1863 reduced the effectiveness of Mosby's raids. *OR,* 19:495; Wert, *Mosby's Rangers,* 105–6.

70. Although not yet the "whipped dog" portrayed by Remmel, Lee did spend the latter half of October withdrawing Confederate forces toward the Rappahannock. Thomas, *Robert E. Lee,* 311.

71. For a description of the military prisons in Richmond see Lonnie R. Speer, *Portals*

to Hell: Military Prisons of the Civil War (Mechanicsburg, Pa.: Stackpole Books, 1997), 89–95.

72. Swift Roback enlisted at Devereaux as a twenty-one-year-old private in Company F of the 97th New York Infantry on September 10, 1861. He contracted a fever and was discharged for disability on June 10, 1862, but enlisted at Danube as a private in Company E of the 152nd New York Infantry on August 29, 1862, and was killed in action at Spotsylvania on May 11, 1864. James H. Monk (sometimes spelled Monks) enlisted at Little Falls as a twenty-one-year-old private in Company A of the 152nd New York Infantry on August 30, 1862, and was killed in action on May 10, 1864. Palmer was apparently a contractor in the tannery-related bark wood industry of Herkimer County, but further identification could not be located. See note 67 above for information about Hiram Cady. Service Records, microcopy 551, rolls 20, 119, 120, and 98; Roback, *Veteran Volunteers*, 74–77, 172–73, 177; Hall, *History of the Ninety-seventh*, 410; Krutz, *Distant Drums*, 74–75, 173–75, 228–29.

73. Born in 1838 to Henry and Malinda Shaver, Eliphelet Shaver died in 1863 and is buried in Stratford Cemetery in Salisbury, New York. Stratford Cemetery Records, Herkimer County Historical Society.

74. Winter quarters generally consisted of canvas-and-log cabins complete with fireplaces and chimneys. Wiley, *Billy Yank*, 57–58; Robertson, *Soldiers Blue and Gray*, 74–77.

75. Monk was absent on sick furlough from March 23 to April 23, 1863. His service record does not indicate an arrest for being absent without leave. Service Records, microcopy 551, roll 98; Krutz, *Distant Drums*, 156–59, 173–75.

76. Lee held a strong position near Rappahannock Station, with rifle-pits on the south side and a redoubt overlooking the railroad bridge. The 5th, 7th, and 54th North Carolina Infantry Regiments defended this position, along with Hays's Louisiana brigade and the Washington Artillery. *OR*, 29:574–76, 578–80, 592–93, 609–11; *OR Supplement*, 46:470, 506; Best, *History of the 121st*, 99–105; Thomas, *Robert E. Lee*, 311.

77. On November 7, 1863, the 121st New York lost four men killed, and one officer and twenty men wounded at Rappahannock Station. Best also cites twenty-five total casualties but notes that three of the wounded received mortal injuries. Company I sustained two casualties during the charge: Pvt. Norman Stone was wounded and Pvt. Asbel Lamont was killed. *OR*, 29:559, 574–76, 578–80, 584–90, 592–93; John R. Adams, *Memorial and Letters of Rev. John R. Adams, D.D., Chaplain of the Fifth Maine and the One Hundred and Twenty-first New York Regiments during the War of the Rebellion, Serving from the Beginning to Its Close* (Cambridge, Mass.: John Wilson and Son, 1890), 131–33; *OR Supplement*, 46:506; Best, *History of the 121st*, 230.

78. Confederate troops crossed the Rapidan River while the 6th Corps advanced toward Brandy Station to again repair the railroad to Centreville. *OR*, 29:610–17; *OR Supplement*, 46:459, 470; Best, *History of the 121st*, 106–7.

79. Although he considered moving back to California at this time, Charley moved instead to Walworth, Wisconsin. Remmel Family Genealogical Files, "Charles R. Remmel"; Remmel, "Harmon L. Remmel," 4–5; Pruett, *Landowner's Index*, 34.

80. There was some expectation of a late-season movement against Richmond. Meade

ordered the 3rd Corps, under the command of Gen. William H. French, across the Rapidan River in an effort to intercept part of Lee's army near Mine Run. This pursuit, however, proved slow and ineffective. *OR Supplement,* 46:459, 470; Best, *History of the 121st,* 107; Thomas, *Robert E. Lee,* 311–12.

81. Maria Empie is apparently William Empie's sister, but the nature of her relationship to Remmel could not be determined. Remmel's letter to her is not part of the Remmel Papers.

82. Certificate of Promotion, April 12, 1863, Remmel Papers, folder 18.

83. Several Russian naval vessels under the command of Rear Admiral Lisovski spent the winter of 1863–64 in New York and San Francisco, influenced at least in part by American diplomatic difficulties with France and England over their support of the Confederacy. In his diary, Secretary of the Navy Gideon Welles does not mention the 6th Corps review attended by the admiral. Howard K. Beale and Alan W. Brownsword, eds., *Diary of Gideon Welles: Secretary of the Navy under Lincoln and Johnson,* vol. 1 (New York: Norton, 1960), 443, 480–81, 484; Albert A. Woldman, *Lincoln and the Russians* (Cleveland: World, 1952), 140–41.

84. The regiment broke camp on November 26, 1863, and crossed the Rapidan River the next day. *OR Supplement,* 46:470.

85. Best suggests that the 3rd Corps crossed the river slowly, thereby impeding the progress of the 6th Corps and causing the pursuit to fail. Copperhead sentiments and newspaper criticisms increased throughout 1863. Best, *History of the 121st,* 107; Elbert J. Benton, *The Movement for Peace without a Victory during the Civil War* (1918; reprint, New York: Da Capo Press, 1972), 10–12; McPherson, *Battle Cry of Freedom,* 590–92.

86. Company Memorial, Remmel Papers, folder 18, item 8.

87. Sedgwick believed the 6th Corps could have taken the Confederate position in front of them. When the 3rd Corps became unexpectedly engaged with Ewell's corps on the morning of the November 27, the 6th Corps moved into a support position on the extreme right of the Union line. The 2nd Brigade led the 1st Division in this movement. On November 28 the 6th Corps moved to the right of the 2nd Corps. They formed four lines on November 30, but firing was limited to an exchange of artillery. The 6th Corps crossed back over the Rapidan River on December 1, 1863, and moved toward their previous encampment near Welford's Ford. *OR,* 29:796–97; Best, *History of the 121st,* 107; Winslow, *General John Sedgwick,* 125–32.

88. Because of their proximity to the railroad, the regiment received regular mail service during the winter. Although money remained scarce, numerous recreational activities occurred that required small amounts of cash, such as purchases from sutlers and small-stakes gambling. Best, *History of the 121st,* 112.

89. Due to the large number of furloughs granted to veteran volunteers during the winter of 1863–64, Remmel did not receive a furlough. Difficulty in obtaining furloughs remained a consistent complaint of the Union soldier. Wiley, *Billy Yank,* 292.

90. The regiment made its winter camp near Welford's Ford on the Hazel River and remained there until late February 1864. *OR Supplement,* 46:459, 470, 506; Greiner, Coryell, and Smither, *A Surgeon's Civil War,* 158.

Chapter 3

1. Remmel received two wounds on May 10, 1864, during the regiment's unsuccessful charge upon a heavily entrenched Confederate position known as the "Mule Shoe." The 121st New York attacked a portion of the Confederate position held primarily by Georgia troops under the command of Brig. Gen. George P. Doles. Remmel returned to the regiment on August 24, 1864. Service Records, microcopy 551, roll 116; Best, *History of the 121st*, 34, 124–33.

2. Although Northern civilians' opinion of military and political leaders rose and fell with the fortunes of the army, soldiers in the field retained a high level of confidence in Grant's ability as a commander, despite the enormous casualties produced during the Overland campaign. Jean Edward Smith, *Grant* (New York: Simon and Schuster, 2001), 338–39; McPherson, *Battle Cry of Freedom*, 718.

3. Having already mailed his initial letter of October 16, 1864, prior to Caleb's arrival at camp, William wrote a second letter to inform the family of his younger brother's safe arrival. William Remmel to Parents, October 16, 1864, Remmel Papers, folder 12.

4. The 121st New York established its winter camp near Hazel River in December 1863 and remained there until commencement of the 1864 spring campaign. *OR Supplement*, 46:459, 470–71, 506; Best, *History of the 121st*, 111–12; Greiner, Coryell, and Smither, *A Surgeon's Civil War*, 158, 177; Britton and Reed, *To My Beloved Wife*, 169, 179, 220–21.

5. Pvt. Michael Russ served in Company A of the 121st New York Infantry. Service Records, microcopy 551, roll 121.

6. The majority of furloughs granted in early 1864 went to veteran volunteers. Wiley, *Billy Yank*, 292; McPherson, *Battle Cry of Freedom*, 719–20.

7. The dimensions and accommodations of Remmel's winter shelter compare favorably to those of other Union soldiers. Wiley, *Billy Yank*, 57–58; Krutz, *Distant Drums*, 190–91.

8. During the Mine Run campaign, which lasted from November 26 to December 2, 1863, Meade attempted unsuccessfully to maneuver Lee into a retreat toward Richmond. Moses Bliss of the 44th New York was wounded in the right hand while on picket duty during the campaign. During the campaign the 44th lost one man wounded and two men captured or missing. *OR*, 29:558, 578–82, 683; Service Records, microcopy 551, roll 11; *OR Supplement*, 43:691, 696; E. B. Long, *The Civil War Day by Day: An Almanac 1861–1865* (Garden City, N.Y.: Doubleday, 1971), 438–42; Krutz, *Distant Drums*, 187–88.

9. The regiment had last mustered for pay on December 31, 1863. The next muster for pay would occur on February 29, 1864. *OR Supplement*, 46:506.

10. Hartwell reported that in early February 1864 two regiments of Mississippi troops attempted to desert en masse but were forced to remain within Confederate lines. In addition, he reported that a squad of Georgians came within Union lines and signed the Oath of Allegiance. Britton and Reed, *To My Beloved Wife*, 194.

11. Remmel may be referring to Pvt. Edgar H. Spencer of the Oneida Indepen-

dent Company of New York Cavalry. This unit, which included recruits from Herkimer County, served in the Army of the Potomac as headquarters escort from April 1862 until it mustered out on June 13, 1865. Spencer died in 1874 and is buried in the Dibble-Tuttle Cemetery in Salisbury. Service Records, microcopy 551, roll 133; Dyer, *Compendium,* 3:1383; Dibble-Tuttle Cemetery Records, Herkimer County Historical Society.

12. On February 6, 1864, the Union's 2nd Corps and cavalry under Generals Judson Kilpatrick and Wesley Merritt crossed the Rapidan River to assess Confederate troop strength in the area of Culpeper, Germania, and Ely's Ford. After a limited exchange of fire, they returned to the Union side of the river on February 7. *OR,* 33:114–18, 139–41.

13. Pvt. John McDougal mustered out with the rest of the 34th New York Infantry on June 30, 1863. He reenlisted as a private in Company C of the 16th New York Heavy Artillery and mustered out as a corporal on June 30, 1865. In February 1864 the 16th New York Heavy Artillery was stationed at Fort Monroe in Newport News, Virginia, as part of the Department of Virginia and North Carolina. Service Records, microcopy 551, roll 92; *OR Supplement,* 42:306; Krutz, *Distant Drums,* 189.

14. Capt. John S. Kidder of Company I and Capt. John D. Fish of Company D, 121st New York, led a detachment of ten men back to the Herkimer area to enroll recruits. Captain Fish commanded Company D from August 23, 1862, until May 12, 1864, when he was killed in action at "The Bloody Angle" during the battle of Spotsylvania Courthouse. Service Records, microcopy 551, rolls 76 and 46; Britton and Reed, *To My Beloved Wife,* 199; Best, *History of the 121st,* 145, 203–4, 235; Krutz, *Distant Drums,* 196.

15. Dr. Holt also noted the depleted ranks. Greiner, Coryell, and Smither, *A Surgeon's Civil War,* 171.

16. Soldiers who reenlisted received a federal bounty of $402, paid from a fund of twelve million dollars collected through commutation fees, as well as the title of "veteran volunteer" and a thirty-day furlough. Local bounties were often added to federal bounties and could reach a thousand dollars or more. Due to the anticipated expiration of many three-year enlistments and the need to meet local draft quotas, such bounties became more common by the spring of 1864. James W. Geary, *We Need Men: The Union Draft in the Civil War* (DeKalb: Northern Illinois Press, 1991), 47, 91, 112–13, 132; McPherson, *Battle Cry of Freedom,* 605–6; Krutz, *Distant Drums,* 188.

17. The 121st New York participated in brigade reviews on February 21 and 22. Generals John Sedgwick and Horatio Wright reviewed the 6th Corps on February 23. Hartwell identifies the soldier and his wife by the surname "Gunnings," but no soldier by that name could be located in the regiment. It appears that the soldier is most likely Pvt. Burdell Ganung of Company I. Remmel does not identify the generous lieutenant in question. In February 1864, Delevan Bates served as first lieutenant of Company I, while Frank W. Foote served as second lieutenant. On March 16, 1864, Foote succeeded Bates after the former accepted the colonelcy of the 30th Regiment of United States Colored Troops. Service Records, microcopy 551, roll 50; Britton and Reed, *To My Beloved Wife,* 200, 208; Best, *History of the 121st,* 114, 237; Thomas P. Lowry, *The Story the Soldiers Wouldn't Tell: Sex in the Civil War* (Mechanicsburg, Pa.: Stackpole Books, 1994), 168–71.

18. Hartwell states that Company C received their pay on February 19, 1864, while

the remaining companies received their pay on February 20. Although Company H received pay on February 20, it appears that most of the regiment was paid on February 29. Britton and Reed, *To My Beloved Wife,* 200; *OR Supplement,* 46:476, 502.

19. Jerome Walter served as a private in the 1st New York Independent Artillery Battery and received a reenlistment bounty in 1864. Service Records, microcopy 551, roll 147; Krutz, *Distant Drums,* 189.

20. Pickets of the 3rd Corps relieved the 6th Corps on the evening of Friday, February 26, 1864. Hartwell concurs with Remmel's description of the weather and the arduous nature of the journey, which saw the regiment march through Culpeper Courthouse toward Madison Courthouse, where they camped for the night at James City, Virginia. Britton and Reed, *To My Beloved Wife,* 201–4; Greiner, Coryell, and Smither, *A Surgeon's Civil War,* 173–76.

21. The 6th Corps served in support of cavalry raids conducted in this area by Generals Judson Kilpatrick and George A. Custer. Although Custer's troops gained some success against J. E. B. Stuart's cavalry, Kilpatrick's attempt to free Union prisoners at Belle Isle proved an utter failure and resulted in the controversial death of Col. Ulric Dahlgren. Robertson's River is a tributary of the Rapidan River. *OR,* 33:161–63, 182–83, 781, 786; *OR Supplement,* 46:506; Best, *History of the 121st,* 113; Greiner, Coryell, and Smither, *A Surgeon's Civil War,* 175–76; Britton and Reed, *To My Beloved Wife,* 201–4.

22. Neither Hartwell nor Dr. Holt mentions receipt of pay, but Hartwell purchased a half-dozen eggs and bread on March 3, 1864. *OR Supplement,* 46:502, 510; Britton and Reed, *To My Beloved Wife,* 202.

23. Many soldiers in the Army of the Potomac expressed great faith in Grant, due to his aggressive and successful campaigns in the western theater. Grant consolidated the army into three corps, with the 2nd, 5th, and 6th commanded by Winfield Scott Hancock, Gouvernour K. Warren, and John Sedgwick, respectively. *OR,* 33:4, 638–39, 663, 669, 717, 722–25; Best, *History of the 121st,* 115–16; Britton and Reed, *To My Beloved Wife,* 219; Greiner, Coryell, and Smither, *A Surgeon's Civil War,* 177; Geoffrey Perret, *Ulysses S. Grant: Soldier and President* (New York: Random House, 1997), 287–90; Brooks D. Simpson, *Ulysses S. Grant: Triumph over Adversity, 1822–1865* (New York: Houghton Mifflin, 2000), 257–61.

24. Remmel described this mission in a letter to his parents on March 1, 1864. See notes 20 and 21 above.

25. Allan Jennings enlisted at Stratford as a private in Company H of the 121st New York Infantry on August 21, 1862. He received a discharge for disability while at Frederick, Maryland, on May 11, 1863, which may explain his "uneasy spells." He later enlisted as a private in Company E of the 175th New York Infantry. Service Records, microcopy 551, roll 71.

26. The 121st New York participated in battalion drill and brigade dress parade on March 17 and in battalion drill on March 18. Baseball and other recreational activities were widely practiced in Civil War army camps. Britton and Reed, *To My Beloved Wife,* 208; Wiley, *Billy Yank,* 169–70; George B. Kirsch, *Baseball in Blue and Gray: The National Pastime during the Civil War* (Princeton, N.J.: Princeton University Press, 2003), 28–47.

27. Albert Jennings is listed as absent due to illness between May 6 and October 31,

1864. He mustered out with the regiment on June 25, 1865. Service Records, microcopy 551, roll 71; Krutz, *Distant Drums,* 375–76.

28. The regiment received its pay on March 24. *OR Supplement,* 46:463; Britton and Reed, *To My Beloved Wife,* 209.

29. For a description of Grant's plans at this point see Simpson, *Ulysses S. Grant,* 269–71.

30. Four soldiers by the surname Watson are listed in the 121st New York Infantry. "Mrs. Watson's son" seems most likely to be either Henry or James Watson, but a final identification was not possible. Service Records, microcopy 551, roll 148; Krutz, *Distant Drums,* 370.

31. William H. Bennett lived in Stratford and worked as a commissioner, lumberman, sawmill proprietor, and farmer. *Gazetteer and Business Directory of Montgomery and Fulton Counties, New York, 1869–1870,* 277–79.

32. Military necessities often interfered with traditional Christian observance of the Sabbath, and both armies experienced a general shortage of chaplains throughout much of the war. Rev. John Sage resigned as regimental chaplain of the 121st New York after the Gettysburg campaign. Rev. John R. Adams, who served as regimental chaplain of the 5th Maine Infantry from June 21, 1861, to June 24, 1864, mustered in as chaplain of the 121st New York Infantry on September 17, 1864, and served until the end of the war, mustering out with the regiment on June 25, 1865. Service Records, microcopy 551, rolls 122 and 1; Service Records, microcopy 543, roll 1; J. R. Adams, *Memorial and Letters,* 17–18, 154, 224; Best, *History of the 121st,* 91, 113; Greiner, Coryell, and Smither, *A Surgeon's Civil War,* 168–69, 249; Wiley, *Billy Yank,* 262–74; Phillip Shaw Paludan, *"A People's Contest": The Union and Civil War, 1861–1865* (New York: Harper and Row, 1988), 349; Steven E. Woodworth, *While God Is Marching On: The Religious World of Civil War Soldiers* (Lawrence: University Press of Kansas, 2001), 146–49.

33. Much of the weather in March consisted of cold temperature, rain, and snow. *OR Supplement,* 46:496; Britton and Reed, *To My Beloved Wife,* 204–14.

34. Meade ordered all sutlers and other civilians out of the military camps in preparation for a general movement. In addition, regiments sent all unnecessary military baggage to Washington, D.C. *OR,* 33:659; Best, *History of the 121st,* 116.

35. "M" seems to mean "midnight." Peter and Hannah Van Vorst owned a farm in Salisbury Center. Peter Van Vorst died on December 10, 1869, at the age of eighty-one, and is buried in Dibble-Tuttle Cemetery in Salisbury. Augustus Remmel apparently worked for him at this time. *Gazetteer and Directory of Herkimer County, New York, 1869–1870;* Dibble-Tuttle Cemetery Records, Herkimer County Historical Society.

36. Grant reviewed the 6th Corps on April 18, 1864. *OR Supplement,* 46:496; Britton and Reed, *To My Beloved Wife,* 219.

37. None of the correspondence from the Remmel family to William Remmel survives.

38. Austin Ferrell reenlisted in Company D of the 97th New York Infantry on January 4, 1864. Hospitalized on June 8, 1864, he transferred to Company F of the 24th Regiment in the Veteran Reserve Corps on February 15, 1865, and was discharged on July 29,

1865, in Washington, D.C. Service Records, microcopy 551, rolls 45 and 155; Service Records, microcopy 636, rolls 13 and 14; Hall, *History of the Ninety-seventh,* 386.

39. In April 1864 the 77th New York Infantry, known as the "Bemis Heights Regiment," belonged to the 3rd Brigade, 2nd Division, 6th Corps, Army of the Potomac, while the 121st New York belonged to the 2nd Brigade, 1st Division, 6th Corps. The 77th New York was camped near Brandy Station, Virginia, between November 1863 and April 1864. Dyer, *Compendium,* 3:1435, 1452; *OR Supplement,* 45:28.

40. In the spring of 1864, Gen. David M. Gregg commanded the 2nd Cavalry Division in the Army of the Potomac. In the spring of 1864, Gen. Ambrose Burnside commanded the Union's 9th Corps as an independent unit. *OR,* 3:3, 803, 827–29, 1045–46; Simpson, *Ulysses S. Grant,* 271, 288–92; Warner, *Generals in Blue,* 57–58, 187–88.

41. Because Remmel does not identify Annie's maiden name, it is not possible to identify the brother she lost at the battle of Chickamauga. The battle of Chickamauga occurred on September 19–20, 1863, as part of the campaign to capture the strategically significant railroad junctions at Chattanooga, Tennessee. Several Wisconsin regiments fought in this battle, most notably the 15th Wisconsin Infantry, which suffered tremendous casualties in the fight for the Viniard farm. For a discussion of the battle of Chickamauga and the role of Wisconsin regiments see Steven E. Woodworth, *Six Armies in Tennessee: The Chickamauga and Chattanooga Campaigns* (Lincoln: University of Nebraska Press, 1998); John Bowers, *Chickamauga and Chattanooga: The Battles that Doomed the Confederacy* (New York: HarperCollins Publishers, 1994); and Peter Cozzens, *This Terrible Sound: The Battle of Chickamauga* (Urbana: University of Illinois Press, 1992).

42. During the regiment's charge at Spotsylvania, Remmel was wounded in both arms, including a severe wound to the left forearm. He received initial care at the evacuation hospital at Fredericksburg, Virginia, before being moved to Emory Hospital in Washington, D.C. Emory Hospital consisted of twelve L-shaped patient wards, residential and administrative buildings, and cooking and laundry facilities. Service Records, microcopy 551, roll 116; *Medical and Surgical History of the Civil War,* 15 vols. (Wilmington, N.C.; Broadfoot, 1991), 6:914–15, 12:688–92; George Worthington Adams, *Doctors in Blue: The Medical History of the Union Army in the Civil War* (New York: Henry Shuman, 1952), 98, 154–55; Frank R. Freemon, *Gangrene and Glory: Medical Care during the American Civil War* (Madison, N.J.: Fairleigh Dickinson University, 1998), 171–76; Robertson, *Soldiers Blue and Gray,* 164–65.

43. The hospital muster roll for June 30, 1864, located in Remmel's service file, lists him as being on furlough. Service Records, microcopy 551, roll 116.

44. Amputation theory and practice varied greatly during the war, with advocates both for and against the procedure. As with mortality rates, a great deal depended on the location of the wound. G. W. Adams, *Doctors in Blue,* 115, 130–34.

45. On May 10, 1864, the 121st New York fought in the battle of Spotsylvania, where Colonel Upton led them in a charge of the Confederate rifle pits. Upton received promotion to brigadier general for his role in this valiant but unsuccessful effort. Survivors of this action believed that their eventual retreat from this advanced position resulted from the lack of proper support from regiments on their flanks. In the charge the regi-

ment lost 155 total casualties, including 3 officers and 46 men killed and 9 officers and 97 men wounded. Company I lost 1 man killed and 1 lieutenant (Foote), 1 sergeant (Remmel), and 9 men wounded. During this campaign the regiment also fought at the battles of the Wilderness and Cold Harbor. *OR,* 36:126, 144, 658–59, 665–71; Service Records, microcopy 551, rolls 47 and 116; *OR Supplement,* 46:506; Best, *History of the 121st,* 124–40; Britton and Reed, *To My Beloved Wife,* 226–27; Greiner, Coryell, and Smither, *A Surgeon's Civil War,* 185–86; Ambrose, *Upton and the Army,* 59. For a broader discussion of the Spotsylvania campaign see Gordon C. Rhea, *The Battles for Spotsylvania Courthouse and the Road to Yellow Tavern, May 7–12, 1864* (Baton Rouge: Louisiana State University Press, 1997); and William D. Matter, *If It Takes All Summer: The Battle for Spotsylvania* (Chapel Hill: University of North Carolina Press, 1988).

46. Remmel went home on a convalescent furlough during the summer of 1864. The exact dates of his furlough cannot be determined, but Dr. John Moon of Stratford, New York, wrote a note on June 30, 1864, reporting that Remmel was unable to rejoin his regiment at that time due to an inflammation of the wound. Service Records, microcopy 551, roll 116.

47. The Union's 6th Corps moved into position to meet the threat from Jubal Early's drive toward Washington, D.C. In April 1864, President Lincoln approved the recruitment of hundred-day soldiers in order to free more-experienced troops for front-line duty. *OR,* 37:265–271, 346–49; *OR Supplement,* 46:471–72; Best, *History of the 121st,* 169–74; McPherson, *Battle Cry of Freedom,* 756–58; Geary, *We Need Men,* 132–33.

48. The only photographer listed in Little Falls is William H. Abbott. The individual referred to as "Case" appears to be the same person referred to as "Case the stage driver" in the postscript to the letter of October 15, 1864. This may be Silas B. Case, who leased a farm from Dr. John Moon in Salisbury Center and is buried in Stratford Cemetery in Salisbury, but certain identification could not be made. Charles Wood lived in Stratford on a sixty-acre farm in 1869–70. *Gazetteer and Business Directory of Herkimer County, New York, 1869–1870*; *Gazetteer and Business Directory of Montgomery and Fulton Counties, New York, 1869–1870,* 277–79.

49. Gen. William Tecumseh Sherman maneuvered throughout August to capture the vital rail center of Atlanta, while Grant continued to press Lee's army in the East. Albert Castel, *Decision in the West: The Atlanta Campaign of 1864* (Lawrence: University Press of Kansas, 1992), 67–73.

50. By September 1864 seven Union hospitals were in operation in Alexandria, Virginia. The city's proximity to the U.S. capital and the Orange and Alexandria Railroad made it a convenient location for a "distribution camp" from which patients were transported to other hospitals or back to their regiments. G. W. Adams, *Doctors in Blue,* 110–11, 155, 171, 192–93.

51. By the end of 1864 the pavilion hospital structure had become the standard in the field, emphasizing improved ventilation and lighting, tall ceilings, and specialized rooms organized by function or specific ailment. The average capacity of such hospitals was 614 beds, with an average occupation of 434 patients. The quality and diversity of hospital rations also improved in the second half of the war. Ibid., 150–55, 164–68.

52. For a comparison of wartime salaries for similar civilian occupations see Michael J. Varhola, *Everyday Life during the Civil War: A Guide for Writers, Students, and Historians* (Cincinnati: Writers Digest Books, 1999), 36–39.

53. Remmel's finger did not require amputation. Service Records, microcopy 551, roll 116; G. W. Adams, *Doctors in Blue,* 130–34, 164–68.

54. For a discussion of the history of the Smithsonian Institution and a description of its holdings and displays see Nina Burleigh, *The Stranger and the Statesman: James Smithson, John Quincy Adams, and the Making of America's Greatest Museum: The Smithsonian* (New York: William Morrow, 2003); James Conaway, *The Smithsonian: 150 Years of Adventure, Discovery, and Wonder* (New York: Knopf, 1995).

55. Emory Hospital was located on the eastern branch of the Potomac, on the plain east of the Capitol. Endowed by James Smithson in 1826 and officially founded twenty years later, the Smithsonian Institution houses an enormous and varied collection of natural history specimens. *Medical and Surgical History of the Civil War,* 6:914–15; Burleigh, *The Stranger and the Statesman,* 253–58; Conaway, *The Smithsonian,* 12–13, 62, 69–71.

56. Although forced to retreat at the conclusion of his move against Washington, D.C., in late July, Early continued to threaten the Baltimore and Ohio Railroad and other strategic points in the Shenandoah Valley. In order to relieve this threat Grant created the Army of the Shenandoah and placed Sheridan in command on August 5, with instructions to clear Early from the valley. Sheridan commenced operations in early August. *OR,* 37:149–52, 265–71, 346–49; *OR Supplement,* 46:482, 506; Best, *History of the 121st,* 176–202; Simpson, *Ulysses S. Grant,* 378; McPherson, *Battle Cry of Freedom,* 758; Heidler and Heidler, "Army of the Shenandoah, U.S.A," 103–4.

57. Soldiers returning to their regiments could obtain free meals and lodging at several "Soldiers' Rest" quarters throughout the nation. Robert E. Denney, *Civil War Medicine: Care and Comfort of the Wounded* (New York: Sterling, 1995), 12; Francis Trevelyan Miller, ed., *Prisons and Hospitals: The Photographic History of the Civil War* (New York: Castle Books, 1957), 331.

58. The 121st New York and the rest of the 6th Corps were operating in the vicinity of Charlestown, West Virginia. *OR,* 37:149–52; *OR Supplement,* 46:482, 506; Best, *History of the 121st,* 174–77; Britton and Reed, *To My Beloved Wife,* 268–72.

59. Completed in 1850, the Chesapeake and Ohio Canal spanned the Monocacy River between Alexandria, Virginia, and Cumberland, Maryland. In August 1864, Jubal Early used Winchester, Virginia, as a base from which to threaten the Baltimore and Ohio Railroad and the Chesapeake and Ohio Canal. Robert E. Lee also targeted the canal for destruction earlier in the war, when he ordered Brig. Gen. John George Walker to destroy the canal and seize Loudon Heights preparatory to the capture of Harpers Ferry during the 1862 Maryland campaign. Walker captured the heights and Harpers Ferry but failed to destroy the canal. *OR,* 19:912–14, 37:149–52, 552; Britton and Reed, *To My Beloved Wife,* 269–72; James A. Huston, "Waterways," in *Encyclopedia of the Confederacy,* ed. Richard N. Current (New York: Simon and Schuster, 1993), 4:1691–92; Dennis E. Frye, "John George Walker," in *Encyclopedia of the Confederacy,* ed. Richard N. Current (New York: Simon and Schuster, 1993), 1677; Robert E. Morsberger, "The Battle

That Saved Washington," in *Battle Chronicles of the Civil War,* ed. James M. McPherson, vol. 4 (New York: Macmillan, 1989), 73; Joseph P. Cullen, "The Battle of Winchester," in *Battle Chronicles of the Civil War,* ed. James M. McPherson, vol. 4 (New York: Macmillan, 1989), 87.

60. Wounded and captured at the battle of the Wilderness on May 6, 1864, Olcott rejoined the regiment in late August. Because of his strict and seemingly arbitrary discipline, as well as a penchant for gambling, drinking, and womanizing, Hartwell and Dr. Holt both viewed Olcott with contempt. Service Records, microcopy 551, roll 106; Greiner, Coryell, and Smither, *A Surgeon's Civil War,* 168–69, 239, 267; Best, *History of the 121st,* 119, 178; Britton and Reed, *To My Beloved Wife,* 275, 295–96.

61. On August 21, 1864, Company I lost one man killed in a skirmish. *OR Supplement,* 46:506; Best, *History of the 121st,* 177–78, 230; Greiner, Coryell, and Smither, *A Surgeon's Civil War,* 241–42; Britton and Reed, *To My Beloved Wife,* 274–77.

62. On August 29, 1864, General Early attacked Brig. Gen. Wesley Merritt's Union cavalry at Smithfield bridge. Merritt withdrew toward Charlestown until reinforced by Brig. Gen. James B. Ricketts's 3rd Division, which stabilized the Union line along Opequon Creek. *OR,* 43:9, 40–57.

63. Jacob F. Dengler enlisted at Fairfield as a twenty-four-year-old private in Company C of the 121st New York Infantry on July 22, 1862, and was killed in action at Spotsylvania on May 10, 1864. Service Records, microcopy 551, roll 35; Krutz, *Distant Drums,* 228.

64. Recruits came into the regiment in small groups in August and September. J. R. Adams, *Memorial and Letters,* 155; Best, *History of the 121st;* Britton and Reed, *To My Beloved Wife,* 278, 283–84; Greiner, Coryell, and Smither, *A Surgeon's Civil War,* 243, 245–46; McPherson, *Battle Cry of Freedom,* 758.

65. The surrender of Atlanta on September 2, 1864, rejuvenated the sagging morale of Union civilians and soldiers with the hope that the war would soon end. Philip H. Sheridan, *Personal Memoirs of P. H. Sheridan,* 2 vols. (New York: Charles L. Webster, 1888), 1:483; John B. Gordon, *Reminiscences of the Civil War* (1903; reprint, Alexandria, Va.: Time-Life Books, 1981), 321; *OR Supplement,* 46:465; Heatwole, *The Burning,* 15–16; Lewis, *The Guns of Cedar Creek,* 21–24; Castel, *Decision in the West,* 527–29; McPherson, *Battle Cry of Freedom,* 773–76.

66. Gottlieb Remmel purchased property in Salisbury from Thomas and Elizabeth Kibbie for five hundred dollars on December 13, 1859. *Book of Deeds, Number 75,* Herkimer County Historical Society Collection, 590; Remmel, "Harmon L. Remmel," 2–3.

67. Charles Remmel enlisted as a twenty-four-year-old private in Company F of the 42nd Wisconsin Infantry on September 2, 1864. By 1863 the federal government paid new enlistees a bounty of $302. Lucrative and widely varied bounty offers continued to characterize the recruitment of Union regiments in 1864 and 1865. According to his service records, Charles received a bounty of $100 paid in three installments, but it does not indicate whether this was a local or federal bounty. He mustered out with his regiment on June 28, 1865, with the rank of corporal. Service Records, microcopy 559, roll 25; *Roster of Wisconsin Volunteers, War of the Rebellion, 1861–1865,* vol. 2 (Madison: Demo-

crat Printing Company, 1886), 714; Thomas Walterman, *There Stands "Old Rock": Rock County, Wisconsin and the War to Preserve the Union* (Friendship, Wisc.: New Past Press, 2001), 294–97, 316–17; Geary, *We Need Men*, 112–13.

68. Best cites 4 killed and 14 wounded at Winchester and 5 wounded at Fisher's Hill (also known as the battle of Strasburg). Capt. John D. P. Douw reported that the regiment lost 2 men killed and 1 officer and 11 men wounded at Winchester. Lt. Col. Olcott reported 2 men wounded at Fisher's Hill. The brigade lost a total of 190 casualties at Winchester and 32 at Fisher's Hill. *OR*, 43:173–74, 177–78, 181–82; J. R. Adams, *Memorial and Letters*, 155–58; Best, *History of the 121st*, 177–87, 201, 230; Sheridan, *Personal Memoirs*, 2:1–49; Gordon, *Reminiscences*, 314–26; Greiner, Coryell, and Smither, *A Surgeon's Civil War*, 250–55; Britton and Reed, *To My Beloved Wife*, 286–91; Lewis, *The Guns of Cedar Creek*, 3–60; *OR Supplement*, 46:465.

69. Jubal Early reported a total of 3,611 casualties at the battle of Winchester, including 226 killed, 1,567 wounded, and 1,818 missing. He cites only three lost artillery pieces at Winchester. Early reported 1,235 losses at the battle of Fisher's Hill, including 30 killed, 210 wounded, and 995 missing, but did not report a figure for artillery pieces lost in that engagement. Rev. Adams cites the same losses as Remmel for the Confederates engaged at Winchester and Fisher's Hill. *OR*, 43:554–57; J. R. Adams, *Memorial and Letters*, 156–57; Best, *History of the 121st*, 187–88; Britton and Reed, *To My Beloved Wife*, 286–91; Greiner, Coryell, and Smither, *A Surgeon's Civil War*, 250–55; Sheridan, *Personal Memoirs*, 2:1–49; Gordon, *Reminiscences*, 327–30; Lewis, *The Guns of Cedar Creek*, 3–60.

70. The regiment marched to Harrisonburg on September 26, 1864, and camped on the hills east of town during the night. They broke camp on September 29 and continued their pursuit of the Confederate army up the Shenandoah Valley. Best, *History of the 121st*, 187; J. R. Adams, *Memorial and Letters*, 155; Greiner, Coryell, and Smither, *A Surgeon's Civil War*, 257–60; Britton and Reed, *To My Beloved Wife*, 292–93; *OR Supplement*, 2:46, 466.

71. Caleb Remmel enlisted as a sixteen-year-old private in Company I of the 121st New York Infantry on September 19, 1864. Service Records, microcopy 551, roll 116.

72. The regiment moved repeatedly in October as it pursued the Confederate army in the valley. *OR Supplement*, 46:457–59, 477, 507; J. R. Adams, *Memorial and Letters*, 158–63; Britton and Reed, *To My Beloved Wife*, 294–97; Greiner, Coryell, and Smither, *A Surgeon's Civil War*, 261–68.

73. During the election of 1864, Lincoln received strong support from the military vote. Rev. Adams and Dr. Holt echoed Remmel's views about the upcoming election campaign. Although Hartwell expressed some war-weariness in mid-August and claimed that McClellan was gaining electoral support among the soldiers, he also voted for Lincoln. J. R. Adams, *Memorial and Letters*, 158, 163, 166, 168, 172, 174, 176, 179–80; Greiner, Coryell, and Smither, *A Surgeon's Civil War*, 245; Britton and Reed, *To My Beloved Wife*, 270, 308; John C. Waugh, *Reelecting Lincoln: The Battle for the 1864 Presidency* (New York: Crown, 1997), 340–42; McPherson, *Battle Cry of Freedom*, 775–76, 803–6.

74. Clarissa Cory Bliss died at the age of fifty-seven on September 29, 1864, and is buried in the Dibble-Tuttle Cemetery in Salisbury, New York. Mustered in on Sep-

tember 7, 1864, the 42nd Wisconsin Infantry served in southern Illinois, primarily at Cairo. Service Records, microcopy 551, roll 11; Edwin Bentlee Quiner, *The Military History of Wisconsin: A Record of the Civil and Military Patriotism of the State, in the War for the Union* (Chicago: Clarke and Company, 1866), 858–59; Dyer, *Compendium,* 3:1688; Dibble-Tuttle Cemetery Records, Herkimer County Historical Society.

75. Dr. Holt resigned his commission on October 16, 1864, and returned to his home to try to regain his health. He died on October 15, 1868, due to the deterioration of health that occurred during the war. See note 47 above regarding "Case the stage driver." Service Records, microcopy 551, roll 66; Best, *History of the 121st,* 233; Greiner, Coryell, and Smither, *A Surgeon's Civil War,* 265–71; *Gazetteer and Business Directory of Herkimer County, New York, 1869–1870;* Stratford Cemetery Records, Herkimer County Historical Society.

76. Nothing in Caleb Remmel's service record reveals anything about a crippled hand. Service Records, microcopy 551, roll 116; Marten, *Children's Civil War,* 165–66; Robertson, *Soldiers Blue and Gray,* 81–101, 147–48.

77. Guided by a deserter from Mosby's command, the 13th New York Cavalry captured the four cannons of Mosby's artillery company on October 13, 1864. *OR,* 43, pt. 2:378; Greiner, Coryell, and Smither, *A Surgeon's Civil War,* 267; Wert, *Mosby's Rangers,* 232–36.

78. Caleb Remmel is marked present on company rolls for September and October 1864. Service Records, microcopy 551, roll 116.

79. No military service record was located for Nick Governour. Allan Jennings, who had served previously in the 121st New York, enlisted as a private in Company E of the 175th New York Infantry in 1864. Prior to the Shenandoah Valley campaign, the 175th New York belonged to the 3rd Brigade, 2nd Division, 19th Corps, in the Department of the Gulf and served primarily in Louisiana. In July 1864 the regiment transferred to the Army of the Shenandoah as part of the Middle Military Division. Service Records, microcopy 551, roll 71; Dyer, *Compendium,* 3:1468.

80. The first use of absentee ballots by soldiers occurred in the presidential election of 1864. Waugh, *Reelecting Lincoln,* 339–43, 354–55.

Epilogue

1. The Army of the Shenandoah consisted of approximately forty thousand troops, while Early commanded a force of approximately twelve thousand during the Valley campaign. In his memoir, Gordon wrote extensively of the battle of Cedar Creek and Early's decision to break off the engagement prematurely. *OR,* 43:40–57, 158–61, 284–86, 365–66, 448–54, 522–29, 554–56, 560–67, 677–79; Gordon, *Reminiscences,* 327–72; J. R. Adams, *Memorial and Letters,* 164–66; Best, *History of the 121st,* 176–201; Greiner, *Subdued by the Sword,* 152–54; Heatwole, *The Burning,* 7–19; Heidler and Heidler, "Army of the Shenandoah, U.S.A.," 103–4.

2. The unidentified Federal troops on the left were variously thought to belong to the 2nd Division of the 6th Corps, a brigade of the 19th Corps, or a portion of the 8th

Corps. Olcott reported that the brigade remained in the woods two or three hours and began its advance between 3 and 4 P.M. Olcott commanded the second line and assumed command of both lines after Col. Ranald S. Mackenzie of the 2nd Connecticut fell wounded. Capt. Baldwin Hufty, commanding the 1st Brigade of the 1st Division at Cedar Creek, described the Confederate retreat as "in confusion." *OR,* 43:167–68, 174–76; Best, *History of the 121st,* 191–97; J. R. Adams, *Memorial and Letters,* 164–66; Britton and Reed, *To My Beloved Wife,* 298–304.

3. Although complimentary of Sheridan's celebrated efforts at Cedar Creek, many survivors of the 121st New York believed that 6th Corps commander Maj. Gen. Horatio Wright deserved equal praise for his calm and professional leadership prior to Sheridan's arrival from Winchester. Soon after the battle the Army of the Shenandoah went into winter quarters at Winchester, while Early withdrew his force to New Market. The Federals renewed the offensive on February 25, 1865. Sheridan pushed back Early at Mount Crawford on March 2 and concluded the Valley campaign with a victory at Waynesboro on March 3. J. R. Adams, *Memorial and Letters,* 165–66; Britton and Reed, *To My Beloved Wife,* 298–304; Best, *History of the 121st,* 200, 231; *OR Supplement,* 46:507; Lewis, *The Guns of Cedar Creek,* 198, 201, 236, 250–52, 291–96.

4. The letters collected by Ada Remmel Benson were held in an envelope labeled "Letters rec'd from old soldiers of the 121st NY Vols in reply to letters of inquiry sent out concerning dear William." J. S. Kidder to H. L. Remmel, n.d., John P. Wiltsey to Mrs. J. G. Benson, January 11, 1907, and M. S. Tanner to Brother Benson, January 13, 1907, Remmel Papers, folder 14.

5. For examples of the diverse opinions among the veterans who corresponded with Ada Remmel Benson about William's fate see the following in the Remmel Papers: unsigned and undated letter, folder 14, item 2; unsigned and undated letter, folder 18, item 7; Treat D. Young to Mrs. Benson, January 11, 1907 [misidentified in finding aid as January 11, 1901], John P. Wiltsey to Mrs. J. G. Benson, January 11, 1907, Mr. and Mrs. M. S. Tanner to Brother Benson, January 13, 1907, Charles T. Dowing to Mrs. Benson, January 16, 1907, C. N. Merrill to Mrs. Benson, January 20, 1907, and Celia Westcott to Mrs. Benson, January 21, 1907, all in folder 15; see also Service Records, microcopy 551, roll 101.

6. John Frank Mumford enlisted at Frankfort, New York, as a twenty-one-year-old private in Company K of the 2nd New York Heavy Artillery on November 22, 1861. He served on detached duty with Battery D of the 2nd United States Light Artillery between March and October of 1862, but he returned to the 2nd New York Heavy Artillery by November of that year. Assigned to the 22nd Corps and to duty within the relatively mundane defensive perimeter between the capital and northern Virginia, the 2nd New York Heavy Artillery saw little fighting until the spring of 1864. At that time, General Grant pressed several heavy artillery regiments into emergency service as infantry to reinforce the casualty-worn Army of the Potomac after the battle of the Wilderness. As part of Maj. Gen. Winfield Scott Hancock's redoubtable 2nd Corps, the 2nd "Weighty" fought throughout May in a quick succession of battles at Spotsylvania Courthouse, Harris Farm, and the North Anna River. As a result, casualties among the "heavies" in-

creased. On May 27, 1864, a Confederate force captured Mumford and the rest of a regimental wagon train somewhere in the vicinity of the North Anna River, between the towns of Bowling Green and Port Royal, Virginia. Mumford arrived at Camp Sumter in Andersonville, Georgia, sometime thereafter. Service Records, microcopy 551, roll 101; Delavan S. Miller, *Drum Taps in Dixie: Memories of a Drummer Boy 1861–1865* (1905; reprint, Baltimore: Butternut and Blue, 2000), 9–120, 231; Dyer, *Compendium* 3:1383; Krutz, *Distant Drums,* 18, 227; Freemon, *Gangrene and Glory,* 177–78; Webb Garrison with Cheryl Garrison, *The Encyclopedia of Civil War Usage: An Illustrated Compendium of the Everyday Language of Soldiers and Civilians* (Nashville: Cumberland House), 20.

7. Service Records, microcopy 551, roll 101; Treat D. Young to Mrs. Benson, January 11, 1907, Remmel Papers, folder 15; William Marvel, *Andersonville: The Last Depot* (Chapel Hill: University of North Carolina Press, 1994), 220–24. For a list of other Herkimer County men who died during service, including battle deaths, deaths in captivity, disease, and all other causes, see Krutz, *Distant Drums,* 369–78. Despite the lack of medical treatment for an apparent gunshot wound to the right calf and a hernia, both sustained while on duty with the captured wagon train, Mumford survived his imprisonment. He remained at Andersonville until transferred to the prison at Millen, Georgia, on November 11, 1864. Paroled at Savannah on November 26, Mumford reported to Camp Parole in Maryland on December 3. Upon his return to Union lines, he received a thirty-day furlough and an honorable discharge on January 20, 1865. After the war Mumford settled in Middleville, New York, worked as a barber, and raised a small family. Citing disabilities related to his capture and confinement, which impaired his ability to work, Mumford received a small veteran's pension beginning in 1876. He died at the age of eighty-four on July 24, 1924, and is buried in Middleville Cemetery in the town of Fairfield. "Memorandum from Prisoner of War Records," Service Records, microcopy 551, roll 101; *Herkimer County Directory, 1888–1889* (Valatie, N.Y.: Land and Silvernail, 1888).

8. For documentation of the family's efforts to obtain Remmel's bounty and back pay see Remmel Papers, folder 16, items 1–7; for information on Gottlieb and Henrietta Remmel's pension applications and related materials see folder 17, items 1–6; for information on the family's memorial service see folder 18, items 3, 4, 5, and 8; for burial information see Remmel, "Harmon L. Remmel," 8.

9. William first refers to Charles's return from California in his letter of October 9, 1863. Mary Bliss Remmel died on November 8, 1894, at the age of fifty-four and is also buried in Healdsburg Cemetery. William Remmel to Parents, October 9, 1863, Remmel Papers, folder 6; Service Records, microcopy 559, roll 25; *Roster of Wisconsin Volunteers,* 2:714; Pruett, *Landowner's Index,* 34; Remmel, "Harmon L. Remmel," 4.

10. Louisa Christiana Remmel married William Burdick Empie on March 6, 1862. Remmel, "Harmon L. Remmel," 4–5; James Logan Morgan, ed., *Centennial History of Newport, Arkansas, 1875–1975* (Newport, Ark.: Jackson County Historical Society, 1975), 17, 21, 25–27, 52.

11. Morgan, *Centennial History of Newport,* 14, 19–22; James Logan Morgan, ed., *Di-*

rectories of the Towns and Villages of Jackson County, Arkansas, June 1880 (Newport, Ark.: James Logan Morgan, 1973), 3; Remmel, "Harmon L. Remmel," 10–11.

12. Constructed to accommodate the casualties from the 1864 spring offensives, the depot hospital at City Point, Virginia, was located at the junction of the James and Appomattox rivers with access to railroad lines for evacuating patients to hospitals in the North. In the spring of 1865 this facility served as the evacuation hospital for the 6th Corps. *OR,* 46:297–301, 587, 901–12; Service Records, microcopy 551, roll 116; Caleb Remmel to Parents, May 27, 1865, Remmel Papers, folder 18; *The Medical and Surgical History of the Civil War,* 12:688–92, 958–59; Best, *History of the 121st,* 202–28; *OR Supplement,* 46:458–59, 466–67, 507; Dyer, *Compendium,* 3:1452; G. W. Adams, *Doctors in Blue,* 110–11, 115, 154–55; Freemon, *Gangrene and Glory,* 177, 184, 186; Krutz, *Distant Drums,* 332.

13. Gertrude Goodwin Remmel remarried in 1894, but she continued to collect a widow's pension to help support her and Caleb's minor children until August 1900, when their youngest son turned sixteen. Service Records, microcopy 551, roll 116.

14. Ada Elizabeth Remmel married Rev. John George Benson on October 12, 1898, in Newport. Remmel Papers, folder 14, items 1–7, and folder 15, items 1–6; Morgan, *Centennial History of Newport,* 22–23; Remmel, "Harmon L. Remmel," 8, 10–11.

15. The editor could not locate a Confederate colonel named Stafford who could be identified as Laura Lee Stafford's father. Remmel Avenue and Remmel Park, both in Newport, are named for Harmon Remmel Sr., as is the town of Remmel, Arkansas, located just east of Newport. Remmel, "Harmon L. Remmel," 5–8; Morgan, *Centennial History of Newport,* 22–23, 55.

16. Remmel, "Harmon L. Remmel," 5–8; C. P. J. Mooney, ed., *The Mid-South and Its Builders: Being the Story of the Development and a Forecast of the Future of the Richest Agricultural Region in the World* (Memphis: Mid-South Biographic and Historical Association, 1920), 796–97; *Arkansas and Its People: A History, 1541–1930,* vol. 3 (New York: American Historical Society, 1930), 35–37.

17. Remmel Papers, Finding Aid description of collection.

Index

www.ingramcontent.com/pod-product-compliance
Lightning Source LLC
LaVergne TN
LVHW050603110926
847619LV00018B/142